THE COMPLETE
MARINE RADIO CONTROL MANUAL

The Complete
Marine Radio Control
Manual

HUGH BRIGHT

CHATHAM PUBLISHING
LONDON

Frontispiece:

The radio control of any marine subject from sail to any other form of propulsion, whether for fun or competitive sailing, is limited only by the imagination of the marine worker.

First published in Great Britain in 1999 by

Chatham Publishing,

61 Frith Street,

London W1V 5TA

Chatham Publishing is an imprint of

Gerald Duckworth & Co Ltd

British Library Cataloguing in Publication Data

A catalogue record for this book is available from the British Library

ISBN 1 86176 087 6

Designed and typeset by Dorwyn Ltd, Rowlands Castle, Hants

Printed and bound in Great Britain by Hillman Printers (Frome) Ltd

Contents

Introduction and Acknowledgements

The concept of remote control of full-size boats and aircraft as weapons of war dates back to the First World War, when it was realised that control was possible using radio technology, as the author was surprised to discover whilst researching the historical background for this Manual. Apparently radio-controlled model boats existed before the outbreak of War – 1914! – and both Britain and France had full-size torpedo-equipped launches but with a short radio control range. Both stories are probably apocryphal but nevertheless there is no doubt that a patent was accepted in late 1918 for a system designed by Professor A M Low for control of both boats and aircraft based upon experiments he had started in 1916. The period between the two World Wars saw the emergence of the successful Queen Bee range of remote-control aircraft used for target practice by the Royal Navy and it was one of the early flights of a 'Bee' from the Royal Aircraft Establishment at Farnborough, Hants, witnessed by a nine year-old boy who had climbed over the boundary fence and sat on the top of the famous Farnborough Hill that awakened the author's interest in remote control! As Chapter 1 will show, the pace of development quickened over the last decade of the twentieth century to a point that the early pioneers would have thought totally unbelievable, with sets of equipment able to perform the most complicated control virtually at the touch of a button. It is the variety of choice between these 'all-singing all-dancing' type

and the more basic sets of equipment that this Manual sets out to guide the beginner through so as to make an informed choice and further to ensure he/she acquires enough technical knowledge to get the best and the most reliable and enjoyable use out of their equipment.

The author has written a monthly column for an international marine modelling magazine for over ten years and one lesson he has learnt over this time is that there is always at least one expert, usually a professional engineer, who is all too ready to quickly point out an apparent technical error or a bit of practical advice that offends professional full-size practice. What is overlooked is that all aspects of model boat building and practice relies upon the availability of material and components which in themselves are not required to have the working lifespan of full-size items. Couple this with the fact that the radio control world has grown up with a language all of its own (for example when talking about frequencies, 'forty megs' is used instead of 'forty megahertz'), and this immediately creates the opportunity for expert criticism. This is mentioned as the author makes no apology for the fact that the Manual contains a mix of both old, 'pondside' and correct terminology so that the beginner can converse with other enthusiasts, and both understand and be understood. All the electric/electronic practices recommended here have been tried and tested for marine modelling. These may not be the professional way but they are

A Queen Bee remote-controlled aircraft at Farnborough in June 1935 of the type that awakened the author's interest in radio control.

based upon freely-available materials and facilities the average modeller will have at his/her disposal.

Safe practice both in the workshop and at the pond must be paramount at all times. It is not always recognised that low voltage direct current circuits and equipment have the potential to cause damage and serious injury particularly where high currents are involved. Power supply batteries are capable of inflicting serious injury if improperly used or disposed of. The irresponsible operation of radio control models without thought for other nearby operators and the general public can lead to control being lost and the model becoming a lethal projectile. Frequency discipline and safety operation will be discussed in Chapter 3. All users of radio control equipment are strongly advised to join a club, which not only offers a 'water' to sail upon and like-minded enthusiasts but also usually provides third-party public liability insurance which is essential when operating in a public place. Even the extended telescopic aerial of a

transmitter or the mast of a yacht has the potential to injure a fellow human being so it is essential that the marine worker ensures adequate insurance is in place before public sailing.

This Manual could never have been completed without the help and support of many people, particularly my friends in the 'trade' who have generously supplied equipment and photos on loan so that a broad picture of the choice available could be painted. This is much appreciated and deserves my thanks. However, the majority of photos are from my own library except where acknowledged. My thanks are also due to those marine modellers who have allowed me to 'poke' my lens into their pride and joy! Two people who have supported me also need mentioning – Chris Jackson, Editor of *Marine Modelling International*, and Dave McQue. Chris I have known for over ten years. His support and gentle but positive criticism has helped enormously in creating what style there is in my writing and I shall be forever grateful. Dave I first met over three years ago when I joined the Joint Radio Control Users Committee (JRCUC). He is an accomplished radio amateur as well as a marine modeller and his technical contribution particularly on frequency bands and the JRCUC background has been invaluable. Last and certainly not least I must pay tribute to my wife Doreen whose encouragement and support has made this Manual possible together with her forbearance of my modelling, both aero and marine, activities throughout our marriage. As a small token of my love and appreciation I dedicate this Manual to her. Lastly my thanks to you the reader for acquiring the Manual. I sincerely trust you find it informative and that its help smoothes the slipway to that first launching and successful voyage with you at the helm and in total control.

Abbreviations

Ah/mAh	Ampere hours or milli Ah – a ratio of battery capacity using current and time
AM	Amplitude Modulation
ATV/EPA	Adjustable Travel Volume or End Point Adjustment (Servos)
BBM	Break Before Make
BEC	Battery Eliminator Circuit
C	Common (relay contact)
C/10	Standard charging rate for nicads. Capacity divided by 10
CB	Citizen Band Radio
DPDP	Double Pole Double Throw
DPST	Double Pole Single Throw
DR	Dual Rates (Servos)
DVM	Digital Volt Meter
E or V	Volts in an electrical circuit
EMF	Electro Magnetic Force or Field. Two meanings dependent upon the subject.
ESC	Electronic Speed Control
F	Fast Acting or Quick Acting Fuse
FET	Field Effect Transistor
FF	Very Fast Acting fuse
Fig. 2/1A	Figure in Chapter 2 / Fig. No – sub diagram
FM	Frequency Modulation
I or A or amps	Current or amperes in an electrical circuit
IC	Integrated Circuit
IC	Internal Combustion (engine)
Kg/cm	Kilogrammes per centimetre – the power or pull of a servo, sail arm servo or sail winch
LED	Light Emitting Diode
mA	milli Ampere – one thousandth of one ampere
uF or mF	microFarad (capacitance)
MHz	Megahertz. A measure of a million frequencies of radio transmission
MSC	Mechanical Speed Controller
mS	milliseconds
mV	milli Volt – one thousandth of one volt
mW	milli Watt – one thousandth of one watt
NC	Normally Closed (relay contact)
NiMH/NMH	Nickel Metal Hydride battery
NO	Normally Open (relay contact)
NOR	Servo Normal
PCB	Printed Circuit Board
PCM	Pulse Code Modulation
PPM	Pulse Position Modulation

R	Resistance or ohms in an electrical circuit
RC	Radio Control
RCD	Residual Current Device
REV	Servo Reverse
RF	Radio Frequency
RX	Receiver
SLA	Sealed Lead Acid (battery)
SMT	Surface Mount Technology
SPDT	Single Pole Double Throw
SPST	Single Pole Single Throw
T	Time Delay, Slow Blow and Anti-Surge fuse
TART	Transmitter And Receiver Test
TX	Transmitter
VET	Vessel Equipment Test
W	Watt. One unit of power in an electrical circuit

1

History of Radio Control

In 1929 a radio 'expert' writing in a marine modelling publication stated emphatically that radio control of a model boat would never be possible due to the size of the equipment and the power supply required. Like all modelling disciplines radio control has its roots in full-size practice. The remote control of full-size aircraft and boats between the two World Wars demonstrated what was possible with the fast developing electronic industry so it was not surprising that the 1929 'expert' view was soon to be overturned. The motor industry in America also contributed with the development of car radios running on low DC voltages and with small thermionic valves. The benefits of all this full-size development was quickly recognised by modellers and adapted for model use with the result that *circa* 1937 the Good brothers in America had demonstrated that a miniature aircraft could be successfully controlled by radio. Indeed, they went on to win the National Radio Control Championships by a wide margin for three consecutive years – 1938, 1939 and 1940.

Basic stability

The distinction between model and miniature is important. A model is a scale reproduction of its full-size counterpart and if built accurately to scale will pose many problems when the builder attempts to either fly or float the model, due to the fact that nature cannot be scaled. The Good brothers recognised this fundamental principle and designed a miniature aircraft which was inherently stable before they introduced radio control to guide it. This is just as true in marine modelling. The craft must be stable in all reasonable weather conditions before attempting to control it. Radio control will not correct design faults – if anything it will make them worse. Ship models have a very long history which can be traced back to an Egyptian funerary boat dating from 1850BC, found in a tomb in Thebes, and now part of the vast model ship collection in the National Maritime Museum, Greenwich, London.

The aero influence

The production of reasonably accurate scale models stems from the sixteenth century. These were used by shipwrights as three-dimensional plans in building the full-size vessels. Many preserved models have accurate working details and the desire of the builders to make these work is evident in many of them. A typical example is the *Foudroyant* of 1798, a 74-gun ship built by a prisoner of war. The model has two cords at the

A valved receiver. This would have been broadly tuned with no crystal. Note the early use of the two solid state diodes below the left-hand valve.

stern which, when pulled, would retract the spring-loaded guns.

With this long history of marine modelling it is not surprising that the advent of radio control offered exciting prospects to the marine modeller to bring ships to life on the water, rather more than the aero modeller who was content with the minimum of functions to control his aircraft in flight. This reliance of the marine modeller on RC equipment designed for aero use existed from the early days up to the early 1990s, but as subsequent chapters will show, much of today's equipment is designed specifically for marine use.

The early days

The outbreak of the Second World War in 1939 brought all amateur radio activity in the UK to a halt, including radio control which up to that time could only be practised by licensed amateur radio enthusiasts. With the end of the war interest grew rapidly in aero model radio control, resulting in the allocation of the 26.96MHz to 27.28MHz and 464MHz to 465MHz bands for the radio control of all models, and in the Wireless Telegraphy Act 1949 which now allowed the modeller to operate radio control

equipment on his own as long as he was licensed. The licence lasted for five years and did not require any examination to obtain it. Although commercial equipment started to appear in 1950 most of the early equipment was scratch-built to designs that appeared in magazines and books. Two transmitters are worth re-membering for their popularity and reliability – The 'Aeromodeller' and The Ivy/AM – both one-valve designs. Couple either of these with Eric Hill's Mark II two-valve receiver and the result was remarkable for reliability, ease of construction and operation, and moderate cost. Operation was simple. The operator 'keyed' the transmitter by switching the High Tension voltage, typically 90V DC, which transmitted a pulse of RF energy which the receiver detected, amplified and operated a relay which in turn released an electro-magnetic escapement. These escape-ments were quite ingenious from a simple rubber 'motor' driven type to electric- and clockwork-driven where power was required to move a ship's rudder. Releasing the transmitter 'key' allowed the escapement to return the rudder to midships. However, as the escapement shaft only rotated one way the next 'keyed' pulse would operate the rudder in the opposite direction, which, if this was not the command required, required swift 'keying' to rotate the shaft to the desired position. Users would become very deft at 'button bashing' to achieve quite remarkable control results.

The 1950s and '60s

All the receivers in the early 1950s were super-regenerative and broadly tuned within the model control band which meant that only one model (aircraft or boat) could be operated at any one time. What was needed was a system where several models could float or fly safely. The answer was a super-heterodyne receiver and this coincided in the mid-1950s with the arrival of the transistor. Of the two the transistor was the more significant as it would eventually solve the power supply problems of dual voltage and weight in receivers and transmitters. The super-heterodyne principle was a well-known broadcast domestic receiver technique designed to eliminate interference either side of the tuned transmission. However, it required both the transmitted and received frequency to be 'held' within tight tolerances and this was achieved with crystals. The use of crystals soon brought about the realisation that the 27MHz band could be divided into channels and ultimately, with international agreement, six channels identified by colours came into common use. The first transistors could only be used at audio frequencies so equipment became a mix of valves and transistors. It took a little time for transistors to be developed for use at MHz frequencies – no doubt the Space Programme accelerated this development. What a difference this made. Hand-held transistor radios to receive pop music appeared with the latest ones frequency modulated – FM. These design techniques and associated components soon filtered down to the RC world with the emergence of crystal-controlled all-transistor transmitters and receivers. RC manufacturers who are household names today made their appearance either in their own adverts or as wholesalers. In 1967 Ripmax were advertising MacGregor, Grundig and Graupner RC equipment. The 1960s also saw the emergence of RC boats in their own right rather than an offshoot of RC aircraft and by the end of the decade model shops could offer a choice of equipment 'specially designed for boats

giving rudder control plus electric switching all from any single channel receiver. Complete control for model boats at minimum cost'. The cost? £4.10. However, at the top end of the market a full seven-function digital system was available for £363.

Early proportional control – reed

It was this period, the late 1960s, that saw the beginning of digital control techniques which would lead ultimately to full proportional control. Prior to this many systems had been tried and

A group of early systems with the heavy ground-sitting E.D. and Triang transmitters at the rear and the first transistor sets at the front.

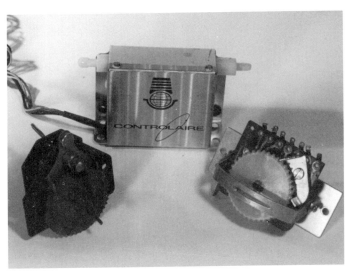

Two escapements and a linear servo containing a motor and circuits to detect when the rack reached either end. The motor polarity would be then be reversed. These servos were used with the reed system.

appeared on the market. Two are worthy of mention. Reed gear used an audio tone system which although not digital came very close to full proportional control of a function, either an elevator on an aircraft or a boat's rudder. The heart of the system was the reed bank which plugged into the receiver output and was essentially a decoder. This output could be one of ten audio tones which energised a magnetic coil and attracted to its core one of ten reeds. Each reed was of a different length and would only vibrate to a specific audio tone. At the end of each reed was a contact and when the reed vibrated it completed the drive to a relay which then switched on a servo motor driving a gear train attached to the control surface. Each motor required two reeds and two relays to change polarity and achieve two-way operation. The transmitter generated ten audio tones which were fed to five two-way switches biased to centre off. Operating any switch either way fed the appropriate tone into the RF circuit for transmission. The system was amazingly efficient but it required considerable skill on the part of the operator to judge the length of tone time to move a servo/control surface

on the model and then apply the opposite tone to bring the surface back to neutral.

Although it was proportional the reed system did not provide the one thing all modellers required – a direct relationship between the physical position of the control on the transmitter and the effect this had on the model. It was the second of the two systems mentioned above which came close to the direct relationship craved for. Designed primarily for aircraft it was known as 'Galloping Ghost' and was a mix of mechanical and electronic techniques. Initially designed for aircraft, the system introduced the principle of pulse proportional control. Previous systems transmitted a continuous tone to operate a motorised actuator. When the tone was switched off all that was left was the carrier wave being transmitted. However, with pulse proportional control the tone signal is continuous and is subdivided into a series of pulses or codes. Pulse rate and pulse width can be varied by the transmitter and detected by the 'decoder' in the receiver. There is now an unbroken control link, albeit via the radio frequency carrier wave, between the transmitter and the receiver/decoder/control surface. It is this principle established in the early days that survives with modern equipment. The GG decoder was a mechanical device driven by a small high-quality electric motor. The pulse rate fed to the motor via a switcher circuit in the receiver caused the motor to oscillate equally about a centre position which when a rudder is connected to the actuator is effectively neutral. Varying the pulse width causes the rudder to stay momentarily longer on one side than the other. By varying the percentage of width variation in either direction, proportional left or right rudder is achieved. Designed essentially for aircraft these actuators were used for boats although they were limited to small craft due to having greater forces being applied to the rudder when turning than on an aircraft. A balanced rudder was essential. Early actuators earned the 'GG' tag by causing an aircraft's tail, or a boat's stern, to 'twitch' when in neutral. The Rand LR3 and the Controlaire Mark II overcame this problem but the 'GG' tag unfortunately stuck. Studying the circuits of this period, the design seeds of the now familiar servo circuits can be seen. Transistors were common at this time but it needed the arrival of the silicon transistor before RC equipment finally became truly proportional.

Into the 1970s and '80s

The 1970s was a period that without doubt benefited electronically from the Space Programme. Solid-state devices working at MHz frequencies became cheaper, smaller and much more reliable. Mechanical decoders gave way to electronic ones which in turn now controlled fully proportional servos. RC equipment was getting cheaper and, more importantly, marine outfits were appearing with electronic speed controllers. Ripmax acquired the Futaba franchise who in October 1977 produced the Medallion Series with four- and six-function sets. In the series range was the Medallion Brick. This unique receiver module contained two servos which as the advertisement said 'just mount up the "Brick" with four screws, connect up the linkages and you are ready to go'. The set was supplied 'dry' – no rechargeable nicads – at £60 complete. With gear getting cheaper, more reliable and with enough options to suit nearly everyone, it appeared that radio control could only go from strength to strength. The original six channels within the 27MHz model control band were extended by some manufacturers to eleven by the introduction of 'splits'. Each split is a frequency approximately half-way between two primary colours and is identified by the two colours. The future seemed bright but there was a cloud on the horizon – Citizens' Band (CB) Radio.

'Rubber Duck calling'

CB radio was appearing in the UK and being illegally used with disastrous results for RC. The CB transmissions were right in the middle of the 27MHz band using audio modulation – AM – so that the older AM RC sets were completely swamped. It was bad

An early example of a valved and transistor receiver (right) compared with a modern receiver (left) and a 20p coin.

One of the first proportional sets of equipment using transistors. The servos were either linear or rotational. The receiver output to the servos was a multi-cable terminating in a distribution block to which the servo leads connected.

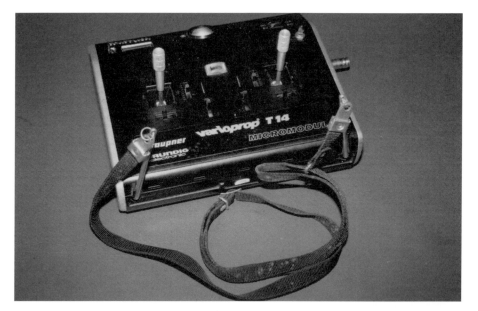

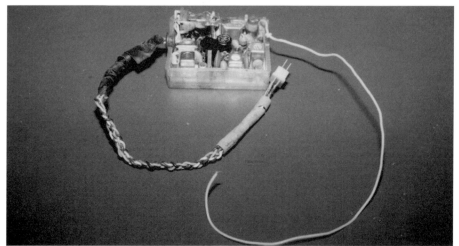

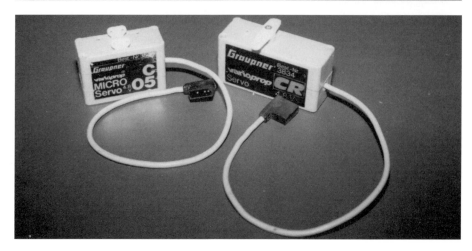

enough to lose control of a boat but with aircraft a potentially serious situation now existed with aircraft being 'shot down'. The late 1970s had seen the introduction of Frequency Modulated – FM – sets and fortunately these were not as badly affected but interference could still happen due to the large difference in radiated RF power of CB sets – 3 or 4 watts compared with the 100 milliwatts of RC sets. In times of crisis those involved come together to help each other and this was true of this crisis. The Joint Radio Control Users Committee (JRCUC) was set up to lobby the Government, comprising members from the trade and the two national bodies representing the aero and marine hobbies. From a safety point of view the aero problem needed priority and eventually the JRCUC reported that the 35MHz band had been allocated for sole aero use. It was not until 18 June 1986 that the Department of Trade and Industry issued a press release announcing that the 40MHz band had been allocated for the use of surface modelling. The original model control band of 27MHz was left as it was until CB radio was finally legalised in the UK and allocated it. However, five of the six original primary colours

were left for model control, including aero use, within the 27MHz band which is the current position.

Two mandatory conditions for the new band was that transmission had to be either FM or PCM. This meant that the 40MHz carrier wave was transmitted either Pulse Position Frequency Modulation or Pulse Code Modulation – PPFM or PCM. However, the greatest bonus was that thirty channels now available compared with the eleven of the old 27MHz band. (Appendix 1

The interior of an early proportional transmitter. Note the finned heatsinks. Thermal runaway was a serious problem for the early transistors. The crystal located at the top left-hand side was awkward to change.

An early receiver and servo compared with its modern counterpart (left).

lists in detail the use of the current three surface model control bands and the 1999 position regarding AM/FM.)

The IC '80s and the Computer '90s

As integrated circuits (ICs) became cheaper and more plentiful and the demand for smaller business computers with more powerful memories grew, once again the RC field benefited. Equipment manufacturers were able to design and produce equipment for a new breed of modellers – the helicopter enthusiast. Transmitters to control helicopters need interrelationships between functions that, at that time, no other model required. The equipment had to be totally reliable and free from internally-generated interference. These higher standards eventually filtered down into more modestly priced sets so that overall everyone benefited. Marine modellers were not slow to recognise the usefulness of multi-function sets and put them to good use with impressive examples of models with working features which today are very much taken for granted. Every aspect of the marine discipline gained, particularly in the competitive field. Yacht sail winches became more powerful and more accurate. The technology of the rechargeable battery – nicads – produced batteries with large capacities for the same physical size which in turn, with more efficient motors and electronic speed controllers, gave birth to 'fast electrics'. But what is possibly the most significant development of the 1990s was the recognition by manufacturers that marine radio control stood in its own right as a commercial market, and they therefore produced equipment specifically designed for marine use. Gone were the function identities of the aero world. It was left to the marine modeller to decide which function was controlled by the transmitter sticks etc. This period also saw the growth of radio-controlled cars which had similar control requirements to boats with the result that equipment became compatible and progress benefited both disciplines.

The latest computerised radios, where different model performance and settings can be stored for recall and adjustments can be performed whilst racing, seem a very long way away from those early days of one-valve push-button transmitters and it is fitting to acknowledge a large debt of gratitude to those early enthusiasts who with very limited resources showed what could be achieved. It would be invidious to name only a few so it is left with a plain 'Thank You' to all those who have justifiably earned a place in the annals of RC.

2

Radio Control Theory, Basic Systems and Fundamental Electronic Principles

Towards the end of the last chapter we saw the evolution of proportional control, establishing the principle of a continuous unbroken radio frequency link between transmitter and receiver. In marine terms, 'the hand is always on the tiller'. This link is called the carrier wave and when continuously modulated is the fundamental principle and common foundation of all modern Radio Control (RC) systems. It is the way in which the carrier wave is modulated – modified – to carry the control information to the receiver that can differ and cause confusion to the newcomer to RC. A basic understanding of permitted carrier waves and types of modulation will enhance appreciation of how RC works and ensure the correct identification of problems when they arise. Whenever discussion occurs within the RC and electronic world the newcomer is likely to be confused by the use of abbreviations and the misuse of terms which over the years have crept into use. Throughout this Manual where a common shorthand abbreviation is first used it will be preceded by the full term

and thereafter that abbreviation used, as RC above. The worst and most confusing is the term 'channel' when used to describe the number of functions a set of equipment is designed to control. Newcomers are understandably confused when a system is described as a 'four-channel' set when in fact it is a four-*function* set working a single channel within a specified Model Control Band. Throughout this book channel will only be used in connection

A basic two-function 27MHz set of equipment. Sets are also available for the 40MHz band but these are usually three-function.

The transmitter. Note the Servo Reverse feature on the lower left-hand side. See Chapter 3.

with a radio frequency band. However, before discussing the theory of RC it would be prudent to first look at the basic elements of the modern system.

The basic architecture

For the newcomer to marine RC the choice of the first system can be difficult when faced with the overwhelming choice of makes, features and technical jargon. The basic system is surprisingly simple – it is only the added features which cause confusion and if the wrong choice is made in the beginning the newcomer quickly becomes disenchanted and gives up. The basic system consists of a transmitter (TX), receiver (RX), two servos, a power supply for the TX, a power supply for the RX and servos and a switch harness to connect the RX and servos. Each element will be discussed in detail in the following chapters, so for now all that is needed is an understanding of the part each plays within the system. In any boat there are only two prime functions that need

controlling to enable the boat to behave in a disciplined manner. One is the rudder to control its direction and the other is the motive power that moves it. The simplest system then is a two-function TX which has a delicate umbilical radio cord with the RX. The TX transmits the control instructions to the RX on a channel in one of the bands available for marine radio control in the UK (see Appendix 1 which also includes USA frequencies and harmonised UK channels in Europe). The RX decodes the signals and moves the servos to the required position. The servos are the workhorses in the system. In the two-function system one will be the rudder control and the other will control the motive force. The various ways in which this second function can operate with the different motive forces will be discussed in Chapter 4. Up-grading from the basic two-function system, a multi-function system can be purchased with four-function being the most common. The ergonomic layout of a RC transmitter has its roots in the aeronautical discipline as we saw in Chapter 1. Full-size aircraft have a control column which can move to any position within a 360° circle. This system is repeated twice on a RC-TX and are known as the 'sticks'. These sticks control the first four functions on a multi-function transmitter, with each stick controlling two servos in the model. Moving the stick either straight up or down will activate one servo and moving it left or right the other servo. Diagonal movement will activate both servos with the movement equal if the stick is at 45°. Any other stick angle will move the servos in proportion to the stick angle from the centre which is the stick neutral and mid-position of the servo. The above is the basic principle of proportional control of all RC systems which can vary in detail and by manufacturer and will be discussed in

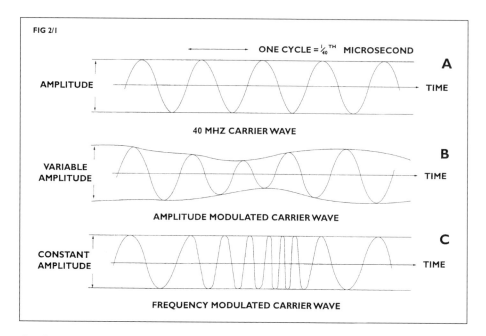

FIG 2/1

ONE CYCLE = $\frac{1}{40}$TH MICROSECOND

A

AMPLITUDE — TIME

40 MHZ CARRIER WAVE

B

VARIABLE AMPLITUDE — TIME

AMPLITUDE MODULATED CARRIER WAVE

C

CONSTANT AMPLITUDE — TIME

FREQUENCY MODULATED CARRIER WAVE

depth in Chapter 3. Every RC system has to equipped with a pair of components called crystals – one for the TX and one for the RX. It is illegal to interchange the TX with the RX crystal within a system and it is inadvisable to use one manufacturer's crystals in another make of RC equipment.

Modulation

This is the technical term for the way in which the carrier wave, Fig. 2/1A, is modified to carry the control instructions. We saw in Chapter 1 that the early systems had the carrier wave voltage in the transmitter rapidly switched on and off to create a pulse which the receiver detected and operated an electromagnetic mechanism. This developed into a continuous crystal-controlled carrier wave modulated by the control instructions. Prior to the introduction of the 40meg band it was technically and economically more viable to modulate the carrier wave by varying the magnitude of the carrier with the control instructions. This is amplitude modulation or AM for short. Fig. 2/1B shows the principle and the waveform where the frequency of the carrier is kept constant while its amplitude or strength is varied. The majority of 27meg equipment available on the second-hand market and currently manufactured equipment is AM.

All 40MHz equipment in the UK is FM – Frequency Modulation (however, see Appendix 1). FM transmissions are of a higher quality than AM and less prone to corruption and interference. FM is illustrated in Fig. 2/1C where the carrier waveform is varied a small amount either side of the centre frequency but the magnitude is constant. The modification of the transmission into control instructions for each output function of the receiver can be one of two systems. The most common system is Pulse Position Modulation (PPM) which will be found on all the AM 27meg sets and all the budget and medium-price FM 40meg sets. A number of higher priced FM 40meg sets will also feature a facility on the TX to switch the transmission from PPM to the second control system,

Pulse Code Modulation (PCM). These two systems each require a compatible receiver, either a PPM or PCM RX. It is not necessary to discuss in depth the technical differences of the two control systems but it is prudent for the reader to appreciate the subtle differences between them so that the choice of a system is an informed one.

With PPM the TX transmits a train of pulses to define the physical position of all functions controls at any one moment in time. The full range of a function control pulse is its width of 1.0 to 2.0mS, with 1.5mS being the mid position. Each function has its own pulse with typically a seven-function TX transmitting a train of seven pulses followed by a long synchronisation pulse of 6 to 8mS. This sequence is repeated continually, sending a stream of control data approximately every 20mS or 50 times a second. The receiver decodes the train of pulses ensuring each output function receives its correct pulse of a length of 1.0 to 2.0mS, reflecting the TX control position, every 20mS. A servo connected to an output will 'read' the pulse length and move its output horn to correspond to the stick position of the TX. Thus each output is continually

altering its position to mimic the originating position of the TX function – Pulse Position Modulation. However, if the data stream is corrupted in any way the whole receiver system collapses and the servos are left floundering in their last position. This is the difference between PPM and PCM. Where PPM is a 'follow-my-leader' system, PCM is a 'do as you are told' system where the function control positions on the TX are sent to the receiver as digital codes, and which are decoded as firm instructions to the servos which move accordingly. PCM can also program the RX to adjust the steering and power controls to a safe position in the event of a corrupted data stream being received.

The minimum basic equipment

A newcomer to marine modelling is surrounded with such an array of boat kits and RC equipment in the local model shop that an ill-informed choice can all too soon lead to frustration, disappointment and an unfinished project. It is understandable that the vision of controlling a large battleship with rotating turrets and firing guns, all controlled by an impressive set of multi-function RC equipment is tempting for the first project. However, a newcomer has to acquire many skills in building and sailing a successful RC model which can only come from a gentle learning curve and experience. The last thing that is required is complicated equipment which can and will cause problems for the inexperienced. The golden rule should be – keep it simple, keep it basic but allow for future growth and, most importantly, plan ahead. This aspect of planning, or not doing so, has been apparent to the author when visiting regattas and observing some superbly-finished models performing in an

A basic receiver with 'On-Off' switch harness, battery box and one servo connected. Note the receiver crystal, top middle. The absence of a charging lead on the switch harness means only dry cells can be used (not recommended). Also note the ball/socket servo connector.

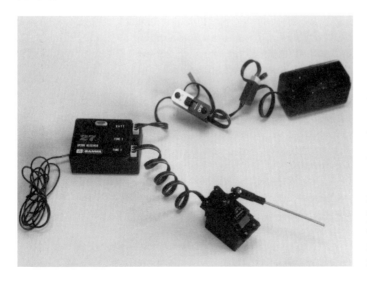

erratic way 'on the water'. Once back on dry land with the superstructure removed the cause is plain to see. The RC equipment and the drive batteries appear to have been held about 3ft above the hull, dropped in and secured where they fell – on some occasions not even secured but left laying loose. A reliable RC system has to be planned right from the beginning and in the case of the beginner, the purchase of first-time equipment must be made in conjunction with the purchase of the first model kit. There are a number of reasons why this is so and these will become evident throughout the following chapters. However, one will suffice to emphasise the point now. One of the major factors that determines the stability of a model boat when afloat is its overall weight and distribution of that weight. Most models require ballast to ensure the hull is down to its designed waterline along its entire length when afloat. The servos, RX and associated wiring harness will not affect this other than in a very small model. However, the RX battery and, if electrically-powered, the main drive battery will make a significant contribution to not only the total ballast required but also the fore and aft stability of the model if they are positioned incorrectly. This Manual is not the place to discuss this in detail other than to illustrate the need to be aware of this relationship at the time of purchase of RC equipment for the first time.

If the choice of entry model into marine modelling is a competitive one, such as yachting or fast boats powered either by internal combustion or electric units, then a minimum of a three-function set is adequate. If, however, the choice is a working scale model then a multi-function set should be considered if the budget allows it. Should there be financial constraints then it is preferable to identify the gear

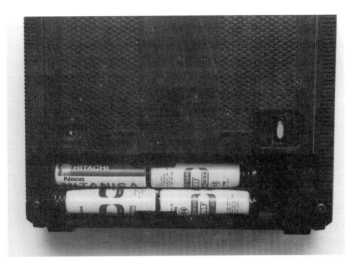

requirements with the model in mind and wait to purchase the RC equipment when funds allow. The model will take time to build to a point when the RC gear needs to be installed which ensures that the ultimate equipment choice has potential for future expansion into more ambitious projects. When purchasing RC equipment for the first time, identify all the makes available in your area and obtain brochures and as much technical detail as you can from the makers/importers so that you can discuss your requirements with your local model shop from a position of knowledge. Most suppliers, for example, will be sympathetic to a request not to purchase all the servos for, say, a seven-function set of gear when you initially only need two. There is a choice of three bands for RC model boats with 27MHz and 40MHz being the most popular (see Appendix 1). Although slightly more expensive 40MHz gear is strongly recommended rather than the cheaper 27MHz equipment, if only for the far wider choice of channels and the less chance of interference within the band. Second-hand gear is not recommended unless its history is fully known. As will be seen in further chapters RC equipment is prone to abuse and

The rear of a basic transmitter showing the battery compartment which can take either dry or rechargeable cells, the transmitter crystal on the right and the charging socket on the left.

maltreatment and can contain possible failures just waiting for the unwary purchaser. On balance, therefore, the purchase of the RC gear should be made well after the purchase of the model kit when the first-time builder is fully conversant with the model's control requirements. This is certainly true for a scale model but is also prudent for competitive boats where, for example, in a yacht the sail is controlled with either a sail winch or an arm fixed to a servo, which unless the boat is small would need to be upgraded in power to be able to control the sail effectively. As will be seen when servos are discussed, they have to be chosen with care for the duty expected of them. It is not always appreciated that a large heavy model needs a more powerful rudder servo, rather than a standard servo, to ensure efficient control when the model turns. If the motive power is electric then the choice of an electronic speed control (ESC) might be preferable instead of a servo. With such a variety of ESCs on the market the correct selection can only be made when the electric motor has been selected and its current requirements are known. From the foregoing it can be seen that all interrelationships need to be identified before equipment is purchased to ensure the budget is wisely spent.

Of course it is quite possible to purchase a simple kit or 'almost ready to float' model boat of whatever type appeals together with a basic set of two-function RC gear and be able to operate almost immediately. However, this leaves no room for progress in the future, particularly if the interest is in scale where the opportunity for the remote control of working features exists. If the interest lies in the competitive side of model boating then a mid-price range set of three- or four-function equipment can be purchased at the outset. Mid-price range means that the TX will have facilities which are not included in budget transmitters as will be seen in Chapter 3. What must be clearly understood is that there is no difference in the efficiency and reliability of the radio transmission and reception of modern budget-price transmitters and receivers and the more expensive sets. However, the first-time purchaser should seriously consider 40MHz equipment rather than 27MHz if only for the larger number of channels available. This is a very real convenience when competing in regattas. How this works will be discussed in Chapter 3.

Fundamental principles

For those with very deep pockets it is quite possible to expand a basic system into multi-function working with additional modules available from the manufacturer. Independent manufacturers of modules are also a source for compatible equipment so it is possible to achieve many working features on a scale boat without delving too deep into electric/electronic theory. However, much more satisfaction and economy can be achieved once basic principles are understood and applied to a project on a 'do-it-yourself' basis. This knowledge will also ensure that the newcomer fully understands the reasons for taking a particular way out of a problem and further ensures the overall system is reliable and safe. Within the discipline of marine modelling it is not always appreciated that although the voltage of the system is low there is a very real possibility of a serious accident occurring due to the high currents which can be obtained from the power supplies used. The relationship of voltage, current and resistance is expressed by Ohms Law which states: $I = {^E\!/_R}$ where I = current, E = voltage and R =

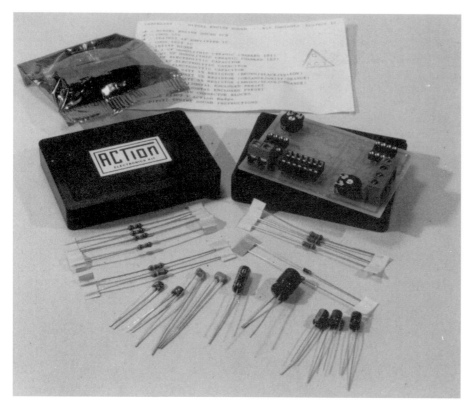

A typical selection of electronic components the marine worker will be working with as experience is gained. Anticlockwise from top left: anti-static bag containing IC chips; case cover; six resistors; four non-polarised capacitors; five electrolytic capacitors ;two diodes; three resistors and PCB with terminal blocks, IC sockets and two pre-set resistors. See Fig 13/3.

Below: Components used in marine electrics. 20mm fuseholders with an electronic fuse alongside the vertical fuseholder. Toggle switch and tag boards. Note the terminal block soldered to the two fuseholders.

resistance. From this simple equation any one of the three values can be obtained if the other two are known. In any electrical circuit think of the voltage as the 'pressure' of water in a pipe and the current as the volume of water and the resistance as the pipe restricting the 'flow' of the water. The unit of electrical pressure is well known as Volts with Amperes being the unit of current flow. Not so well known is the unit of electrical resistance. This unit, Ohms (usually denoted by the letter R in formulae such as Ohms Law above), is the opposition to the flow of current within a circuit. When a current flows through a circuit which has resistance, heat is generated and electrical power is dissipated within that resistance. The unit of electrical power is the Watt usually denoted by the letter W. The relationship between the three units Watts, Volts, and Current (amperes) is expressed by: $W = E \times I$. Since from

A very realistic two-paddle canoe controlled by a basic two-function set. Two servos operate the arms from within the Indian figures. Steering is achieved by individual servo control.

Ohms Law $E = I \times R$ and $I = {}^E/_R$ then power can also be calculated in two further forms: $W = E^2/R$ and $W = I^2 \times R$.

In the domestic environment volts, amperes and watts are mostly in whole numbers. As progress is made within RC it will quickly become evident that values less than one are commonplace. It is vital to fully understand how these values are expressed to prevent misunderstanding. The most common will be milli-volts and milli-amperes written as mV and mA. Milli is one thousand so 200mV is one-fifth of one volt. This can also be written as 0.2V. Milli-amperes are expressed in the same way with 200mA being one-fifth of one ampere. Complete understanding is essential particularly when dealing with power supplies and batteries where battery capacity is expressed in amp/hours or milli-amp/hours.

Fundamental principles would not be complete without discussing polarity, which is the 'way round' a battery is connected into a circuit. A battery has two terminals – one positive and one negative. A lamp connected to a battery will light either way it is connected. An electric motor will run one way when its positive and negative terminals are connected to the positive and negative battery terminals. Reverse the motor terminals and the motor will run in the opposite direction. Electronic equipment is not so accommodating. If connected to a power supply the 'wrong way round' the equipment can suffer instantaneous damage, often terminal, so the old carpenter's rule is essential: 'measure twice and cut once', and even then check again for correct polarity.

Components

Further chapters will discuss the use of electronic components. Some of these are polarity-conscious and where appropriate these will be identified. However, it is a wise precaution to always check for polarity when working with electronics as a mistake can turn out to be very expensive. To keep polarity in perspective, all RC equipment manufacturers ensure that it is impossible to connect the various components of a system together incorrectly. It is when this protection is broken that care is needed to maintain the original integrity of the system by planning and maintaining a record of workshop operations as the work proceeds. A prudent worker will always read the manufacturer's manual and installation instructions before even taking the item out of its box!

3

Transmitters and Receivers

In Chapter 2 basic TXs and RXs were discussed as tools controlling the minimum of functions in a model boat. This chapter will discuss the differences between a 'budget' system and the all-singing-and-dancing systems that have been developed mainly due to the requirements of the competition side of marine modelling. Firstly, however, it is necessary to discuss the parts that are common to all systems whether basic or extremely sophisticated.

Model control bands

In the UK there are four bands for the use of radio-controlled models regulated by the Radiocommunications Agency – an Executive Agency of the Department of Trade and Industry (see Appendix 1). These licence-free crystal-controlled frequency bands are:

26.96 to 27.28MHz General use. (Any RC Model)

40.66 to 41.00MHz Surface use. (Cars, Boats and misc. RC models)

458.5 to 459.5MHz General use. (Any RC Model)

34.995 to 35.255MHz Air use. (Exclusive to Aeronautical modelling)

Three of the four bands are colloquially referred to as 27megs, 40megs and 35megs with the fourth band rarely mentioned as there are very few commercial sets of this equipment in use in the UK. Note the 'use' of the bands. It cannot be emphasised too strongly that it is illegal for radio-controlled aircraft to use the 40meg band and conversely it is illegal for radio-controlled surface models to use the 35meg band. The original 27meg band is still available for model control but interference is possible from CB radio use.

Each band is divided into channels or frequencies. The 27MHz band has five recommended frequencies which 'should provide the best operating frequencies for model control' bearing in mind that the band has been allocated for CB and other use and it is possible that interference may occur.

A mid-range six-function highly specified set for 40MHz with dual conversion receiver. Sets like these are normally supplied with four servos and nicads for both transmitter and receiver. Note the front location for the crystal and the third lead on the switch harness for charging the receiver nicad. A maker's charger, not shown, is part of this set.

Users will find that many of the old frequencies outside the five recommended above are still being used and newcomers should approach using these with extreme caution. 27MHz band channels are identified by colours. Today's 40MHz band is divided into 34 channels and, as it is solely dedicated to surface modelling, it offers the best option for marine use. Each channel is identified by its centre frequency with the first channel being 40.665MHz and separated by 10kHz from the second – 40.675MHz – and so on up the band. In use a 40meg channel is identified on a transmitter with a flag carrying the last three frequency digits – 675, 685 etc. Coloured flags are used in the same way for the 27meg band. The rarely-used fourth band has 38 channels spaced from a centre frequency of 458.5 to 459.5MHz. Note that this band and 27megs is for general use including aircraft, whereas the 40meg band is solely for surface use. Appendix 1 describes in greater detail the use of the 27MHz band for marine RC and the possible interference from CB radio.

TXs and RXs

Whether it is a budget or a multi-function TX or RX the Radio Frequency (RF) element is, and has to be, of a very high quality. The only difference between a budget and a multi-function TX is that the RF circuitry is 'built in' in the budget TX and is usually a separate removable module in the more expensive TX. Whatever type they are, they both have one thing in common – removable crystals. The same principle applies to RXs. The RF element is of high quality and again fitted with a removable crystal. The difference between the budget and the expensive RX is very apparent when handled for the first

time. The budget RX will only have two or three output ports for servos whereas the multi-function RX might have up to eight output ports. Both will have a separate port for the battery power supply. No matter how simple or sophisticated a TX/RX combination is there are two factors which are vital to the successful transmission and reception of the RC signal – the power supplies and the crystals. TX and RX power supplies will be discussed in Chapter 5.

The crystal is literally the heart of either the TX or the RX. From the early days of radio the pioneers recognised that a crystal could be made to 'beat' or oscillate at a frequency and hold that frequency within very tight tolerances. This is why each band is able to accommodate a number of channels, keep the transmitted signal within each channel, and not interfere with its neighbouring channel either side. Conversely the RX will only receive its TX crystal-controlled signal and will remain unaffected by other signals. However, if a rogue signal is powerful enough it can 'blast' its way into the RX and cause interference which will be discussed in Chapter 6. It can be seen then that the system is not immune to failure and it is vital that crystals should be handled carefully and only those recommended by the manufacturer used if the equipment is going to work correctly and be in a position to reject interference if it occurs. For technical

A pair of 40MHz crystals. Note the identity is by frequency with the last three digits being the channel number 765, and the fact that the receiver crystal (left) is dual conversion.

reasons outside the scope of this Manual, each of the pair of TX and RX crystals operate at a different frequency. However, they are matched as a pair and identified as either TX or RX with the channel frequency or the channel number or the channel colour. Crystals should be handled very carefully and if either one is dropped on a hard surface both should be replaced. If a crystal is damaged internally it may appear to work satisfactorily but it is a failure just waiting to happen. If damaged and working it could be the cause of interference to other channels. Most marine workers, particularly if into competitions, will over a period of time acquire a stable of crystal pairs so that they can adjust their equipment for a particular slot or 'peg' when a number of boats are sailing at the same time. The use of the word 'peg' originates from the system of TX discipline used during competitions where each competitor is allocated a channel or frequency 'peg' for a round or heat. Only those with 'pegs' are permitted to switch their TXs on whilst the 'peg' is in their possession thus preventing interference and a possible accident. These 'pegs' are just spring clothes pegs either coloured for 27megs or numbered with the last three digits for 40megs. The 'stable' should be kept in a crystal 'tidy' box which is available from most model shops or advertised in marine magazines. Prior to the purchase of a first set of RC equipment the beginner is urged to find a local model boat club and join it. Most clubs run a members' frequency register for 40megs and consequently will advise a new member of a 'slot' personal to him or her. (Most clubs also have their own 'water' and so membership automatically provides somewhere to sail.) This first purchase should not occur until the user has a clear idea of what he intends for his modelling career and of

the difference between the various options and makes available. As emphasised in Chapter 2, unless there are severe budget restraints 40MHz equipment is to be preferred even as a basic set. It gives much more flexibility with its 34 channels, is exclusive to water- and land-based models and is far less prone to interference from any source. Ergonomically there are three types of current production designs in the mid- to multi-function range and two in basic TXs.

Basic twin stick – two function
The most common type is a TX which is held in both hands at an angle of some 30° to the horizontal with the thumb of each hand resting on the top of a 'stick' either side of the TX. In a basic economy TX the two sticks only move in one direction, the right-hand stick, Number 1, left and right and the left-hand stick, Number 2, up and down (most current production seems to be adopting this configuration but nevertheless a beginner could come across a make which is the other way round). Each stick has a spring-centred or neutral position which can be moved by adjacent 'trim' levers. However, which way round the sticks are does not alter the fact that the up-and-down stick is naturally the 'throttle' or sail control and the left-right stick is the rudder. Most makes provide for at least one of the sticks to be modified by removing the spring control and fitting a ratchet plate usually on the throttle. This feature enables the user to sail 'hands off', is less tiring and provides a much more precise movement of the stick in steps. Most TXs also have an external adjustment to the spring tension, using a screwdriver via a small hole in the casing.

Numbering the functions 1 and 2 enables the user to identify the correct socket on the RX to plug the servo or speed control into. It is here that the confusion regarding function/channel referred to at the beginning of Chapter 2 occurs as most manufacturers seem to persist in marking the sticks Channel 1 and Channel 2. Above the sticks and in the centre there is usually an indicator of the state of the TX batteries. This can be either a meter with coloured segments or a row of coloured lights – red-yellow-green. Once yellow/red is indicated, sailing should cease and the batteries either recharged or changed (see Chapter 5). Above the battery state indicator and fitted into the top of the TX will be the telescopic aerial which has to be fully extended when sailing. Midway between the sticks will be the neck strap attachment point with the TX power switch below it. Most budget TXs have their RF sections built into the internal circuit board and consequently the removable crystal will be sited somewhere on one of the case faces – usually near the bottom on the front.

A feature that is becoming common to budget equipment is Servo Reverse. This is probably one of the most useful facilities to have appeared in recent years. In its 'Normal' condition a servo output disc will rotate clockwise when the TX stick is moved to the left and anti-clockwise when moved to the right. Without Servo Reverse the worker is stuck with fitting the servo one way round. With a large hull and plenty of room this is not a major problem but it can become one when space is limited. The control of a throttle on an IC engine is another instance where reversing the servo solves the direction the TX stick is moved to increase forward speed. The facility on the TX is usually a small slide switch set below the surface of the case to prevent accidental operation. It will have two positions – NOR and REV – and the function (Channel) number.

The back of the TX will have a removable cover for access to the power supply which more than likely in a budget TX will be dry batteries. Some makes offer the option for upgrading to rechargeable nicads and consequently a charging socket will be provided usually on one end of the TX. Battery options and management will be discussed in Chapter 5.

Pistol grip or steerwheel two function
Originally introduced for model cars this design is becoming popular with fast electric and IC (Internal Combustion [engines]) boat competitors. The user holds the TX in the left hand with the index finger 'locked' into a double-sided spring-loaded trigger. Squeezing the trigger will cause the

The six functions have servo reverse and four have servo response adjustments. Note the identification of the functions using CH1, CH2,) etc. See the beginning of Chapter 2.

boat to move forward and pushing it away causes the boat to move astern. This design makes spring-loading mandatory so ratchet conversion is not available. In the steerwheel design, the right hand steers the boat via the steerwheel in the conventional way as if standing at a ship's wheel looking forward. Some users claim the system is more 'natural' than the twin-stick layout while others say there is little or no difference. It is a matter of personal choice. One advantage the steerwheel has is that in use the aerial, when fully extended, naturally assumes an approximately 30° angle to the horizontal which is the optimum for efficient reception by the RX. A TX aerial must never be pointed directly at the boat as this is the weakest RF 'coupling' between the two. The one major difference between the two types is the steerwheel telescopic aerial which when not in use is detachable and 'parked' in a slot within the TX body. In all other respects a budget steerwheel TX usually has the same features as a twin-stick TX, such as Servo Reverse, upgrading to rechargeable nicads with a charging socket

and coloured light indication of battery state. Because it is a steerwheel design the trims will be rotary knobs and not levers. The neck strap attachment is of course not required with a pistol-grip TX.

Mid to multi-function twin stick

It is this group that offers the most choice with three ergonomic designs and a variety of function options that can be very confusing to the first-time user. To the Twin Stick and Steerwheel TXs described above must be added the Console TX which is more popular on the Continent than in the UK where to the author's knowledge only one importer offers it. The fundamental difference of the Console TX is the way it is supported by the user and its shape. It still has twin sticks, meter and power switch etc, but no neck attachment facility. It can be held in both hands with the thumbs operating the sticks. However, the preferred method is to use a moulded fitted tray, available from the manufacturer, which has a two-point fitting strap hung around the neck of the user. This leaves the hands free to operate the sticks and the many auxiliary switches etc, as required. These switches are located in an angled upstand at the back of the TX as it lays flat in its tray. This upstand also carries the telescopic aerial at an angle of 35° to the horizontal, which never changes during operation, with the benefit of the best RF coupling between TX and RX.

The more common Multi-function Twin Stick TX has the same fundamental layout as the basic TX but with different stick numbering. The major difference is that each stick can move freely in any direction. The right-hand stick when moved left to right will control Function 1 and moved straight up and down will control Function 2. However, if it is moved in any other direction both functions will respond.

A console-type eight-function transmitter which can be expanded to an additional eight servo and eight switched functions when funds allow. The transmitter is equipped with a twin-stick unit (see Chapter 9).

The display screen of a sophisticated three-function computer transmitter intended for high level competition (see Chapter 20).

For example if 1 and 2 controlled rudder and throttle, moving the stick to the top left-hand side would cause the boat to accelerate ahead whilst turning to the left or port and if moved to bottom right the boat would move astern whilst turning to the right or starboard. The arrangement is known as gimbal mounted and enables the user to 'mix' functions 1 and 2 in any proportion required or operate them individually. The left-hand stick is the same but is now numbered 3, up and down, and 4, left to right. This four-function (channel) is probably the most common TX in use. However, fast becoming popular is the three-function (channel) basic TX which has the third function (Auxiliary) in the form of an On-Off switch or a rotary control controlling, for example, a boat's siren, lights or a second sail.

The four-function TX is also available extended up to seven functions in some makes and eight in others. These additional functions are available either as two-way 'On-Off' switches, three-way 'On-Off-On' switches, rotary controls and linear slider controls. Chapter 14 will discuss in detail how all these additional functions can be used by the marine worker to operate many working features in a scale boat. For those whose interest lies in the competitive side of the hobby, three- or four-function equipment will suit all their needs as long as the TX has further refinements as discussed in Chapter 4. It is these refinements that can cause so much confusion if the beginner has not fully understood the foundation on which any RC system is assembled and operated.

Receivers – assembly and operation

The modern Receiver (RX) is simplicity itself, having nothing to adjust and requiring only a power supply, its aerial installed for reception and the servos plugged into it. However, the way in which this simple black box works needs to be understood before a system is assembled and operated. In Chapter 1 mention was made of the introduction of the superheterodyne principle in the early 1950s. This 'superhet' technique enables the RX to satisfy three main requirements for satisfactory reception, namely (i) high sensitivity to the reception of a weak signal, (ii) good selectivity for the selection of the correct channel from among the other channels, which could be stronger, on adjacent frequencies, and (iii) rejection of spurious signals, *ie* interference.

The incoming signal is very small in value and has to be amplified to a level where it can be used by the servo electronics to perform 'work', for example moving the rudder. Amplifying the MHz carrier is possible but is expensive requiring close tolerance components and manufacture. 'Superhet' works by converting the incoming 40MHz RF carrier into a much lower frequency. The modulation then has to be abstracted from the carrier and amplified to a level where it can be used by the servo electronics to perform 'work'. This will be achieved with at least two stages of amplification, making the superhet design of high-gain amplifiers economic and reliable. Converting to one lower intermediate frequency, usually 455KHz, is Single Conversion and is the majority system in modern RXs. One of the benefits of conversion is the rejection of interference and when this is really troublesome at some waters Dual Conversion RXs, with two intermediate frequencies of 10.7MHz and 455KHz, are available which usually solves the problem. However, for reasons outside the scope of this Manual a Dual Conversion crystal is required for the RX. The TX crystal will be the same for either a single or dual RX system. Most manufacturers/importers will offer Dual Conversion RXs within their 40meg range with a single crystal or paired with a TX crystal. It is worth reiterating the earlier advice to only use manufacturers' recommended crystals and not those 'bargain buys' sometimes to be found on stalls at regattas. What may appear to be a 'bargain' could end up as a very expensive accident when control suddenly fails and a fast boat becomes a lethal projectile heading for the bank and a small child. All manufacturers identify their crystals usually with a tag carrying an alphanumeric code. Frequent use will weaken this tag and it is worthwhile to create an inventory and add your own identification in the event of the tag breaking and becoming lost. Each Dual Conversion RX crystal will be identified either by a coloured band on the tag or as part of the code.

A RX aerial is always a multi-stranded single insulated cable approximately 1mm in diameter and about a metre long, dimensions which may vary between manufacturers. It should always be treated with care and generally should never be shortened although there are exceptions which will be discussed in Chapter 16. It will exit from the crystal end through at least 40mm of sleeving to give mechanical strength and protection. Tight bends and kinks should be avoided at all times to prevent breaking the internal strands. The crystal is plugged into the RX and is not polarised. Some makers provide the crystal within a carrier which although not waterproof does provide some degree of sealing, while others use a soft plastic cover for the crystal which fits snugly within the RX. The other end of the RX has the numbered function socket outputs plus one other marked B for the power input. These sockets are polarised with each make having its own method of achieving this. Each socket has three pins, carrying a positive and negative supply and the 'signal' information, which mates with a plug attached to a three-core flat cable connected into, initially, a servo.

All current production of 27MHz equipment is basic two-function with a transmission system of PPAM – Pulse Position Amplitude Modulated (see Chapter 2). Current production of 40MHz basic two- and three-function-equipment is PPFM – Pulse Position Frequency Modulated. However, a number of three-function computer sets, to be discussed in Chapter 20, have appeared with a switched facility of PPFM/PCM – Pulse Code Modulation.

It is the multi-function group that offers the greatest choice either as manufacturers' sets or creating your own set from a catalogue. Although marine-orientated sets are available, the majority of the equipment is still biased towards aircraft so the possibility of assembling a set for marine use is attractive. The basic operation of any function is to move a servo arm from centre to maximum throw either way. Latest RC technology can now offer the user a number of options of changing that basic movement either during operational use or by pre-setting the TX. The understanding and use of these and other options will influence the final choice of the TX/RX combination and will be discussed in the next chapter on servos. However, to conclude this chapter, assuming the budget only runs to a basic set of equipment, how is this assembled and operated straight from the box?

All basic two/three-function sets are sold for dry battery operation although, as previously discussed some TXs have the facility to upgrade to rechargeable nicads. All dry single cells, when new, have a terminal voltage of 1.5V. Due to their different chemistry single-cell nicads when fully charged and under load have a terminal voltage of 1.2V. A basic two/three-function set will have a battery box to take eight AA size cells inside the TX and a RX battery box and lead taking four AA size cells. Both boxes are wired with the cells in series producing $8 \times 1.5 = 12V$ for the TX and $4 \times 1.5 = 6V$ for the RX when dry cells are used. If individual nicads are used then $8 \times 1.2 = 9.6V$ for the TX and $4 \times 1.2 = 4.8V$ for the RX. Two things arise from these simple sums. Firstly, it demonstrates the wide operational voltage of RC equipment and secondly, it introduces the first-time user to the two foundation rechargeable nicad packs within RC which will be discussed in Chapter 5. The physical arrangement of TX power supplies can vary from make to make. Some favour a 'built-in' box to take dry cells only or 'built-in' with a charging jack to take separate nicads. Others will have a separate removable box which is replaced with a nicad pack. Supplied with a basic set is a RX switch harness which will have two leads if the set is dry and three if it is rechargeable. Initial assembly and testing should be done with fresh sealed alkaline dry cells or fully-charged nicads. When using separate cells, carefully check the polarity as they are inserted. No harm will occur to the equipment if some are the wrong way round. It just won't work!

Testing can be done on the 'bench' with the TX aerial retracted but with the RX aerial fully unwound. Assembly of the RX, switch harness, battery power supply and servos is straight-

Six-function equipment makes multi-sail control possible.

forward following the maker's manual. Mistakes cannot occur as all the connections are polarised and it is worthwhile to understand how this is achieved on the make purchased. On no account should any plug/socket connection be forced. The RX switch may be marked ON-OFF either on its top face or on a removable fixing plate. If not, or the plate is the wrong way round, the OFF position is always the battery end of the switch. Before connecting the harness into the RX make sure the supply is OFF. When testing RC equipment for the first time, get into the habit of always switching the TX on first then the RX. After testing switch the RX off first then the

TX. This safety regime prevents out-of-control boat accidents if the reverse procedure is used.

That first test

Lay out the RX, servos, switch harness and battery box on a piece of, say, 5mm board securing the items with 'Blu-Tack' or a similar product which can be removed later without damage to the item. Using the discarded cardboard tube from a used kitchen roll wind the aerial on to it securing both ends with 'Blu-Tack'. Secure this to the board. From the horns supplied select a disc and fit it to the servo. Hold the disc between forefinger and thumb when tightening the retaining screw. Be very careful not to strip the thread in the servo spindle. 'Just Tight' is about right. Identify and set both stick trims to the mid position. Switch on the TX then the RX. *Do not extend its aerial.* Move each stick in turn and note the direction the servo disc moves. Move each trim in turn and note how, although the overall servo movement does not change, one end can increase at the expense of the other end. If servo reverse is available operate it and note the effect. These initial tests should not take longer than five to ten minutes as fully fresh/charged batteries are needed for the next test which you will need some assistance for and is best conducted outside. Operate one of the sticks and note with your assistant the servo disc position. With the TX aerial still collapsed, walk slowly away from the RX until your assistant sees the servo disc moving intermittently. In RC terms this is 'glitching'. Measure the distance – it should be beyond 10 metres – and note it for the future. This is a Range Test and should be carried out on a regular basis (see Chapter 19). Extending the aerial will cure the glitching.

4

Servos

The *Oxford English Dictionary* defines a servo as 'a powered mechanism producing motion or forces at a higher level of energy than the input level'. It is this definition that is frequently overlooked when choosing a servo for a particular task in a RC boat. All too often too much is expected of the 'Standard' servo which has been chosen for a task beyond its designed parameters and it is condemned when it inevitably fails. The maker comes in for it as well, being heatedly castigated for producing 'rubbish' when in fact the fault lies with the marine worker in not selecting the right 'tool' for a particular job. Once again the root of the problem lies in the aero influence upon the design parameters of servos in the past. Compared to marine work the power, *ie*

torque, required to move a control surface in an average model aeroplane is small. This aero influence created the 'Standard' servo supplied with the majority of sets of RC equipment. This is adequate for rudder control in small to medium-sized boats, auxiliary duties in scale boats, and sail control in small yachts. However, as model boating has become more popular manufacturers have recognised its needs and developed more powerful servos for specific tasks. These tasks and the servos available for them will be discussed in this chapter but before that it is necessary to understand how a servo works, its installation and common principles to ensure a trouble-free working life.

The Standard servo

As was seen in Chapter 2, present at each of the RX output sockets will be a continuous signal mimicking the position of the relevant control on the TX. What is now required is to turn this signal into 'work' to control the boat. This is achieved by a servo which comprises a small Printed Circuit Board (PCB), an electric motor driving a chain of gears and a potentiometer, all terminating in an output shaft. This shaft is splined to accept a variety of disks and arms also known as horns. These all have 'take off' points mechanically connected to the function to be controlled. The purpose of the gear train is to convert the high

A Standard and Micro servo compared with a 20p coin. The Micro (left) is 28mm long.

revolutions of the motor down to a practical speed, moving the 'horn' through an arc which can vary, according to servo type, from 90° to 180° and continuous for a number of turns on the drum of a sail winch. The total arc will mimic the total movement of the TX control including trims. The potentiometer, variable rotary resistance, is driven by the gear train and compares the horn position with the signal which is defining the TX control position. When both match, the motor is stopped with the horn repeating the control position. Most manufacturers publish their servo technical specifications which will list the servo speed over the arc degrees. Most will quote half the arc, *ie* from centre to extreme movement. For example: 0.5sec/60° or: Speed/45°-0.20sec. When considering servo speeds it is important to also know two other factors, the voltage at which the speed was measured and the load which is always assumed to be the published torque of the servo. Without exception all modern RXs and servos are designed to work over a voltage range of 4.8V to 6.0V. This is to accommodate both rechargeable and dry power supplies. Some listings will state the voltage at which the figures were taken. If not, always assume it was 4.8V bearing in mind that at 6.0V both the speed and torque will increase. The torque will be quoted in kilograms/centimetre (kg/cm). General-purpose servos, *ie* the so-called Standard, will have a total arm deflection of twice the speed degrees – taking the above examples 120° and 90°. However, specialist servos will often list a total deflection figure, *eg* 1 × 180° (incl Trim) or 1×130°–180°.

Servo motors, bearings and gears

Motor type, output shaft bearings, gear train material and waterproofing are also features where a choice has to made. The standard or general-purpose servo will be fitted with a three-pole motor, plastic gears usually nylon and plain bearings. These three design features will dictate the accuracy of the output arm position, reflecting the transmitted signal position, and the price of the servo. Most reputable makes will have a degree of water-tightness in the form of gaskets between the case joints. Some makes also offer servos with full water-proofing. Other unknown makes offering cheap servos will not even have fitted gaskets. The Middle Class range will have five- to seven-pole motors with metal gears and miniature ball bearings. Special Application or Pro-fessional servos will feature coreless motors, metal gears, ball bearings and extreme accuracy with high speed and high torque. This is why there can be a price differential of ten to twelve times between Standard and top of the range servos.

Servo potentiometer

The last technical feature that is worth discussing is the method of drive to the potentiometer ('pot'). This component is probably the most important part of the servo as it determines the position the output arm takes up as the electronic 'match' occurs. It has a rotary carbon track over which sliding contacts feed a value back to the PCB. The value between each end of the track and the contact is very high so a small movement of the contact could represent a relatively large movement of, for example, the rudder. It is essential therefore that there should not be any vibration on the 'pot' that could cause unwanted movement between contact and track. What is required is an indirect drive from the gear train to the 'pot', thus decoupling the motor

Two examples of using servo trays – vertical and horizontal. Note the mechanical connection to the rudder tiller. This is not recommended as it is difficult to adjust and prone to failure.

vibrations. The majority of modern makes are indirect drive but some cheap servos are not. The use to which a servo is put will determine the choice of motor, bearings and gears. These options will be discussed in the detail usage that follows this general overview. However, there is no choice for the 'pot' drive so it is down to the user to enquire of the maker what system is used. Indirect drive is strongly recommended for all servos regardless of what duty they are required for. Most makers/importers will be only too happy to provide this information.

Servo case size

As far as the author is aware there is no formal agreement between manufacturers regarding the size of a servo case. However, most of the major makes are producing case sizes which are compatible with each other within a millimetre or two. Certainly the overall design with fixing lugs at either end is now common with fixing centres compatible with each other. The output shaft dimension to one end is also

approximately compatible but does need checking when considering alternative makes either in the design stage or as maintenance replacements. The fixing lugs are designed to accept two rubber grommets with brass inserts at either end. This fixing system is anti-vibration and again originates from the aero discipline. Generally speaking it is not required for marine work and should only be used if there is the possibility of severe vibration occurring. Bolting a servo down firmly will make for a more accurate movement of rudder, sail and power control. If, however, the grommet is used the brass insert should be inserted with its lip next to the mount with a washer underneath the head of the mounting screw. The purpose of the insert is to ensure the grommet is not screwed down too tightly.

Mounting servos

Secure mounting of any servo is vital to prevent future failures, particularly rudder and power control servos. With these last two it is essential that the mounting platform material is stiff enough to prevent movement. Wood is far from ideal as the 'meat' around the screw fixings is minimal due to the closeness of the 'cut-out' for the servo body. It is therefore far better to use 3mm sheet plastic or 16g alloy sheet which in turn can be fixed to wood bearers. Double-nutted metal screws are preferred to secure the servo to its mount. All the major makers offer servo trays in a variety of designs and are worth considering.

An exploded view of the internal parts of a servo.

Servo linkage

The position of the servo and the linkage to the function is crucial to ensure the maximum accuracy of function movement that the system is capable of. If the linkage has too much play in it this will reduce accuracy and if too tight it will increase the servo current and waste RX battery power. Wherever possible servos should be mounted parallel to the linkage so that the servo fixings are the maximum distance apart to counteract the torque in operation. The linkage is connected to, say, the rudder in a similar way to the connection to the servo horn using one of a series of holes in the tiller arm. The selection of which hole to use at each end has to be done with care so that the servo does not 'over-drive' the function and strain the whole assembly. Examining a typical horn, it can be seen that the further away from the centre a hole is the greater the linear

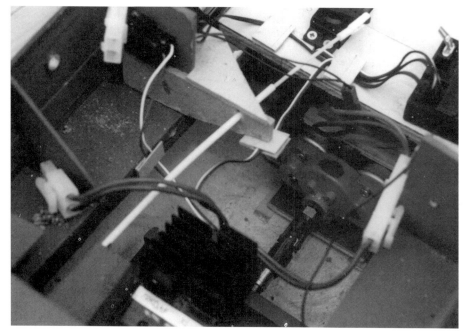

A Bowden cable connection from the top right servo curving down to bottom left. Note the haphazard wiring and the RX aerial laying across power wiring. All the ingredients for possible operational 'glitching' and ultimate failure.

Double mechanical connections are favoured by some workers for added strength and accuracy. The 'Z' type connector shown here is not recommended. Note the servo-operated micro switch and the close proximity of the 'clean' to the 'dirty' wiring. See Chapter 6.

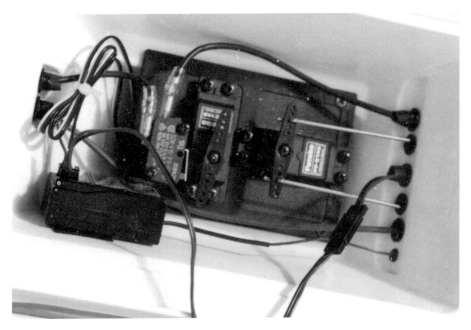

movement of the linkage rod will be. By careful selection the servo arc of 120° can be reduced to a rudder throw of 70°. The amount of total servo movement can also be adjusted electronically in the TX by a process called Adjustable Travel Volume (ATV), but this feature is only available in the more comprehensive and expensive equipment. This and other servo control features will be discussed later on in this chapter. Regardless of ATV etc, it is more prudent initially to set up the servo/function relationship correctly in the beginning and use ATV etc, as a bonus rather than to correct a poor design and installation. The majority of servo/function linkage can be a single arm but with a large rudder a double linkage, a rod either side of centre, will provide a balanced system with better control. The overall length of the linkage should be kept as short as is practical, within the design of the hull, to prevent whip and subsequent poor control. A solid metal rod not less than 2mm in diameter with a ball and socket connection each end is preferred as this system will have

little or no slack in it. The rod is threaded at both ends and each end cuts a thread into the plastic sockets as they are screwed on. A ball is fitted to the servo horn and the function connection with a metal screw and double-nutted. Each socket 'snaps' on to the balls. This system produces a linkage without any slack but is free in operation without adding to the servo current. The rod length should be such that either plastic socket can be screwed in or out to 'fine tune' the final distance between servo and function.

Alternative fixings

The alternative fixings of either a clevis which has a pin sprung into the horn hole, or a simple Z bend formed into the rod and inserted into the horn, should be avoided as in use these will twist and bind adding to the servo load resulting in an increase in servo current. Any twist in the ball and socket system will be taken up by the ball/socket at each end without such an increase in servo current. For really difficult installations where it is impossible to achieve a straight line run between servo and function, a Bowden cable can be used. This is a stranded cable within a tough, usually nylon, sheath with a metal thimble bearing at either end. Each sheath end has to be firmly secured with the ability to swivel, as the cable will move off its centreline during the horn arc. Each end of the cable is soldered into a brass connector which can itself be soldered onto a short piece of threaded rod connected to a ball/ socket horn fixing. This system enables a curved 'run' between servo and function and can achieve a 90° turn as long as the curve is gentle. Sharp bends will inevitably lead to high servo current and complete failure when the cable binds solid. In use, each end should be inspected frequently and kept well lubricated with thick grease. Bowden cables, ball and socket connectors and threaded steel rods can all be obtained from model shops.

Servo leads

It is not often realised that the most vulnerable and failure-prone area in a RC/RX installation is the point where each servo is plugged into the RX. If these connections are at all suspect then failure will surely follow. This area is the one that is most used and abused with all the plugging-in of the servos during the lifetime of the RX. The RX battery which is providing power for all the functions is also plugged in here and it will become a very crowded area when up to nine leads are involved. The difficulties and damage arise when a plug has to be removed. This should be done by holding the lead between forefinger and thumb about 2in above the plug and pulling up in a straight line with a firm movement. Never pull to one side or attempt to ease the plug out

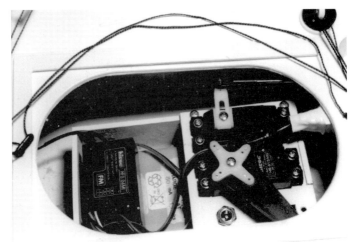

with a tool. The connection is three round pins mating inside three square sockets which can easily be strained on all four sides making a loose connection which will be subject to failure. Of the three within each plug one is the signal conductor and the other two are positive and negative power to the servo. Whatever the make, the plugs are polarised to prevent a wrong connection. This polarising is by physical design of the plug/socket with either a rib on one side to mate with a slot in the RX or a chamfer on both sides again mating with the socket for correct insertion, or an irregular-shaped plug which only fits one way.

The three conductors are arranged as a flat cable 3.5mm wide × 1.15mm. The signal conductor is usually one of the outer conductors and coloured white or yellow. The other two are always coloured red and black, positive and negative, but differ between makes on their relationship to the signal conductor. The most common is the 'Futaba' type with the red, positive, in the middle and the black, negative, on the outside. Other makes have the negative in the middle. Each conductor is stranded and crimped, never soldered, into its individual socket. These square sockets are each secured

Ball and socket connection on the top servo. Note the adjustment available for decreasing the servo horn arc. The two mating surfaces are serrated and lock together for security once the horn screw is tightened. The other servo is a sail arm type.

within the plug by three 'fingers' moulded into the housing. By careful use of a thin bladed jeweller's screwdriver each 'finger' can be raised, the socket released and the three conductors pulled clear of the housing. They can now be re-arranged to suit a different signal-positive-negative-relationship. However, this must be done with great care, planned on paper first and only as a last resort as any error can prove very expensive.

It is a worthwhile exercise for a beginner to remove one socket to appreciate the clamping action to the pin and how any lateral force on the socket will damage this internal clamp. Any electronic connection will offer resistance, however small, to the passage of current. A loose connection increases resistance with consequential loss of power and performance. Standard and Middle Class servos are fitted with tin-plated sockets which if properly treated and maintained will give years of service. To achieve even lower contact resistance one manufacturer offers Professional servos equipped with gold-plated sockets which ideally should be mated with gold-plated pins in the RX. It is doubtful if the use of gold-plated equipment is of any advantage to the marine worker and is only mentioned for completeness.

ATV and Dual Rates

Adjustable Travel Volume (ATV) or End Point Adjustment (EPA) and Dual Rates (DR) are features which have been available with computer TXs for some time and are now appearing in more modestly-priced equipment in increasing numbers. ATV, or EPA which explains the feature rather better, is an electronic alternative on the TX for reducing the total movement over the servo arc equivalent to selecting appropriate holes in the horns at either end of the linkage. In other words the maximum travel of the servo is reduced whilst the two end points of the RX stick travel remain the same. DR follows the same principle but in this case the user has an additional optional setting, selected by an adjustable potentiometer, of reduced servo travel which can be selected at the flick of a switch. This feature virtually desensitises, say, a rudder control in a very tight turn when racing at high speed, thus preventing possible capsize. The DR 'pot' can be either a preset which has to adjusted with a screwdriver blade prior to use on the water or the 'pot' is connected to a wheel which can be accessed during sailing. Pistol Grip or Steerwheel TXs (described in Chapter 2) are now becoming available fitted

Two examples of connectors which are not recommended. These lack adjustment which is vital in this model which is steam-driven. Note the RX switch and battery left lying in the bilge (top) and the RX aerial laying across hot steam areas (bottom). All potential failures waiting to happen.

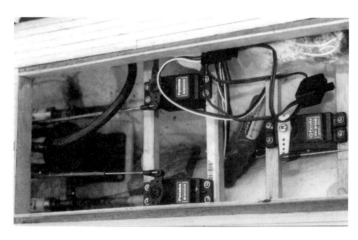

with a DR wheel which can be operated by the thumb holding the pistol grip. The DR 'IN-OUT' switch is also located adjacent to the DR wheel making instant adjustment and use very efficient.

Mixing

A newcomer will come across this feature when comparing specifications of equipment in the Mid to Multi Function Twin-Stick group discussed in Chapter 3. Mixing is the ability to control two servos from one function of the TX. It is usually programmable with the ratio of movement of one servo to the other variable. Although designed specifically for aero use Chapter 14 will discuss how this very useful feature can be used in marine work.

Servos in detail

For scale

There is no doubt that whatever the type, size or motive power the most important servo in any vessel in marine modelling is the rudder servo. If the vessel's direction cannot be controlled there is no point in sailing. However obvious this truth is, what is not always accepted is that this servo still needs to be chosen with care so that it is compatible with the duties expected of it. Once a mass is moving in a straight line considerable force is required for the mass to change direction, force which is further affected by weather conditions. This force is made up of many components and to analyse them mathematically is outside the scope of this Manual. However, as long as it is recognised that a relationship exists between the displacement, *ie* the total weight of the model, the type of craft it is – slow-moving tug or fast patrol vessel etc – the area of the rudder and

the servo power, *ie* torque, a judgement can be made regarding servo choice using a very approximate 'Rule of Thumb'. Before going any further a word or two is needed regarding published performance figures for servos. What may be the torque figure for one maker's 'Standard' servo will not necessarily be the same for another make. The following torque values are used as benchmarks as an aid to making an informed choice and not as an indication of the power needed to control a particular mass or sailing circumstances which are changing all the time.

For slow-moving scale boats not exceeding 5kg with a total rudder area not exceeding 15cm² a Standard servo with a minimum torque of 3.0kg/cm will be more than adequate. For larger slow-moving boats and fast boats exceeding 5kg with rudder areas greater than 15cm² it is prudent to upgrade the servo to a torque of at least 5.0kg/cm plus ball race bearings. Upgrading the servo will not only improve the sensitivity of the steering but during the turn considerable back pressure is exerted through the linkage into the servo motor which responds by drawing more current to maintain its position. In extreme conditions the servo will be driven backwards as the back pressure overcomes the torque creating a large rise in servo current which could lead to unnecessary depletion of the RX battery capacity at best and at worst total failure.

With displacements over 5kg not only are ball race bearings recommended but linkages themselves should be of a stronger quality and stiffness with appropriate stronger connections. Bear in mind that when upgrading servos the torque figures are those achieved at 4.8V and sometimes increased torque for borderline cases can be obtained by upgrading the whole RX system to 6.0V or even higher as will be seen when servos for sail are discussed. All the above recommendations are for single rudder boats so it is not unreasonable to ask 'how about multi-rudder boats'?

Experience has shown that displacement will probably be the determining factor in upgrading the rudder servo and as it is likely that multi-rudder boats will be above 5kg the additional rudder areas can be ignored. Rudder servos in scale boats normally work in a dry environment but there is always the possibility that ingress of water can occur especially in models with a low freeboard and a high scale speed, such as naval vessels. It is hard to justify the use of a waterproof servo on cost grounds as these can be up to five times as expensive as a non-waterproof servo. The answer is regular inspection, immediate removal and drying-out in an airing cupboard in severe cases and replacement if performance indicates all is not well. Remember that any doubtful servo can be stripped down, cleaned, re-greased and used on other non-safety duties (see Chapter 19).

Where a scale boat is powered by an electric motor it has to be controlled to achieve a realistic 'on the water' performance. This will be covered in detail in Chapter 9, including a group of electric power controllers which are mechanical and require a servo to operate. This servo, together with the controller, is usually mounted as close to the motor and the power supply as is practical within the design of the hull. Mechanical Speed Controllers (MSC) comprise of a resistive PCB with contacts moved through an arc by a servo. The PCB is either mounted directly on top of the servo or remote with a linkage similar to a rudder installation. As with a rudder servo the MSC servo must be mounted firmly with quality linkage to reduce slack to a minimum. If using a remote MSC the servo mounting can be lengthened to include the PCB. The design of the mounting should also provide for the remote type PCB to be fixed flat to prevent warping. Considerable care is required to set up the amount of movement and the centring of the MSC contacts. This is where the facility of ATV discussed earlier in this chapter is invaluable. See Chapter 9 for more detail on warping and setting up.

For sail

Sail is the oldest form of marine model activity and ironically is the one that possibly tests RC equipment to its maximum in both performance and reliability. The force and stress imposed upon the rudder servo and a sail arm servo or a servo winch by a highly tuned racing machine in severe weather conditions are considerable. Couple this with the need to keep the electronics within the equipment dry to ensure reliable operation and it can be seen that the correct choice of equipment is vital. However, this does not apply right across the board in sail but it serves to establish a high benchmark which can be scaled down as the need arises. All sail vessels need a rudder servo so, starting with competition yachts, the first parameter to satisfy is to ensure the servo is watertight. This will rule out the Standard servo and increase the servo cost by a factor of more than four, so some budget-conscious workers prefer to use a Standard servo and replace it if and when performance falls off or it fails. There are other advantages in using a watertight servo – they are usually better equipped internally to withstand the stress of use with a more powerful motor, ball bearings, high resolution and a torque of 5.0kg/cm. For those yachtsmen who do not compete, preferring just to

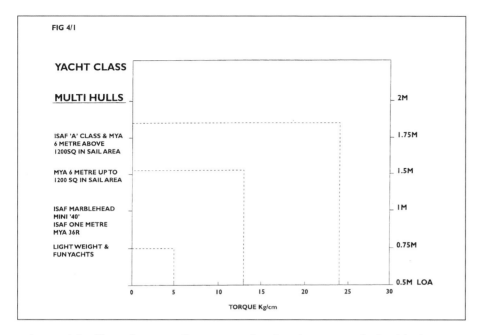

FIG 4/1

enjoy social sailing, the cost of a water-tight servo is hard to justify and a Standard servo will fill the bill for yachts up to 5000cm² sail area. Above that it would be prudent to use a servo with a torque of 5.0kg/cm. Scale sailing is becoming increasing popular with many examples of Thames barges, similar work boats and multiple-masted sailing ships appearing at regattas. For this group the Standard servo for the rudder is ideal although if the hull length is in excess of 1.5m a servo with a torque of 5.0kg/cm is advisable.

All sailing vessels require control of the sails and it is in this area where tremendous progress has been made in the design and production of economic sail servos and drum winches by RC and small specialist manufacturers since the emergence of the first servo-driven drum winch in the mid-1970s. A Sail Servo or Lever Arm Winch has a long arm fitted to its output shaft instead of the usual horn or disc. The arc of movement is usually the same as a servo – 120° – although one manufacturer, 'hitec', offers a sail arm servo with 140° arc. A servo drum winch has a drum

fitted to its output shaft with the servo electronics modified to rotate the drum a number of turns, which on some servos can be set by the user by external adjustment. The drum can be either a one spool, single line system, or a double spool, continuous loop system, according to the line, or sheet, control favoured by the worker. The power that both drum and arm winches now achieve is remarkable with a range between 3-24kg/cm. The development of RC sail control has also shown the need for metal gears and ball raced output shafts with some high powered units shafts double ballraced. To obtain both high torque figures and speed of operation it has become necessary to increase the power supply to many winches to 6V and this should be remembered in the design and purchase stages. How this is achieved will be discussed in Chapter 5.

The correct choice of the sail servo or drum winch for a yacht is complicated due to the complexity of yacht classes, the range of possible sail areas within the classes and the wide selection of sail control equipment

A superb RC equipment installation in a steam-driven model. Note the use of a separate insulated compartment, bellows and ball/socket connectors.

available with torque figures from 3.1kg/cm to over 24kg/cm. However, one parameter can be settled easily. The choice of sail arm or drum is determined by the available space within the hull to accommodate the arc of the arm and is easily checked by drawing the servo outline on the deck plan. Remember to allow for the depth of the servo in relationship to the curve of the hull. The deeper the servo is then the nearer to the fore and aft

Another example of the wrong connector being used. The metal to metal clevis can cause interference to the RF circuitry of the receiver.

centreline it will be positioned. Once the available space has been determined, either sail servo or drum winch, Fig. 4/1 can be used as a guide for the power likely to be required for the class of yacht being contemplated. However, it must be emphasised that Fig. 4/1 is just that, a guide, which in most cases will provide a starting point for the correct choice. Should there be any doubt it would be prudent to seek guidance from either your local model shop or from either of the two specialist suppliers listed in Appendix 2 to whom I owe a debt of gratitude for supplying most of the data on which Fig. 4/1 is based. The mounting of the sail arm servo/drum winch should be designed and installed with particular care, bearing in mind the stress and forces involved, particularly when using the high-torque units. The unit should ideally be bolted down using metal thread screws with locking washers and double nutted for additional security. The mounting must be stiff enough to prevent any flexing which will compromise the precision of sail setting. The electrical connections should be firmly secured and routed well clear of the control lines and the arc of the arm when this type is used.

For steam and fast electrics

Although the combining of Steam and Fast Electric servos under one heading might appear strange, they do share a common working environment – heat and moisture. This is obvious with Steam but it is not always appreciated with Fast Electrics, which generate considerable heat from the motor and the power supply in a virtually watertight compartment during each race. The system design is such that the drive batteries have just enough capacity to complete one race and need fast charging before racing again. To do this the watertight access to the hull interior is broken releasing the heat and leading to rapid cooling which creates condensation in the interior including the servos. Condensation, like steam vapour, is invasive and will penetrate a servo unless it is sealed so this type of servo is recommended for both types of propulsion. Although space is limited within a Fast Electric hull the rudder servo should be located as far away from the motor and ESC as is practical as these are usually water-cooled. The same attention should be given to quality of servo mounting and linkage as discussed previously to eliminate any slack to achieve the sensitive steering system required at high racing speeds. With steam-powered vessels not only is there the ever-present steam vapour and heat but also the residue fumes, possibly more invasive, from the burner heating the boiler. The rudder and throttle servos should ideally be housed within a separate compartment with the linkage rods exiting via miniature bellows. These bellows are usually obtainable from specialist model submarine suppliers (see Appendix 2). Particular and regular attention should also be

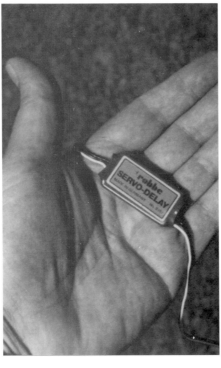

The small size of the 'robbe' Servo Delay. This can be installed in the 'clean' wiring cable run.

given to all plug/socket connections for the onset of corrosion when using steam power (see Chapter 19). Automatic Boiler Control (ABC) units are now available using servos to control the flow of gas to the burner and water to the boiler. Of necessity these

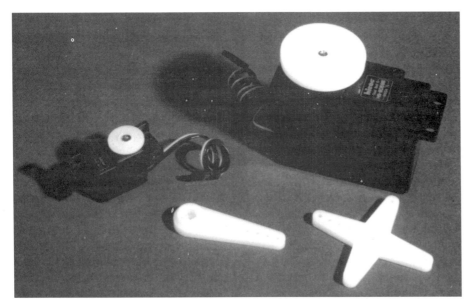

An example of a very small servo, the 'hitec' Super Micro – 26 x 13 x 24mm. It comes with two vertical mounting brackets.

servos are located close to the power plant. They should be watertight and regularly inspected/serviced.

For special use
The servos discussed previously have all been 'safety' servos which if any failed would inconvenience the model at best and at worst cause an accident. This last group with one exception are all non-safety, the exception being servos used in RC model submarines. All the RC equipment is housed within fully water-tight modules so good-quality Standard servos are adequate for steering and hydroplane control with the linkages exiting via bellows. Standard servos can also be used for control of whatever system is used for submerging.

Non-safety functions which can be servo-operated are many, limited only by the worker's ingenuity. Many working features can very easily be controlled by servos. The most common ones are functions that need to be rotated and raised up and down. These include fire monitors, cargo cranes and gun turrets by rotation and raising/lowering of water cannon/cargo

hook/gun barrel and the firing and release of towing lines. The required action is obtained by replacing the servo horn plate with a coarse-toothed wheel which chain-drives another toothed wheel on the function. Scale speed of operation is achieved by a suitable choice of diameter ratio of the two wheels. Every servo comes complete with a selection of output horns and discs. These discs are suitable for creating or attaching cam plates. A cam plate can have either a hump or an indent on its circumference. Switching of functions is achieved by the use of a number of micro switches, position-ed around the circumference, with fingers which are operated by either a hump or an indent. To achieve a more realistic operation one manu-facturer, 'robbe', has produced a unit, plugged into the wiring between the RX and the servo, which slows down the servo speed. Servos are crucial to the successful operation of marine RC and if correctly selected for a particular task and regularly serviced will give years of failure-free service. The choice and responsibility is the marine worker's.

5

Transmitter and Receiver Power Supplies and Management

In Chapter 3 battery supplies were touched upon in discussing the basic rechargeable nicad voltages required to power RC equipment. These were established as 4.8V for RXs and servos and 9.6V for TXs. It is more than likely that the first-time buyer of RC equipment will purchase a 'dry' basic set which will require a number of AA size primary batteries. A primary battery or cell is one which is discarded once its capacity is discharged by chemical reaction. A secondary battery or cell is one which once its capacity is discharged the chemical reaction can be reversed by charging and the cell reused.

There are three technical features which are of importance to the understanding of the efficient use of batteries in RC equipment.

1. Nominal Voltage. All the common primary cells available for RC use have a nominal voltage of 1.5V per single cell off load. With secondary cells, however, the nominal voltage is dependant upon chemical type of which there are two for RC – Nickel Cadmium (Nicads) and Lead Acid. All Nicads have a nominal voltage of 1.2V per single cell. Lead Acid batteries used in marine modelling are of the sealed maintenance-free type for drive motor power supplies and have a nominal voltage of 2.0V per single cell. These batteries will be discussed in Chapter 8.

2. Discharge Curve. This is a line on a graph which has the cell load voltage plotted against time. It illustrates the voltage stability of the cell over the period of discharge to a point when the cell is considered 'flat'.

3. Capacity. The lack of appreciation of ensuring the correct capacity of a cell or pack for a particular current load and duty is possibly the most likely cause of failure of RC equipment. Capacity is expressed in either Ampere Hours (Ah) or Milli-ampere Hours (mAh). It is extremely rare for capacity to be shown on primary cells, but all quality rechargeable cells will carry this information which will be

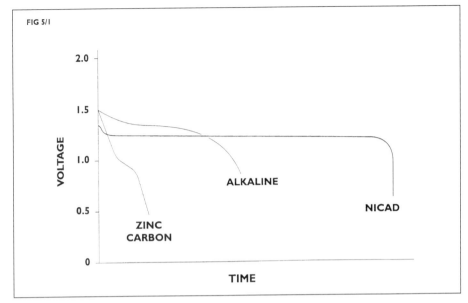

FIG 5/1

ZINC CARBON

ALKALINE

NICAD

VOLTAGE

TIME

Common types of nicad packs with three types of connectors. The top pack and Tamiya-type connector is often used for powering sail winches. The second pack has a servo-type connector. The third pack comprises of four individual 850mAH 1.2V cells making a 4.8V receiver supply. Its spring-loaded carrier is not recommended for marine receiver use. The connector is a manufacturer's 'special' which restricts its use.

discussed when capacity choice and charging is explored later on in this chapter.

Batteries for operational use

Although basic 'dry' equipment can be operated with primary cells they are not recommended for operational use for two very good reasons – the user has no control over choice for cell capacity and they exhibit erratic current discharge with falling voltage throughout their discharge cycle. Rechargeable nicad cells, on the other hand, can be chosen for the correct capacity suitable for the workload and in use they maintain their nominal voltage irrespective of current load up to the point of complete discharge. The disadvantage is that there is little or no warning of complete discharge. These characteristics are shown in the discharge curves in Fig. 5/1. The two most common dry cells have a falling voltage curve which means that the cell has an ever-decreasing ability to drive the current required through the circuit – hence the diminishing light output from a dry cell torch. Nicads, however, have a virtually flat discharge curve which ends in a sudden voltage collapse. Not shown in Fig. 5/1 is the very new Rechargeable Alkaline Manganese (RAM) cell developed in Canada and now available in the UK. The discharge curve is similar to the dry alkaline cell with the difference of a larger initial capacity almost twice that of a nicad. However, over 25 charging cycles the capacity will fall to equal a comparable

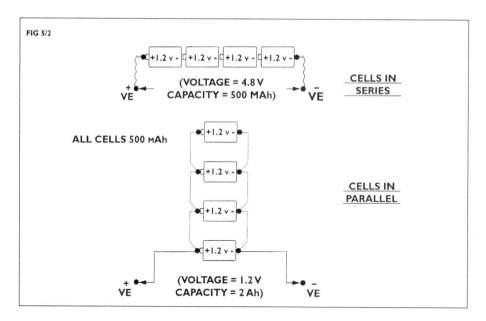

FIG 5/2

+1.2 v - +1.2 v - +1.2 v - +1.2 v -

(VOLTAGE = 4.8 V
CAPACITY = 500 MAh)

+
VE

−
VE

CELLS IN SERIES

ALL CELLS 500 mAh

+1.2 v -

+1.2 v -

+1.2 v -

+1.2 v -

CELLS IN PARALLEL

+
VE

−
VE

(VOLTAGE = 1.2 V
CAPACITY = 2 Ah)

nicad which will continue to deliver its capacity up to and beyond 200 charging cycles while the RAM cell capacity will continue to fall. RAM cells require their own specifically designed charging system and are not recommended for fast charging techniques and continuous high output currents. They are a viable alternative for TX and RX use but the marine worker is advised to carefully explore the cost of a RAM system before spending any money.

The very basic dry TXs will have an integral battery compartment designed for a number of single primary cells or secondary single cells if a charging socket is fitted. Some manufacturers use a removable battery box which is replaced with a rechargeable nicad pack.

What can cause confusion for a beginner is the question of total voltage both in the TX and the RX packs when converting to a rechargeable system. A simple sum shows that when a TX is fitted with eight 1.5V primary cells the total voltage equals 12V. However, when fitted with eight 1.2V nicads the voltage equals 9.6V. The same thing happens

with the RX conversion from 6V 'dry' to 4.8V nicad. This is perfectly in order as the TX, RX and the servos are designed to work within these voltages. A TX has a virtually constant current requirement of its power supply so time is the only parameter of interest to the user when converting to nicads. All nicads will have their capacity shown on them in mAh. A TX nicad pack will vary in its capacity

A rechargeable alkaline 12V transmitter pack. This is suitable as a budget alternative for transmitter use only as long as the spring and end connections are kept well maintained using EML200 - see Chapter 19.

FIG 5/3

EQUIP	QUIESENT CURRENT	MINIMUM LOAD CURRENT	MAXIMUM LOAD CURRENT
RECEIVER SINGLE CONVERSION	@ 4.8 v 8.5 MA	ON SIGNAL 8.5 MA	N/A *
RECEIVER DOUBLE CONVERSION	@ 4.8 v 12 MA	ON SIGNAL 13.5 MA	N/A *
STANDARD SERVO	@ 4.8 v 9.5 MA	270 MA *	640 MA *
ELECTRONIC SPEED CONTROL	@ 4.8 v 23.5 MA	ASTERN 30 MA *	FORWARD 30 MA *
SWITCHER	@ 4.8 v 27 MA	N/A *	65-122 MA *
SAIL SERVO	@ 4.8 v 9 MA	⊡ 300 MA *	△
SAIL WINCH	@ 7.2 v 28 MA	⊡ 880 MA *	△

* SEE TEXT
⊡ NO SAIL OR CORDAGE ATTACHED.
△ WILL VARY ACCORDING TO SAIL & WEATHER.

from maker to maker, usually from 500 to 700mAh. This indicates that the pack will provide 500 to 700 milli-amps of current for one hour before discharge is complete. As most TXs' current requirements are considerably below these figures a fully-charged pack will comfortably provide for a day's sailing which will be intermittent due to the limitations of the RX supplies. It should be noted that if using single nicads in an integral battery box they should all be of the same mAh rating, either 500 or above. It is useful to further note that when batteries are connected in series the voltage of each cell adds together, as discussed in Chapter 3, but the rated current and the mAh of each cell remains the same. However, when connected in parallel the voltage equals that of any individual cell but the rated current and mAh add together as shown in Fig. 5/2.

The capacity range of RX nicad packs is considerably wide, from 500mAh to 1.7Ah, as these could power a large number of servos and other modules. A recently introduced, more environ-mentally-friendly alternative to the nicad is the NiMH (Nickel Metal Hydride cell). Apart from their freedom from cadmium and other toxic materials they offer 50 per cent more capacity of a similar-size nicad cell. One manufacturer is currently offering a 4.8V RX NiMH pack with 2.5Ah capacity. However, they have other characteristics which differ from nicads which will be discussed later on in Chapter 10. The reason for the availability of a wide capacity range of RX rechargeable 4.8V packs is to enable the marine worker to match the battery capacity to the requirements of the equipment he/she intends installing in the boat. This equipment will range from the basic minimum to steer and control the power to the maximum number of functions the TX is capable of controlling. The current consump-tion of each piece of equipment needs to be known so that these can be added together to establish the drain on the battery for any one of three conditions. These are:

1. Quiescent;
2. Minimum load;
3. Maximum load.

Manufacturers do not publish this information and although it is possible for the advanced worker to establish the figures it is unreasonable for the beginner to do so. However, with very few exceptions most makes of equipment have much the same current consumption values so that a reasonable answer can be arrived at using the values in Fig. 5/3. These are average values over a wide range of makes of equipment and are intended not as definitive values but for use at arriving at a reasonable total current consumption enabling the choice of battery capacity to be made on a fail-safe basis.

In operation a basic minimum set of RC equipment comprising RX and two servos has three states it can be in at any one time:

State A Quiescent – Equipment switched on but no function operating.
State B Min Load – Equipment switched on and a minimum of two functions operating.
State C Max Load – Equipment switched on and a minimum of two functions operating.

From Fig. 5/3 the RX quiescent current is 8.5mA. This is for a Single Conversion RX. A Double Conversion RX will sink slightly more current, up to 12mA. Note also that the SCRX current remains the same both when quiescent and when processing a control command. However, the DCRX current does rise slightly when processing a control command. This will have little or no consequence to the final capacity choice and is only included to show it is unwise to take anything for granted. Each quiescent

servo will sink 9.5mA making a total of 19mA. Adding the RX 8.5mA makes a total of 27.5mA for State A. Assuming both servos are operating in State B (the rudder and a mechanical speed control) adds 540mA to the RX 8.5mA making a total of 548.5mA.

Now this is not a continuous current but flows intermittently as the RX responds to transmitted signal commands and the servos move to their new positions. Once there, the current falls to the quiescent state. However, if an ESC is used for electric power control the maximum load current falls to 308.5mA in the forward direction but rises to 380.5mA as the boat goes astern. The reason for this difference is that the majority of ESCs have a relay which operates to change the polarity of the motor supply for astern movement and it is this relay coil which accounts for the increased current.

Any mechanical movement can be brought to a stop and servos are no exception. This is the Stalled State and on average is around 700mA which will quickly drain a RX power supply to the point when all control is lost. In most installations the only affected servo fed from the RX supply is the rudder servo and it is rare for this to be stalled but it can happen. When sailing, if directional control is lost every effort should be made to recover the boat in case a servo has stalled, threatening the possibility of complete loss of control. It is for this reason that the RX supply should only be used for steering, power control and non-safety servos with auxiliary functions fed from a separate fused supply discussed more fully in Chapter 8.

What is now known is that in operating the two servos the current from the RX battery could rise to a maximum of 1288.5mA with maximum mechanical load on the servos. In practice this is unlikely but it demonstrates the principle of ensuring that an adequate power reserve is available should it be required, including in case of a stalled servo. As capacity is measured in mAhs a 900mAh pack would be the preferred choice for a medium-size scale craft with a total weight of around 5kg, with a running time of well over three hours with no emergencies. The pack is quite capable of supplying a high current in an emergency but at the cost of a fast-reducing Ah timescale. These values are for the Standard Servo discussed at the beginning of Chapter 4 which also discussed rudder servo choice, all-up weight, Middle Class Servos, Professional Servos, Sail Servos or Lever Arm Winches and Servo Drum Winches which have increased torque and higher maximum currents which must be taken into account when calculating the mAh requirements of the RX supply. Also mentioned in Chapter 4 is that a higher-voltage power supply is often required for many sail winches and how this is achieved will be discussed later on in this chapter. It is not recommended to drop the RX supply for smaller boats below 700mAh rating for general sailing. However, with competition electric racing boats where heats are of short duration and ESCs are forward motion only – no relay – the RX supply can be dropped to a 500mAh pack or a Battery Eliminator Circuit (BEC) used, as favoured by many workers.

A BEC is an electronic device which will accept a range of input voltages and ensure the output is a stabilised voltage required by the RX and servo, irrespective of voltage fluctuations in the higher supply. This supply can be the propulsion battery which drives the motor controlled by an ESC or an auxiliary supply. Many forward-only ESCs developed for racing have the BEC built into them and it is only necessary to connect the usual signal lead to the RX throttle function to

power it and the steering servo as the power supply is fed via the red and black conductors. No other supply must be connected to the RX battery socket. Most ESCs with an internal BEC will also have two additional external leads to switch the RX supply On-Off. However, boats racing in National competitions are mandatorily required to have an emergency loop fitted on the port side of the hull which can be pulled off 'to cut the connection between the motor and the propulsion battery'. This will still leave the ESC and the RX supply intact so it is left to the worker to decide whether or not to fit a RX supply isolating switch. Although at the time of writing the fitting of such a switch is not a requirement by either the UK National body Electra or the European body Naviga, the prudent worker is advised to check the current regulations at the time of construction. A BEC can also be used external to the ESC. The device usually takes the form of a small sealed unit inserted in the middle of a servo-type lead which is plugged into the usual RX Batt socket. The other end of the lead is left to the worker to terminal connect to the main drive supply via a switch if required. When using BECs, more than usual attention must be given to interference suppression, dealt with in detail in Chapter 6.

Most sail arm servos and winches will require an increased voltage supply. Where this is 6V the battery pack can be plugged into the RX battery position and the RX and rudder servo will operate quite happily. However, if the winch power requirements are above 6V, usually 7.2V, then a BEC system must be used. This can be a separate unit or built in either to the RX itself or the winch. Whichever system is used, great care is needed before testing, as irreparable damage can be caused if the principles are not understood and an incorrect connection is made. Always follow the maker's instructions and double-check before switching on.

Where a separate nicad RX supply is used, switching arrangements, mainly for convenience, are required to provide for the charging of the pack. Towards the end of Chapter 3 a switch harness was introduced which can be either a two- or three-lead harness, depending on whether the set was sold as dry or rechargeable. Most manufacturers supply a common switch harness irrespective of which modelling discipline will use it. Consequently although adequate for either aero or car environments it is not suitable for reliable long-term marine use, being a sliding switch with 'open' contacts being used in a potentially corrosive atmosphere. It can be used for short-term duty as long as the contacts are regularly inspected and maintained as discussed in Chapter 19, but in any event it should be replaced after two years' service. This supplied harness will have either two or three leads attached to the switch. The two-lead harness is for dry batteries only with one lead equipped with a servo-type plug which connects into the RX Batt socket. The other lead will have the maker's preferred power connector which will mate with the battery box provided. The three-lead harness has the third lead fitted with a socket for connection to the maker's charger exiting from the same end of the switch as the battery lead. The switch is a double-pole switch which means it controls both negative and positive outputs from the battery by switching them either into the RX via the servo type plug – the ON condition – or into the charging socket – the OFF condition. In use this third lead is left parked neatly within the boat away from possible water contamination and when charging is required the charger is simply plugged into it. Of

necessity, any switch harness must be fitted in a dry location within a boat which means that access can be difficult and damage result in removing a complicated superstructure when either switch operation and charging is required. Many workers hide the RX switch under hatch covers etc, to avoid the corruption of the scale appearance. However, access is still required within the boat for charging, so dispensing with the maker's harness and constructing a custom-built switch/charging assembly where access to the boat interior is only required in an emergency is an attractive option.

Soldering

Soldering is a skill a beginner marine worker needs to acquire early on in his/her modelling career. The tools and techniques required for making successful electronic solder joints are covered in depth in Chapter 11 which needs to be studied before embarking upon making up the alternative switch assembly shown in Fig. 5/4. The switch is a Sub-Miniature Toggle with a Double Pole Double Throw (DPDT) ON-OFF-ON, locking both ways with centre off, action. Rated 5amps at 30V DC it is more than adequate for its purpose. It has an added advantage of a commercially-available Waterproof Toggle Switch Cover complete with a sealing O-ring which is fitted between the cover and the mounting surface.

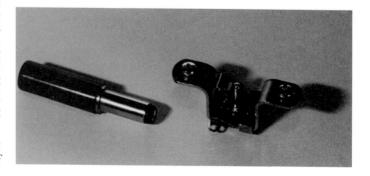

A long-reach 2.1 DC power plug and chassis socket.

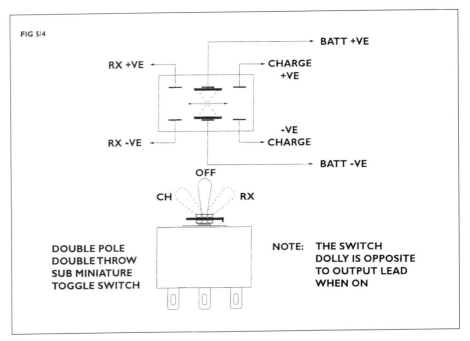

FIG 5/4

BATT +VE

RX +VE

CHARGE +VE

-VE CHARGE

RX -VE

BATT -VE

OFF

CH   RX

DOUBLE POLE
DOUBLE THROW
SUB MINIATURE
TOGGLE SWITCH

NOTE: THE SWITCH
DOLLY IS OPPOSITE
TO OUTPUT LEAD
WHEN ON

A maker's charger for transmitter and receiver nicad packs. Note the unusual connections peculiar only to this maker. However, these are available from Maplins to make up leads to use other charger/analysing equipment.

Most of the major makers offer servo extension leads of several lengths, usually up to a maximum of 1 metre. These leads have a servo plug on one end and a battery socket on the other. These can be used to form the new switch assembly by cutting them off once the lengths are known and the surplus lead used for the charging socket. Use heat-shrink sleeving to provide mechanical strength. Double-check the polarity before connecting up the assembly to test. All the parts are available from any good electronic component store such as Tandy or Maplins in the UK, who also supply by mail order, or Radio Shack in the USA.

Battery requirements of additional features

So far the discussion has centred on the basic minimum RX supply requirements of steering and propulsion control. When servos and switchers are added, for example in a scale model where additional functions are required, the supply mAh rating has to be increased to accommodate the higher load current. Generally a 1.2 or 1.7Ah nicad pack is adequate for five additional functions. However, if a higher current pack is necessary the new NiMH packs offer a 2.5Ah rating. This is especially useful where a high torque sail arm servo is operated from the common 4.8V RX supply and is quite capable of drawing high currents under adverse weather conditions. This last point brings the discussion nicely to the area of charging batteries, battery connections and chargers. Initially it is essential to identify the charging regime required for a particular type of battery. The old fashioned 'wet' lead acid battery charger used for automobile batteries should never under any circumstance be used for charging any battery used for marine modelling. This is a very simple charger which has no regulation of either its voltage or current. Nominally designed for 12V the current flow during charging will start with a high amperage and fall to milli-amps, the trickle charge state, when the battery is fully charged. This high initial inrush of current will destroy a nicad, NiMH or sealed lead acid battery. At this point all that is necessary is to identify the use of a constant-current charger for both nicad and NiMH TX and RX packs. The charger supplied with a set of RC equipment is adequate for safe charging over a long period of equipment use but will not necessarily ensure the user obtains the maximum capacity from the packs as they age. This and the principles of charging for all types of batteries used in marine modelling will be discussed in depth in Chapter 10. Using the maker's charger does not present any problem with connections as the charger is equipped correctly so that it is just a matter of connecting the charger to the third lead of the maker's harness for charging the RX battery. However, if the worker has elected to custom-build his/her own switch assembly a choice has to be made for the charging connection system.

One of the most common types of DC power connectors in RC equipment is the 2.5mm plug and jack socket. The 2.5mm is the diameter of the positive polarity centre pin of a 5.5mm diameter

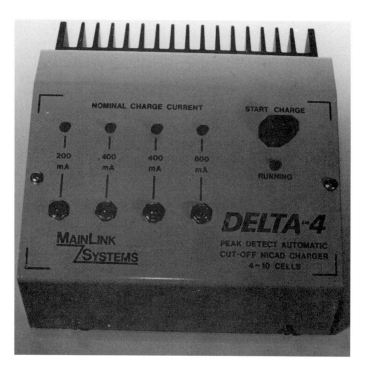

The versatile MainLink DELTA~4 charger. See text.

socket which is fitted in the charging position of the TX. The plug has a hollow metal insert, to fit the socket pin, insulated from a metal 5.5mm diameter outer which is usually the negative polarity. These plugs are available in standard and long-reach versions. The maker's charger will also have a TX charging lead and this will carry one of these 2.5mm long-reach plugs to fit the TX socket. It is prudent then that a custom-built charging system should be TX-compatible and furthermore use the smaller pin version for the RX charging connectors. Using the smaller pin type will fail-safe if mistakes are made when connecting for charging. The socket can be hidden behind a porthole or a hatch cover which hinges up when required. These plug/socket components are in common use in cassette recorders, pocket calculators and other domestic consumer items and are easily available from Maplins in the UK and Radio Shack in the USA. All nicads require a disciplined charging regime if they are to provide their full capacity and

The practical
application of Fig 5/4.
The charging socket is
mounted out of sight
alongside the switch.
See text.

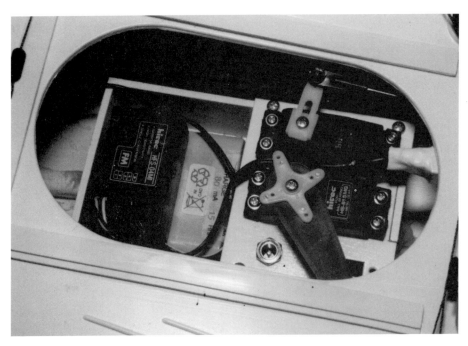

reliability over a full boating season year after year. The reasons for such a system and the equipment required are discussed in Chapter 10. The system employs a controlled discharge, capacity analysis and charging of nicads with equipment that uses the 2.5mm plug/socket connectors which will be compatible with the custom-built RX system in the boat. The need for efficient management of the charging regime employed with the power supplies of TXs and more importantly RXs cannot be overemphasised. No matter how complicated the boat functions are or how simple or sophisticated the RC system is, if the RX battery fails through poor or mis-informed management the marine worker has only him/herself to blame. Modern RC equipment is extremely reliable and virtually failure-free and in the author's experience most RC failures are battery failures brought about by a less than thoughtful approach to charging. Not all failures are terminal, where all control is lost. A badly charged battery can cause 'glitching' when called upon to supply a high current. This 'glitching' will appear to be a momentary loss of control which more often than not the operator will blame someone or something else, which could be so as the next chapter will show, thus hiding the real culprit.

6

Interference and Earthing

There are three types of interference within radio control, two technical and one human! Technical interference can at best cause 'glitching' of the servos and at worst a complete corruption of the transmitted signal. With human interference it can be the worker him/herself who unwittingly creates the conditions where interference can occur, or the well-meaning but ill-informed 'expert' who will cheerfully proceed to take other workers' equipment to pieces to find a fault before checking to see whether in fact the equipment is switched on!

External interference

The first cause of technical interference is that generated externally to the boat and detected by the RX aerial, corrupting the transmitted signal and leading to loss of control. One subtle point that needs to be made is that interference cannot in itself cause a failure within the TX, other than a massive amount of electromagnetic radiation which is very unlikely to be encountered. When the power of the external interference is far greater than the transmitted signal it swamps the TX signal to the extent where the RX cannot respond. The most common cause is when another operator switches on a TX which is on the same channel.

This causes the RX to respond with massive glitching of the servos. The need for channel discipline at all times cannot be overemphasised, even when apparently sailing alone. If other operators are 'live' always check the channel being used before switching on the TX first, followed by the RX. Always carry out a basic check of propulsion and steering control before the boat is put into the water and always carry the channel identification flag on the TX aerial (see Appendix 1). Always retrieve the boat whilst the system is 'live' and switch off the RX first then the TX.

In the UK, where marine modellers have a choice of RC bands, there is a very real possibility of 'legal' interference when using one of them. This is the 27MHz band which is officially allocated to Citizens' Band Radio. The band is still available for all model control with five spot frequencies which are not operational channels for CB. However, marine workers should be aware that even using the five

A 40MHz identity flag supplied by David Swain. See Appendix 2.

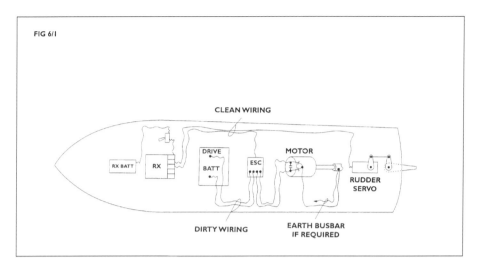

FIG 6/1

'spot' frequencies there is a very real possibility of 'legal' interference from other modelling disciplines. With regard to the possibility of CB interference, the marine worker needs to select his 27MHz channel with great care as a number of channel crystals are available for use which are CB operational in the UK. Appendix 1 lists these in depth and study is recommended before purchase. One channel

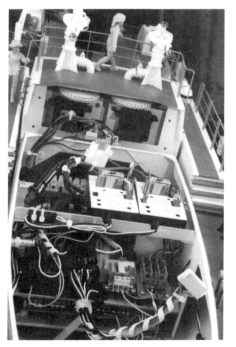

Forming cable looms goes a long way to ensuring the separation of 'clean' and 'dirty' wiring.

in particular – Blue – needs special attention. This was one of the original six spot frequencies, 27.245MHz, in the early days of the band, which subsequently became 27.255MHz. Both are now CB-operational frequencies. The permitted radiated RF power for a CB TX is 4 watts which is forty times greater than the permitted power of a RC TX. So any 27MHz RC transmission in the vicinity of a CB transmission on the same frequency may suffer heavy interference. One redeeming factor is that CB transmissions are mandatorily required to be FM where most second-hand and current production 27meg equipment is AM which reduces the possibility of interference. However, a close CB transmission will totally swamp a RC transmission due to the radiated power difference regardless of the different methods of modulation (see Chapter 2). With careful planning and attention to detail during installation of the equipment in the hull, the marine worker can virtually eliminate his/her own contribution to interference, and this will also drastically reduce the possibility of internal interference generated by electric motors and other causes which is the second technical cause of interference. Planning ideally should start before construction of the boat begins. Not in specific detail but enough to give the worker a reasonable indication of where the major items of equipment will be installed. There are two reasons for this – Clean and Dirty Wiring and Earthing.

Internal interference – clean and dirty wiring

Wiring carrying a large current can induce interference into other wiring running alongside. The technical reasons for this are outside the scope of this Manual but it does happen and the prudent worker will separate his/her wiring looms into Clean Wiring running one down one side of the boat and the Dirty Wiring down the other side (see Fig. 6/1). 'Clean' wiring is any lead that connects into the RX. All other wiring should be classed as 'Dirty'. Which side is used for which is determined by where the rudder servo is placed so that its lead to the RX runs naturally down the nearest side. Servo leads should be kept as short as is practical but if over 1 metre, by using extension leads, it is prudent to use an extension lead which incorporates a filter to reduce interference, particularly

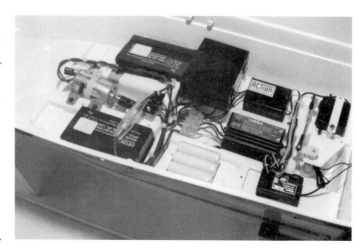

Note the clear-cut separation of 'clean' and 'dirty' wiring with the 'clean' on the right and the 'dirty' on the left. The receiver aerial at the bottom right has yet to be terminated.

if using high-frequency ESCs. When planning the location of an ESC, mount it across the hull so that the power and the motor 'dirty' leads are run onto the 'dirty' side and the RX connecting lead again runs naturally onto the 'clean' side. Cable runs can be formed by using self-adhesive bases which have slots to accept nylon self-locking cable ties. These items are available from any good electronic component store such as Tandy or Maplins in the UK, who also supply by mail order, or Radio Shack in the USA. This system will produce a neat and tidy installation together with the knowledge that the worker has reduced a

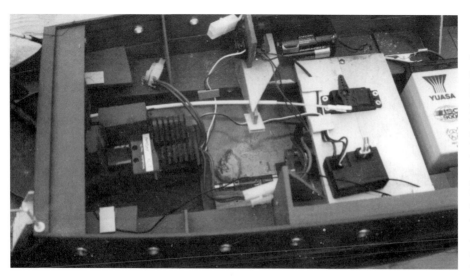

This photograph shows many potential problems and failures waiting to happen. Note the mixing of all the wiring regardless of 'clean' and dirty', the use of dry cells, for the receiver and servo, in an unsecured spring-loaded battery holder, the crocodile-clip connector, and the aerial draped over the power wiring and waiting to be entangled by the shaft coupling.

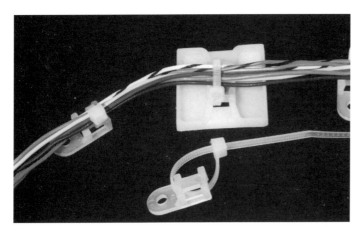

Two types of cable loom bases. The large base is self adhesive. The smaller base can be secured using either cyanoacrylate or two part resin adhesives. The nylon ties are self locking and are not reusable. Note they can be fed either way through either base.

number of possible causes of interference which could lead to RC failures.

Earthing ✗

At first glance this term and the necessity for it may appear incompatible with a model boat and RC equipment. Many would have experienced the uncomfortable 'shock' when alighting from a motor car as static electrical potential is discharged. Static electricity is an electric charge that has built up on an object, either because rubbing it has dislodged some of its electrons, or because a charge has been induced by an opposite static charge nearby. Any sudden discharge of static will be picked up by the RX and could corrupt an incoming signal. The use of metal connections in servo linkages should be avoided for this reason and all large masses of metal, including IC motors, within a boat need to be connected to a common point. This is the earthing busbar or rail which is connected to either the metal prop shaft casing or

the metal rudder stern tube, whichever is the most convenient although the shaft casing is to be preferred. This connection must be soft-soldered and not clamped to ensure the long-term lowest potential state of the earthing busbar. The busbar can be located in any convenient position near to the equipment and can be either a series of terminals common on one side or preferably a short length of heavy gauge copper wire which the 'earths' are soldered to. There should be only be two soldered connections on the prop shaft casing/stern tube, the busbar and where required the earthing of the electric propulsion motor as seen further on. All 'earths' must be separate connections and earth loops must be avoided at all costs to prevent any interference not discharging itself by circulating within the earthing system.

With IC and Fast Electric boats the worker will have realised that the prop shaft casing or the rudder stern tube is effectively the earthing busbar and it is unnecessary to install anything else. However, for the scale worker, where there will probably be other electric motor functions together with moving metal functions, cranes and turrets etc, the installation of a busbar will make wiring that much more convenient. Regular inspection should be made of all earthing connections for soundness. Any potential seeking 'earth' will take the least resistive path, therefore screw terminal connections should examined for corrosion and the screws tightened on a regular basis, bearing in mind that they 'live' in a vibratory and

Self-adhesive cable ties. Useful for small looms but must be used with protective sleeving, as shown on the right, to avoid insulation damage and possible serious short-circuits.

The Earth bus-bar made by twisting the tags through 90° and threading a solid conductor through each one and soldering. Note the two other methods. The 6 and 12V negative bars are formed by binding each pair of tags to a solid conductor and then soldering. The 6V positive has a solid conductor laid against each tag and soldered.

corrosive atmosphere. Failures due to interference are extremely difficult to identify, especially those caused externally to the boat. There have been occasions in the UK where unthinking and misinformed 27MHz band users have reversed TX and RX crystals in the mistaken belief they can create additional channels within the band. This is not only illegal in the UK but it can cause interference radiation from the RX aerial which adjacent boats will detect, 'glitching' their servos. Try proving this to the perpetrators and it can be seen how difficult the problem of interference can be. All that the responsible worker can do is to take as many precautions as he/she thinks are appropriate for their particular use. However, one precaution is vital unless the worker has abundant funds – electric propulsion motor suppression. If not carried out it can be an expensive lesson to learn. Where appropriate the ensuing chapters will recommend the necessity for suppression and earthing other auxiliary functions. It is a quick and simple thing to do, with the worker left secure in the knowledge that nothing has been left to chance.

7

Electric Motors

There is no doubt that when Michael Faraday (1791-1867), the English physicist and chemist, discovered the principle of Electromagnetic Induction and invented the dynamo in 1831 he laid the foundation for not only the electricity industry but also the electrical and electronic life which is taken very much for granted today. Aptly enough the unit of capacitance – the farad (F) – honours his name for evermore. What Faraday discovered was that if a coil of wire on a shaft is rotated within a magnetic field, a current would be generated in the coil and a voltage would appear at the terminals – an electric generator. It did not take long to realise that if a voltage was applied to the terminals of a generator the shaft would rotate and it would become a machine capable of work – an electric motor. This fact, that both machines have the same principle of working, needs to be borne in mind when dealing with DC electric motors. The use of DC motors in marine modelling is widespread and there is no intention for a detailed discussion of their working principles and types in this manual. However, it is necessary to establish certain basic facts to enable the marine RC worker to understand the reasons for applying techniques

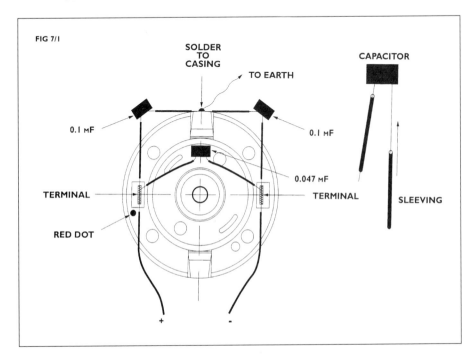

FIG 7/1

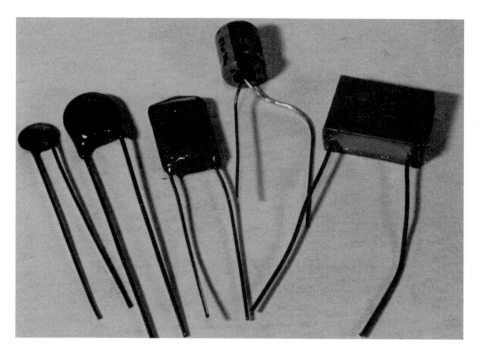

Three types of capacitors suitable for suppressors. Note the electrolytic type fourth from the left with the black band and negative symbol which must never be used as a suppressor.

for their use in conjunction with RC equipment.

Interference

The DC electric motor is of the most prolific and damaging sources of interference. Its design is such that it not only has the ability to manufacture very high levels of interference to the RF system but also to create a large back electromagnetic force (EMF) when the motor current ceases, and it becomes a generator, which if not controlled will immediately destroy an electronic circuit. The major mechanism for interference is the brush to commutator where arcing occurs as the motor draws current into its windings as the armature rotates. The higher the current then the higher the arcing and the consequential interference 'spikes'. These spikes have no power but can be hundreds of volts in magnitude which if allowed into the system via the wiring have the ability to destroy solid-state components. They will also radiate and be detected by the RX aerial and can

cause signal corruption. However, most modern RXs have protection built into the RF end of their circuits to combat this type of interference. Nevertheless, the RX aerial must be kept well clear of any electric motor. The best defence is to suppress the interference at source and this is achieved by fitting suppressors across the motor terminals. This is shown in Fig. 7/1, which uses capacitors. These have the property of being able to store a charge of electricity and consist of two conducting plates separated by an insulating medium called a dielectric. When charged there is a voltage difference between the plates which is immediately 'bled' away to the earthing busbar discussed in Chapter 6. Fitted across the motor terminals they act like a sponge soaking up the interference spikes and safely dumping them into 'earth'. There are two main types of capacitors – non-polarised and polarised. As the polarity of the motor supply can be reversed it is essential that non-polarised capacitors are be used as suppressors. A polarised capacitor is

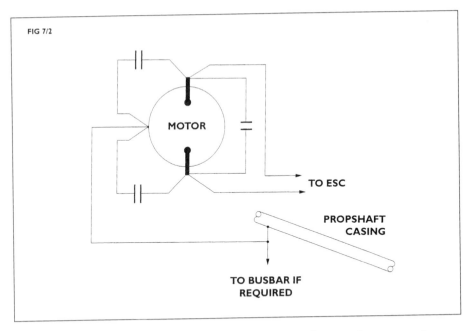

FIG 7/2

MOTOR

TO ESC

PROPSHAFT CASING

TO BUSBAR IF REQUIRED

Fitted suppressors. Note the large dot above the left-hand capacitor denoting the positive terminal. See text.

known as an Electrolytic Capacitor and will have the positive and negative connections clearly identified.

As previously discussed these spikes can reach high voltages which will in time break down a low-voltage working capacitor. The prudent worker will fit as high a working voltage capacitor as obtainable. Listed in the Maplins UK catalogue is a range of 630V working High Voltage Metallised Polyester Film capacitors of the values required – 0.047mF and 0.1mF (microFarad). Note that capacitor values can also be expressed in two other ways – see Appendix 3. Fig. 7/2 shows the earth connection from the motor casing to the prop/rudder shaft casing where it is soldered together with the earthing busbar connection if required (see Chapter 6). When fitting suppressor capacitors, ensure the leads on the motor terminals are wound round the terminal making a secure mechanical joint prior to soldering. Do the same with the other leads by twisting them together. When soldering, heat each joint sufficiently to ensure a good flow of solder without overheating and damaging the capacitor. If in doubt use a heat shunt. The capacitor connection to the motor case should have the earth wire twisted into it and the case tinned prior to soldering (see Chapter 11). The motor may have a flux ring, which is a metal band sprung onto the case.

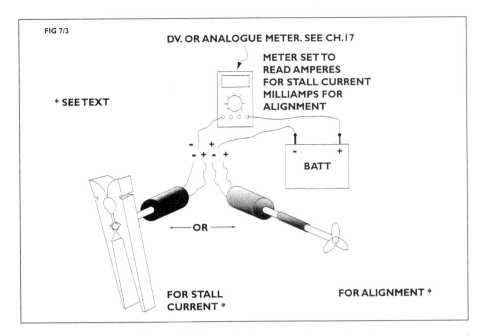

FIG 7/3

DV. OR ANALOGUE METER. SEE CH.17

METER SET TO
READ AMPERES
FOR STALL CURRENT
MILLIAMPS FOR
ALIGNMENT

* SEE TEXT

- + - +

BATT

—— OR ——

FOR STALL
CURRENT *

FOR ALIGNMENT *

Do not attempt to solder to it. Instead ease it out of the way and solder to the case proper. Keep all leads as short as possible. If the motor has a plastic outer case take the capacitor connection straight to earth. Generally the higher the motor build quality the less likelihood of heavy arcing from the brushes. This is also true of the number of poles the motor has. A five-pole motor is less likely to arc than a three-pole one. Although the first priority is to suppress interference at source, what also must be achieved is to prevent it from entering the main power supply chain and becoming a 'virus' affecting individual electronic circuits.

If used strictly in accordance with the maker's instructions and just for the control of propulsion and steering, modern RC equipment will very rarely give any cause for concern. If other working functions are added using the maker's preferred additional pieces of equipment then irritating glitching or worse failure would again be rare. However, difficulties may occur when independent manufacturers' electronic items are integrated into a system because the worker has no means of knowing how the internal circuitry can cause problems or be affected by the one common part of the system – the power supply. One example is that many independent manufacturers' electronic speed controls have a common negative 'rail' where the propulsion battery negative is common to the RX battery negative. Usually this does not cause any problems as the maker would have tested his ESC with a number of makes of RC equipment but it does not always follow that compatibility is automatic. Although the propulsion motor is the main probable source of interference, the same attention must be paid to other electric motors, however small, that are introduced into the system. Being light duty and possibly of cheap manufacture they can still cause serious interference problems if not adequately suppressed and their wiring is allowed to come in contact with 'clean wiring'. The worker should bear in mind that there is no substitute for a high-quality five-pole fully suppressed motor to ensure minimum brush-originating interference if the budget

Four types of motors. The smallest (left) is a robbe with an integral gearbox suitable for radar scanners etc. The next left is the widely popular 545. The motor to the right of the 545 has a flux ring fitted. The large motor (far right) has flying leads which necessitates the use of a tag strip for fitting suppressors.

allows. The 'poles' of any motor can be ascertained by counting the coils on the rotating armature. Usually these can be seen through the ventilating slots at either end of the motor casing.

Stall current and shaft rotation

There are two other propulsion motor procedures which can be usefully carried out prior to final installation in the boat. These are identifying the stall current and the shaft rotation. The motor stall current will be required when designing the main power supply, fusing and selecting the correctly rated speed control. The stall current is the maximum current a motor with no other fault will draw from its power supply when its shaft is prevented from rotating, *eg* if the propeller is jammed by debris. The motor is secured in a temporary mounting which must be firmly fixed either to the workbench or held in a vice. Two hardwood strips approximately 1in × ½in × 8in are joined together with a hinge at one end. A 'V' slot is filed in each inside face about 1½in from the hinge end. The depth of the slots should be such that the motor shaft can be gripped tightly to prevent it turning. A multi-meter set to its highest DC current range, ideally 20 amps, is connected in series with the motor, switch and the designed voltage battery. With the motor running the wooden-hinged tool is squeezed onto the shaft until the motor just stops. Read the stall current and release

immediately – Fig. 7/3. Repeat the procedure twice more to confirm the figure. There is, however, one note of caution. This method of arriving at the stall current should never be used on high-performance specialist electric motors designed specifically for racing as these motors can sink upwards of 100 amps when stalled. With these high currents it is all too easy for an accident to occur. The method should be confined to motors intended for scale use and of moderate cost. High-performance racing motors are in a class of their own and many current marine magazines and books devote space to their safe testing and use.

Whilst any motor intended for installation is on the bench it is wise to identify and mark the polarity of the terminals, note the direction of rotation and fit the motor leads. With auxiliary functions such as water pumps etc, a check on the rotation required is prudent prior to fitting the leads. With the exception of the propulsion motor these should be red and black unless this conflicts with a polarity reversal to obtain the rotation required and a terminal already marked by the maker. In this case use orange and white leads. Unidentified terminals should be marked for future reference. Most quality propulsion motors will have the positive terminal identified with a red dot. This indicates the maker's preferred long-term direction of rotation and efficient power performance of the motor design. Unfortunately there is no convention of rotation, clockwise or anticlockwise, when the motor is connected as recommended by the red dot, so it is up to the worker to check it as this is vital so that the correctly-handed propeller can be fitted. First fit the motor leads (see Chapter 8 – Power Wiring and Chapter 9 – MSCs, ESCs and Fusing). These leads should be coloured orange and yellow if not already part of the speed controller, to remind the worker when connecting a speed controller to double-check the connections. Run the motor on a low voltage to ensure the rotation, clockwise or anti-clockwise, can be easily detected. Propellers are either left hand or right hand when viewed from astern and driving ahead. A left-hand prop will rotate anticlockwise and a right hand prop clockwise. The easiest way to 'hand' a prop is to hold it up as if viewing from astern with one blade upright. If the leading edge of the blade is on the right it is a left-hand prop and if the leading edge is on the left it is a right-hand prop. It is outside the realms of this Manual to explore further the choice of material, diameter and pitch of props but it is necessary to ensure the worker has enough information so that the motor shaft rotation is known in relationship to the polarity and lead colours when finally installing the chosen speed controller. This is vital particularly when twin drives are used, where one shaft must rotate clockwise and the other shaft anticlockwise. A moments' reflection will show that with twin drives there are a number of combinations of rotation/propeller 'hands'/motors polarities, and as will be seen in Chapter 9 on the setting-up of speed controllers, the process of ensuring the most efficient and economic power set-up can become complicated. It is essential that the worker makes accurate notes

of connections, wiring colours and rotations as it is more than likely that polarities will have to be changed to achieve the desired result. It is much more convenient to do this at the speed controller interface than attempt it at the motor terminals where space is at a premium and a hot soldering iron is unwelcome, par-ticularly if the hull is plastic!

Mounting

The correct mounting of any motor is essential for its maximum efficient running and to ensure that no power is wasted through poor alignment which causes binding within the motor and prop shaft bearings and unnecessary higher current consumption. Poor alignment will also quickly lead to worn motor bearings which at the brush end will increase arcing and interference. To align a motor is very simple and starts with ensuring the mounting arrangement enables the motor to be adjusted laterally. Ideally motor and shaft should be a single unit with a solid coupling. However, this can put an unreasonable load on the motor bearings leading to excessive wear which again in turn increases arcing interference. Over the years the author has found it better to use a flexible coupling as illustrated below. Note that this type has splines which allow a certain amount of fore and aft movement for expansion. The design of the motor, its mounting, shaft

A quality coupling which allows for fore and aft movement of the propeller shaft. See text.

An example of water cooling fitted to a fast electric motor.

and coupling assembly should be such that the shaft can be withdrawn at any time in the future without disturbing the motor. The whole is assembled using a temporary solid coupling with the motor held just 'finger tight' in its mounting and the shaft able to turn freely. Connect the motor to as low a battery voltage as will just run it. Now connect a multi-meter (see Chapter 12), set on a low current reading range in series with the battery, switch and motor – Fig. 7/3. The motor is now run and adjusted to achieve the lowest current reading. When satisfied that no more adjustment is possible the mounting fixings should be gradually tightened without increasing the motor current. Should the current rise this indicates binding in the assembly. Stop, investigate and remove the cause. More often than not it is in the vertical plane, which only becomes evident as the mountings are screwed down. This can be cured by packing up the mounting with thin washers. Recommence the procedure and finally tighten the fixings, preferably either side in turn. The temporary coupling can now be replaced with the final coupling choice. The reason for reducing the motor voltage is to lower the motor current to, if possible, milli-

amps as this will give a much more sensitive indication of misalignment.

So far the discussion has dealt with direct-coupled motors. There is no doubt that for scale boats to run at displacement speeds for a more true-to-life appearance the output propeller shaft needs to revolve at a low speed. This is accomplished using a gearbox between the motor and the prop shaft. There are available from many marine kit manufacturers as complete drive systems with an integral gearbox or alternatively the worker can incorporate his/her own gearbox between the motor and the prop shaft. Whichever method is used, all the requirements so far discussed are still needed, and furthermore the worker should note that the final output shaft rotation can be opposite to the motor rotation and under no circumstances whatsoever must the motor stall method described above be carried out on the gearbox output shaft. If this is attempted the gearbox will suffer fatal damage.

Brushless motors

This chapter would be incomplete without mention of the latest development in electric motors available for marine work. These are brushless motors and as the name implies are without brushes and a commutator. Where a brush motor has windings wound onto an armature revolving in a magnetic field created by magnets secured around the inside of the casing, the brushless motor is completely the opposite with the magnets revolving inside the windings secured inside the casing. The angular position of the shaft in relation to each winding is detected by electronic sensors coupled to an electronic controller which switches the driving current on and off to produce rotation. The main advantage is no brush arcing causing interference and a higher efficiency compared to a brush motor. The motor is virtually maintenance-free with no replaceable components to buy during its life. Their major disadvantage is the high initial cost of the motor/controller and the high replacement cost of the controller if damaged. At present their marine modelling use is confined to fast electric racing but there is no doubt that costs should fall once the present production sales begins to offset the development costs. Should a worker be tempted to invest in a brushless motor and controller, more than usual attention should be paid to ensuring the controller is waterproof in view of the high replacement cost.

Speed Controller

Start of a fast electric heat at Princes Park, Eastbourne, 1998.

8

Main Power Supplies and Fusing

The integrity of the main power supply and its well-being is of equal importance to the boat, when it is in the middle of the lake, as the RX power supply. It is no use being able to steer back to port if the propeller cannot turn! Also there is little the helmsperson can do if the boat suddenly bursts into flames, again in the middle of the lake! What is not always realised is the inherent danger within high-capacity rechargeable batteries to cause significant damage. They should be treated with respect at all times, especially fast-

charging nicads which will be dealt with in detail in Chapter 10. Even a Sealed Lead Acid (SLA) battery of modest capacity is capable of producing a discharge over a short duration of over 100 amperes with disastrous results both to the boat and the operator. The possibility of an accident can be considerably reduced by the initial design of the power supply, correct fusing and appropriately rated wiring. Once again the worker should remember that operating in a public place carries third party risk and responsibility to ensure that all steps have been taken

Sealed Lead Acid Batteries. Note the vents between the terminals.

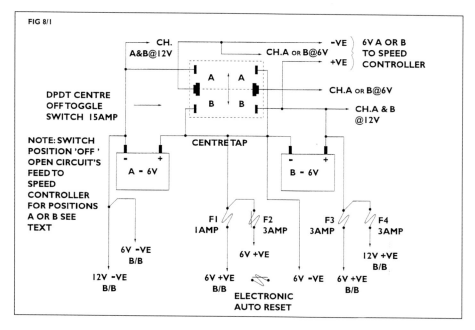

FIG 8/1

to minimise the possibility of an incident. Insurance will not cover negligence if the design and operation of the equipment is doubtful.

Sealed Lead Acid batteries

The majority of scale RC boats require a reasonable amount of power to move them and also weight to act as ballast. The SLA battery fulfils both requirements with a range of capacities to suit most needs. The most common are 6V and 12V with capacities ranging from 1Ah @ 6V to 65Ah @ 12V – a massive battery weighing over 22kg! A middle of the range choice would be a 7Ah capacity which would supply motive power well beyond the Ah rating of the RX supply as well as supplying auxiliary functions. It is essential to be aware of the overall design requirements of the power supply even before building commences so that the worker can be sure that there will not be any catastrophic changes required to the hull when it is finished and it is found that the opening for the battery is too small! This happened to the author with his first

model trawler – a plank-on-frame kit – which was painstakingly built to the kit manufacturer's instructions which, almost as an afterthought on the last page, suggested the time was now right to ballast the model and fit the RC equipment including the drive battery. This meant cutting through the finished deck and working in a very confined space. It was a valuable lesson to learn. In designing a power supply the first job is to define the physical limits that the design must conform to, *ie* the space available within the hull and the overall weight of the finished model. Most marine kits now list the weight or displacement on the box and often in the maker's catalogue. A very approximate weight can be obtained by weighing the kit contents prior to construction and deducting 10-15 per cent building scrap from the result. Whilst the scales are available weigh all the RX equipment including the battery and motor. Total all the results and deduct this from the overall weight of the finished model. This value is the ballast required to bring the model down to its correct waterline level.

Usually up to 90 per cent of the ballast weight can be the drive battery leaving the last 10 per cent for fine-tuning the model's trim. At this point a tentative evaluation of available space and position in the hull is made, bearing in mind that the majority of ballast should be located as low as possible within the hull, on the fore and aft centre-line and amidships.

An analysis is now required of the voltage and current requirements for the system. This should include all the auxiliary functions and noting also any function which is polarity-conscious. It might well be that it is unavoidable that there is a mix of 6 and 12V requirements, but there is no need for concern as it will be seen that a dual voltage supply is perfectly feasible. Each function is now analysed to achieve the lowest possible current requirement. For example, 'grain of wheat' tungsten lamps are often used for deck lighting and port/starboard sidelights. These lamps usually consume 50mA at 6V. Say there are also eight deck lights also consuming 50mA each. If fed individually the total current required would be $10 \times 50mA = 500mA = \frac{1}{2}$amp at 6V. If, however, the ten are fed as five pairs, each pair in series, then the total current would be $5 \times 50mA = 250maA = \frac{1}{2}$amp at 12V. Remember that to series feed functions the voltage and current must be equal for both to operate satisfactorily. See Chapter 13 and Fig. 13/1 (p114).

Once all the voltages and currents are known a start can be made on the design of the power supply. If there are a number of auxiliary functions and the propulsion motor requires a 6V supply it is prudent to design for two 6V batteries with as large an Amp/hour rating as the hull space and weight will allow. Separate fused busbars can feed groups of functions making fault-finding much easier when failures occur

and also providing a much more flexible power supply for the future. A typical supply along these lines is shown in Fig. 8/1. Two 6V batteries are connected in series and centre tapped to give a choice of 6 or 12V outputs. Note the inclusion of a 15amp toggle switch. This is to even out the high current consumption of the propulsion motor so that both batteries are drained down to a common level so the pair can be charged in series at 12V. Also provided is the option of charging each battery singly at 6V if one battery has been drained heavily. The Double Pole Double Throw (DPDT) switch is centre MOTOR OFF – or A or B battery ON – and single charging at 6V. There is a separate socket for series charging both batteries at 12V. However, for the whole system to work efficiently it is essential that both batteries are new from the outset for charging in series, as with age and use, a battery's resistance will rise and if these are too different charging in series becomes unreliable. For sailing the worker selects A or B battery with the option of switching batteries if desired. The output from the switch feeds whatever speed control is used and the 6V charging socket. No propulsion motor fuses are shown as this will be discussed in Chapter 9. The auxiliary outputs can be a variety of 6 and 12V with polarities as required. They are fused as shown with the fuses feeding busbars. The main advantage of the design is that a short-circuit failure of an auxiliary function will blow its respective fuse and protect the integrity of the whole supply. It also makes for easier fault-finding in a complicated multi-function system. Note that the centre tap can be either positive or negative relative to either battery and this can be economic in 'return' wiring by creating common 'return' busbars in other parts of the boat. F2 is shown as an electronic auto reset fuse. These are

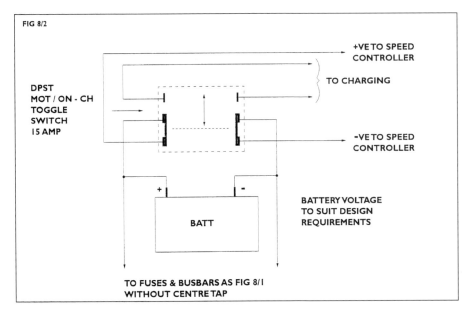

FIG 8/2

+VE TO SPEED
CONTROLLER

TO CHARGING

DPST
MOT / ON - CH
TOGGLE
SWITCH
15 AMP

-VE TO SPEED
CONTROLLER

+   -

BATT

BATTERY VOLTAGE
TO SUIT DESIGN
REQUIREMENTS

TO FUSES & BUSBARS AS FIG 8/1
WITHOUT CENTRE TAP

very useful devices for electronic circuits such as sound effect units and will be considered later on. If the worker is content that a single battery is adequate, the same principles should be followed as above with, however, a DPST MOT/ON-CHG switch as shown in Fig. 8/2. In principle SLA batteries can be installed in any position to suit their environment, but for model marine use it is advisable to always ensure that the top of the battery where the terminals are should be clear of obstruction in the very unlikely event of the automatic low pressure venting system opening to release excessive internal pressure (see photo on p74). In deep wide-beam hulls they can be mounted upright which makes for easy access to the terminals. In narrow hulls this can cause the model to become 'tender', *ie* having a high sensitivity to rolling in a slight sea. In these cases the battery should be mounted flat to get the weight as low as possible. The majority of SLAs are fitted with moulded-in blade terminations accepting 6.35mm (¼ in) push-on connectors with one exception of the YUASA batteries listed in Appendix 3. The 12V 0.8Ah 350g battery comes

with a 195mm fly lead intended for PCB connection. It is a matter of personal choice whether to use push-on connectors or soldered connections to the battery blades. If 'push-ons' are chosen adequate space should be allowed for regular inspection and maintenance (see Chapter 19).

Fusing

The principle of fusing is one of the most common misunderstandings, even in daily life. During my professional life I never found two engineers who agreed on the subject of fusing although there are certain common-sense principles which have stood the test of time. What has to be appreciated is that there are two disciplines, electrical and electronic, which require different results from a fusing technique. It is when they meet that problems arise as in the case of the large drive batteries and Electronic Speed Controllers (ESCs). When electrical equipment develops a fault it fails in seconds, relatively slowly compared with an electronic circuit which fails in milliseconds or faster. It is this time element which is the crucial difference between the two fail scenarios. What must now be obvious is that a fuse suitable for electrical use may not provide enough protection for electronic use, because a fuse 'wire' needs time to react to excessive current flow, become hot and finally melt and break the circuit. A fuse in either discipline is not only there to prevent damage from excessive current in the equipment but primarily to protect the power supply and its wiring to the fuse. A large fault current could in the worst case create enough current to melt wiring insulation and eventually cause a fire with damage to the boat and possibly people. This is important to remember as most boating activities take place in a public place where public liability is the responsibility of the worker.

Not all faults are of the short-circuit type where the fuse 'blows' within its designed time. There can be a build-up of current with a slowly binding prop shaft or a partially fouled prop which is not enough to immediately 'blow' the fuse but is enough to damage the motor and fatigue the fuse to a point where in the future it ruptures for no apparent reason. All fuses should be renewed on an annual basis to guard against possible rupture caused by fatigue or ageing after carrying large currents for long periods. The selection

of the correct fuse can be very difficult when confronted with the vast selection in a supplier's catalogue. But what becomes clear is that current and time are the prime factors to be considered when making a choice. Furthermore, over the last few years attempts have been made to agree classification standards which in Europe are IEC 127 and BS 2905A and in the USA and Canada UL198G and CSA22-2, No 59. The point of mentioning this is that the characteristics differ between European and USA/Canada standards and fuses manufactured to either standard are not interchangeable.

For electronic circuits, if a fuse is to be of any use in protecting components it must rupture very fast indeed when a fault occurs. This is the response time of a fuse and modern fuses are grouped into three time classifications. The first class (FF) – Very Fast Acting – will blow in two milliseconds or less at ten times the rated current. These are only required within electronic circuits and normally the marine worker has no need to use them. The next class is (F) – Fast Acting or Quick Acting – which have a slower blowing time of around 20 milliseconds at ten times the rated current or 30mins for double the rated current and should be used to fuse winch, radar, crane and anchor motors and low-current propulsion motors. They can also be used for fusing sound modules but the Electronic Fuse in Fig. 8/1 is better. The last class is Time Delay, Slow Blow and Anti-Surge Fuses and is designated class (T). This is by far the largest and most bewildering class of fuses listed in suppliers' catalogues and for the marine worker the most important as it is from this class that a selection has to be made for fusing the propulsion motor supply. In use the conditions the fuse has to contend with are harsh and what is not required is 'blowing' for no apparent reason,

Open clip type fuseholders. The 20mm fuseholder at the bottom can be fitted with a commercially-available clip-on cover.

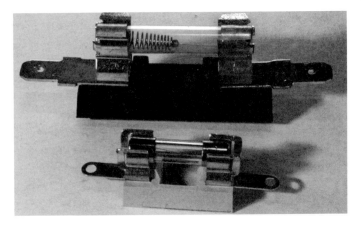

leaving the boat dead in the water. The continuous running current can be anything from a few amps to upwards of 30amps. With a large displacement model the starting current can surge well beyond the fuse rating which it must withstand. It must also withstand inappropriate use when the helmsperson decides suddenly to go astern from full ahead but at the same time fail safe and rupture when a genuine emergency arises. The mechanical construction of a (T) class fuse can be either a straight wire, spiral wound or spring type enclosed within the usual glass envelope or a ceramic body which is preferred. The Time/Current characteristics required for marine use are upwards of an hour at 1½ times the rated current to reduce ageing, to 'blow' in under a second at four times the rated current for safety and approaching 500 milliseconds at ten times the rated current to cope with surge currents. A fuse meeting these requirements can be found in the RS Components Ltd catalogue whose address is listed in Appendix 2. The foregoing shows the basic principle of fuse selection combining time with the current rating which can be used when no other information is available. However, modern fuses now becoming available have their designations further broken down into groups of current ratings with three letters indicating the fuse duty. For example, a Maplin (see Appendix 2) 31mm (1¼in) 10amp or 15amp ADL Glass Time Delay (T) fuse recommended for high starting currents or surge currents will rupture between 12 seconds and 2 minutes at 200 per cent overcurrent or rupture within 1 hour at 135 per cent overcurrent. The 1-hour rating also tells the user that continuous high current through a fuse will age it and eventually rupture it without there being a fault. As discussed above this is a fact com-

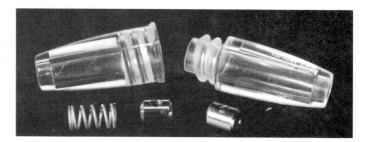

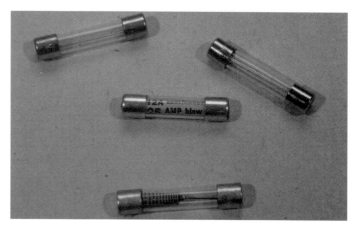

monly overlooked, leading to chasing a non-existent failure which could have been avoided by the correct choice of fuse initially and regular maintenance.

There are two other parameters, voltage rating, which does not normally concern the worker, and temperature. Generally speaking fuses are rated over an ambient temperature range of 20-25°C. If the ambient temperature rises where the fuse is located the effective current rating of the fuse will come down. For example if the temperature rose to 35°C then the fuse should be derated by 10 per cent. This effect should be remembered when apparent nuisance blowing of fuses occurs.

Fuses can be held either in an open clip fuseholder or enclosed in a sealed in-line fuseholder. The most common types are glass-bodied 20mm or 31mm (1¼in) long. Unfortunately the 31mm types are only easily obtainable up to 15amp rating which means that for higher currents the marine worker has no alternative but to use a professional

Top: A high-quality Bulgin 1¼in (31mm) 'In Line' fuseholder. Note the position of the spring behind the connection collar. This is where it should be when installed. Never in contact with the fuse.

Above: 1¼in fuses and a slightly shorter auto fuse (centre). These should be used with care in fuseholders because of the reduced length.

range from a specialist supplier or the car range of fuses for which no details are available other than the 'blow' and the 'continuous' current printed on the fuse body. These fuses are slightly shorter than 31mm and this should be noted when using them particularly in an in-line fuseholder as intermittent contact can occur if the spring does not maintain adequate pressure on the wire thimble or ferrule which should be between the fuse and the spring. However, these car fuses are being replaced by the Euro blade type which are colour coded Blue 15amp, Yellow 20amp and Clear 25amp.

Fuse selection

Propulsion motor circuits should always be fused according to the type of speed controller and motor in use. For a simple resistance-type controller controlling a low-current motor a Class (F) Quick-Acting fuse rated as near to but above the stall current of the motor should be fitted (see Chapter 7 for determining the stall current). For medium and high current motors controlled by an ESC a Class (T) Anti-Surge fuse rated at 1¼ times the stall current is required. Always be prepared that your initial choice may have to be modified in the light of practical experience as the performance of the motor/ESC/boat can occasionally cause nuisance 'blowing' for no good reason. Upgrading the rating to no more than 1½ times the stall current usually cures the problem. Fuse positions in motor circuits has been the subject of debate over a number of years and this will be further discussed in Chapter 9. Auxiliary circuits should be fused with Class (F) fuses. The rating is determined by adding up all the continuous currents and deducting a percentage for diversity as not all the functions will be working at the same time. What the percentage is has to be is decided by the worker but the final figure is the fuse rating. If anything err on the high side.

The latest blade type of European auto fuses. Available in ten ratings from 3amps to 30amps. There is also a Mini Blade in eight ranges.

3 and 5amp electronic fuses compared with a 20mm fuse. An electronic fuse will automatically reset once the fault has been cleared.

Below: A supply distribution and fuse board. Note the voltage busbars and the F2 electronic fuse.

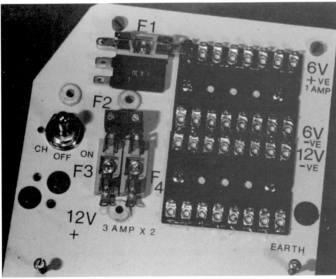

Power wiring

The design of the power wiring should be carefully thought through, paying attention to ensuring it is correctly rated and particularly that the common return wiring to the negative battery terminal is the correct size for the overall current it has to carry. Any conductor has resistance to the flow of current and if it is too small for that current it will create volt drop along its length as well as becoming warm. The motor wiring from the battery should be beyond reproach and rated at least 1¼ times the motor fuses. If these fuses are 15amps the correct wiring to use would be 2.5mm^2 (Appendix 3). Many ESCs already have the power input wiring built in and these usually are coloured red and black and will be correctly rated. Any additional wiring should be of the same quality and size.

Soldered terminations are preferred to terminal blocks particularly if the terminations are behind switch panels. Soldering is a technique worth mastering for the marine worker (see Chapter 11). The auxiliary power supplies are cabled in the same way as the propulsion power, using stranded coloured equipment wire rated as before. For easy fault-finding, use orange and pink as well as red for the different positive voltages. Use black, blue and brown for negative and green for the earth busbar connections.

9

Controlling the Power

The one component within the RC system which has developed beyond all recognition over the last two decades is the speed controller used to control electric propulsion motors. In the very early days of marine modelling the power choice was between an IC engine or an electric motor, with the IC engine probably the most popular, for a number of reasons. An IC engine had a more efficient power/weight ratio and was easier to control using a servo coupled to the carburettor and was also more realistic as the majority of model prototypes were also IC powered, while electric motors were large and not as efficient as modern types. Batteries were also large and potentially dangerous, being 'open' wet acid types. However, as the IC engine developed it became extremely noisy and environmentally offensive leading to it being banned from many club sailing waters. At the same time lead acid batteries became sealed and, together with motors, more efficient with a good power/weight ratio. Rechargeable nicads appeared and soon marine workers realised that electric power was a viable alternative to IC power.

Prior to the appearance of transistors, RC equipment circuits were assembled on tag boards and connected with solid wires. However, transistors needed an alternative system to achieve the benefit of the small compact circuits they offered and soon the printed circuit board (PCB) appeared. A PCB is a sheet of insulated board with a thin layer of copper deposited on one side. The circuit is printed onto the copper using an acid-resistant ink. Holes are drilled through the board where the component wires are to be connected into the circuit. The unwanted copper is then acid-etched away and the resistant ink removed leaving the copper circuit intact. Each component is inserted through the board from the non-coppered side and soldered onto the copper circuit 'lands' creating a compact space-saving unit. (The current technology is for double sided copper clad boards with components on both sides. This is Surface Mount Technology (SMT).) RC manufacturers and others soon realised that a PCB combined with resistors and a servo could become an electric motor controller.

Mechanical Speed Control

A DC electric motor will develop its full power when the designed voltage for that power is present at its terminals. When a resistance is introduced into the path of the voltage to the motor its speed and power will be reduced. If two resistances, R^1 and R^2, mounted on a

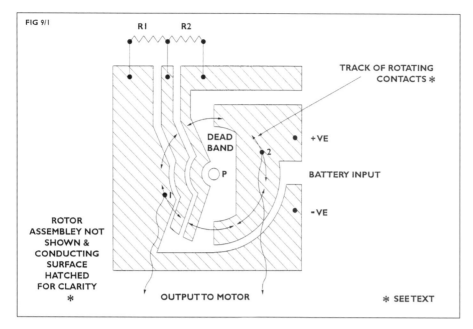

FIG 9/1

PCB, are used with the ability to select either none, one or two in series, and are arranged in an arc over which a sliding contact (1) on a pivot P is moved by a servo, then a three-step speed control is achieved (Fig. 9/1). This is repeated on the opposite arc with a second sliding contact (2) on the same pivot. The two contacts, insulated from each other, are connected to the motor and the negative and positive power supply connected to each arc respectively. The contact pivot plate has a horn which is connected to the servo in the same way as a rudder installation with the 'none' or DEAD BAND position the mid point of the servo and the TX 'stick'. When the stick is pushed forward contact (1) has resistance inserted in its path to the motor and is negative whilst the second contact (2) is connected directly to the positive power supply and the boat goes forward. Pull the stick back and the reverse happens with contact (2) having resistance inserted and is now negative and contact (1) is now connected to the positive supply. With this change of polarity the motor now runs in the

opposite direction and the boat goes astern. Although using electronic components and principles this form of control is known as a Mechanical Speed Control (MSC).

'Bob's Boards'

If lands on a PCB are narrow they will have a resistance along their length.

A 'hitec' mechanical speed controller. See Fig 9/1.

A 'Bob's Board' mounted on top of a servo. The power input wiring is absent for clarity. In time the board can warp, and should be supported from the beginning. See text. Note the need to keep the output wiring clear of the moving wipers which are shown at maximum power/speed.

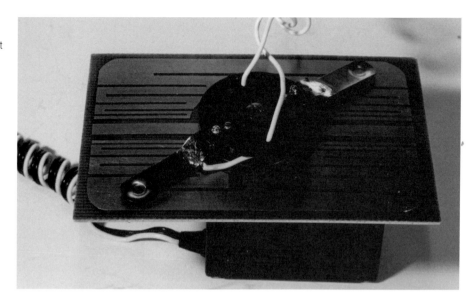

Different widths will have different resistances. If a continuous land starts with a very narrow width which grows to a large width in the middle and then reduces to the same narrow width at the other end then a variable resistance has been created along its total length with virtually no resistance in the middle and maximum resistance at either end. Design two of these lengths onto a PCB either side of a pivot with positive and negative contacts connected to a motor and wiping the lands and a double resistance controller is created, which is what happened in the mid-1970s with a Company in Birmingham (UK) creating a range of Varispeed Motor Control Boards colloquially known as 'Bob's Boards' (see Appendix 2). These are still in production and have been sold virtually world-wide. A 'Bob's Board' varies from the first example above and Fig. 9/1 in two ways. Firstly, the board is mounted directly onto the servo with copper contact wipers attached to either a circular or 180º 'horn'. The servo output spindle is the pivot P. Secondly, the four quarters of the PCB have equal resistance, with one pair positive and the other pair

negative, so that each motor lead wiper has maximum resistance introduced as it moves from the horizontal Dead Band onto each resistance land. As each wiper moves towards top and bottom of each diagonal arc there is less and less resistance to the supply and the motor speeds up until with the wipers at the top and bottom of the PCB there is maximum voltage at the motor terminals. The servo has moved to its maximum from its mid position which is also the TX stick mid or neutral position. When the TX stick is returned to neutral and then moved in the opposite direction the wipers now track across the other two diagonal resistance lands but this time each wiper has changed its polarity and the motor is now rotating in reverse. The system is surprisingly efficient but it does need careful installation and setting up, regular inspection and maintenance. The tinned copper substrate which forms the printed circuit is stuck to a glass-fibre board which in turn is attached to a thin aluminium substrate with an overall thickness of just under 1mm. The board is supplied with a self-adhesive pad on its underside which is pressed on to the top of the servo with the board length-ways to the servo length. Before fixing two actions are required. First, the pilot hole in the board's centre has to opened up to clear the mounting boss of the servo output shaft so that the maximum fixing surface on the servo top is used. The best way to enlarge the pilot hole is to carefully rotate a large diameter round tapered file backwards and forwards to its maximum diameter and finishing off by filing to the required size. Do not under any circumstances attempt to enlarge it by drilling as this will tear the thin board and worse still cause an accident to the worker. Secondly, the servo has to be mounted on a sub plate as its fixings cannot be accessed once the PCB is in place. The sub plate should be either thin aluminium or plastic (see Chapter 4 on mounting servos), and wide enough to accept a tag strip fitted at a later stage.

For the next stage the servo needs to be operational. Select the function on one of the sticks that will be the eventual throttle which should ideally be on a ratchet. (The owner's manual will have instructions on how to it convert from spring-loaded.) It is usual for this function to be up and down with up being the forward speed. An appropriate disc or double arm horn is selected and fitted with the two copper wipers. Each is secured underneath the disc with two self-tapping screws through slotted holes with each wiper 180° apart. Exact positioning of the wipers is essential to the ultimate success of obtaining the smoothest motor control the system is capable of. Temporarily assemble the horn/wiper onto the servo. The wipers should be positioned with each wiping dimple almost at the extreme end of the dead band track. With the TX stick and its trim-centred switch on, move the stick to its maximum up, boat forward, and

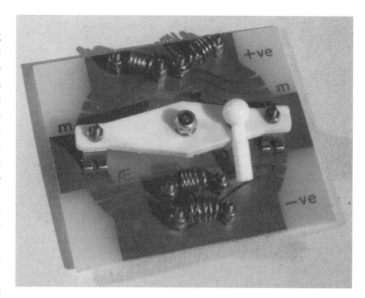

check the servo wiper assembly moves so that with a normal 45° servo arc each wiper is positioned in the centre of the wide minimum-resistance track when full power is called for. This adjustment is a combination of using the slotted adjustment holes and 'setting' each wiper into a 'dog leg' form so that it not only maintains pressure but the top surface is virtually parallel to the board. Now move the stick to neutral and then down, boat astern, and check the wipers are in a similar but opposite position to maximum up – boat forward. Remove the wiper assembly, carefully mark each wiper position on the disc and remove them. Fit a four-tag strip onto the sub plate well clear of the PCB. Solder the lead supplied on the underneath of each wiper, clear of the retaining screws head positions – in the first bend of the dog leg is ideal. Replace them on the disc in the marked positions, fully tighten the wiper screws and secure with a dab of quick-drying paint – or old nail varnish is ideal. Each lead is threaded through a spare hole in the disc from the underneath so that it is clear of the board and soldered onto the tag strip. This is to prevent fouling

Another type of MSC where the servo is remote. Note the wire wound resistances which will get very hot in use. The servo connection is to the ball fitting to the right of the pivot.

Two 'hitec' Electronic Speed Controllers. The left-hand one has an integral BEC which can be switched in or out using the slide switch in the middle. Note the terminated power connectors which should be discarded for marine work. See text. The left-hand ESC has aluminium heat sinks fitted to the FETs.

of the board as the assembly moves in use. The battery supply leads are each soldered onto the top surface of the board in the middle of each of the maximum width tracks on the pivot centreline. These are neatly positioned well clear of the board and soldered onto the other two tags of the above tag strip.

The PCB aluminium substrate serves two functions – a heat sink for any generated heat when in use and providing stiffness to prevent warping and consequential poor wiper contact and arcing. Never drill through the PCB for fixings as this will inevitably cause a battery short and probably a fire. The assembly should be mounted in the boat so that reasonable ventilation is achieved. The PCB should be regularly treated with a contact cleaner/lubricant (see Chapter 19), and checked for warping and arc burns. Treated in this way a 'Bob's Board' will give years of reliable service, but the worker should appreciate that unlike the fully enclosed ESC any MSC is open to the environment, which in a boat is hostile, and can deteriorate

and ultimately fail without regular attention.

Electronic Speed Control

At the beginning of the chapter mention was made of the vast development of electric motor controllers and it is the Electronic Speed Control (ESC) type that this refers to. Although the preceding MSC offers an alternative to the budget-conscious worker the present-day ESC, in the medium current range, becomes attractive when considered price-wise with the cost of a resistance type controller and a servo to drive it. The ESC range is now vast with a current-handling range and price to suit most pockets. The choice varies from self-build budget kits to sophisticated computer-type high current controllers, with a price to match.

The major fault with a resistance controller is the waste of power dissipated within the resistance when slow speed is called for. This results in low torque within the drive motor to move the boat's mass. With an ESC maximum torque is available regardless

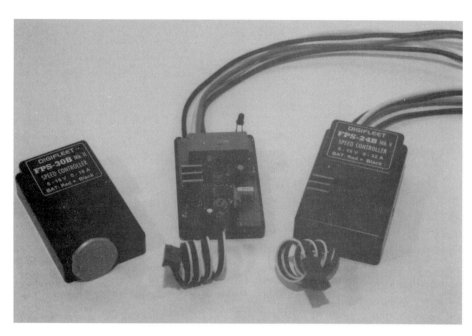

Two British ESCs by Fleet. Conservatively rated and highly reliable with good soft start performance. Note the LED middle top right to indicate relay 'pick up'.

of speed. This is achieved by pulsing the motor with 'squirts' of power on and off, the mark-space ratio, at a chosen frequency. At slow speed the mark, the time the power is on, is small, with a large space between each pulse. When the mark is gradually increased, with a corresponding decrease in the space, the motor has power for a longer time and accelerates up to full speed when the mark is continuous and the space non-existent. Each pulse during the process is at full voltage and with apparent negligible resistance the motor draws full current and thus maximum torque. It is the quest for 'apparent negligible resistance' which accounts for the development and the high price of some ESCs. The 'front end' circuit of a conventional ESC is virtually the same as for a servo except that its output has to tell the power circuitry when to switch on and then to speed up. It also has to tell the power circuitry when to reverse the polarity of the supply to the motor for reverse. Polarity reversal is done with a relay which is energised when the front end circuit detects the stick has moved from centre downwards. The motor supply is fed over the relay contacts from FETs (Field Effect Transistors), controlled by the mark-space circuitry, which are fed from the drive battery supply. FETs are electronic switches and the early ones suffered from a small resistance to DC current as they switched. It has been the reduction of this internal resistance and their ability to handle higher and higher currents that has marked the development of FETs and their use in ESCs. In the past some extravagant claims have been made for the maximum currents some ESCs could handle, so workers should approach this part of an ESC specification with care. Apart from the specialist worker using the latest high-performance motors, the current ESCs in production have negligible resistance to motor current and the scale worker has no need to be concerned about the choice of makes. The choice should be based on long term or continuous current handling only and this should be at least twice the stall current of the motor (see Chapter 7 for determining the stall current). Although many workers

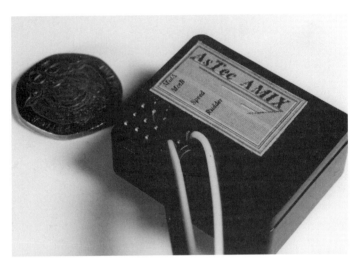

The sophisticated British-designed and manufactured AsTec AMIX mixer allows the marine worker to mix rudder and throttle operation using microprocessor technology and memory. See text.

believe that motor circuit fusing should be as close to the motor as possible the author, after many years of experience, has come to the view that the battery positive supply to both types of controllers, MSCs and ESCs, must be fused in accordance with the principles in Chapter 8. If one of the motor leads is fused it will not detect a fault in the controller and will not protect the wiring back to the battery supply. Most ESCs' positive leads are usually long enough to be cut and the fuse holder inserted in series.

ESCs should be mounted close to their motors with plenty of space around them for ventilation of the FET fins which usually protrude through the top of the case. One make, Electronize, does not have these protrusions, and instead the base of the ESC is a metal heat sink which should be bolted between runners so that ventilation can flow underneath. Most require setting up via adjustment holes and adjacent LEDs usually in the top surface which must be kept clear for access. The author prefers to solder all controller power leads on to a heavy-duty tag strip adjacent to the controller and connect the supply and motor leads to it. This ensures that the controller can be removed easily in the future without

causing heat damage to the suppressor components and internal parts of the hull. It also ensures that the motor leads cannot be shorted together, the supply inadvertently connected and serious internal damage caused. Follow the maker's instructions for setting up and take care to ensure that the reversing relay is de-energised for forward movement. This keeps the relay coil current demand on the RX supply to a minimum. Once the worker is confident that with the relay de-energised and the polarity of the motor leads known for forward movement, this information, plus that obtained during the bench work described in Chapter 7 (motor rotation and establishing the prop hand), can be integrated into the final installation.

Twin motor installations

So far this discussion has focused on a single motor installation. Twin motor installations using one speed controller are practical in several ways. Two 6V motors can be wired in series and fed with 12V using one controller and function. The series motor current will be the same as for one motor fed with 6V and the fuse value will also be identical. One function and controller can feed two motors wired in parallel but the motor current, the controller current rating and the fuse value will be double that of a single motor. Although feasible, both methods suffer from the possibility of unequal revolutions from each motor causing erratic straight-line movement. Turns are much wider as motor revs are roughly the same when ideally the inner motor should slow down with the outer motor speeding up. It is far better to allocate a separate up-and-down stick throttle function to each motor on the TX. This gives independent motor control enabling the operator to balance each motor for equal revolutions using the stick trims, thus achieving straight-line movement and tighter turns. It does require dexterity on the part of the operator as one of the stick functions left to right will also be the rudder. However, a system is available on the UK market, Astec-Amix multi motor mixer, which mixes the rudder signal with each speed controller signal so that the degree of rudder movement will automatically slow the inner motor down and at the same time speed up the outer motor in proportion. This system requires the normal rudder function and servo and one throttle function. Each motor has its own ESC. Both ESC signal leads are connected to the mixer unit which has two signal leads, throttle and rudder, connected into the usual RX outputs. The rudder servo is plugged into the mixer. If the craft has triple motors the centre motor ESC can be plugged into the mixer pass through port and respond to an un-processed throttle signal whilst the mixer controls the wing motors. The mixer is a combination of microprocessor and memory and runs an embedded program that dictates what action it should take and when. Details of this can be found in Appendix 2. Whatever method is used for twin-motor working the props must be contrarotating so great care is needed to ensure the motor polarities and the propellers are of the correct hand to achieve this (see Chapter 7).

The 'robbe Futaba' range of RC equipment includes the F14 Navy Twin Stick TX which has a dual stick unit fitted in place of one of the single sticks. The dual sticks can be mechanically latched together for parallel operation or each can be operated singly. This twin stick unit is available as a separate item for retrofitting to existing F series equipment (see Appendix 2 – Gee Dee Hobbies & Models). This ability to control two TX functions with one hand should not be overlooked for the control of mainsail and jib on sailing boats. However, both stick positions give a visual indication of either motor speed or sail position with just a glance down. Twin stick facility is also available on a converted 'hitec' Ranger III 40Mhz TX ordered new as a special order from Tony Abel Racing Yachts (see Appendix 2).

Reversing an electric motor

A technique that the marine worker is constantly in need of is the knowledge of the options of reversing an electric motor. However, before looking at the options in detail, certain principles must be understood not only to ensure reliable operation but more importantly safe operation. As previously discussed the worker can be involved with high currents which have the potential of causing damage and possibly a fire if they are mis-routed. MSCs and ESCs, when correctly installed, wired, fused and operated will reverse a motor without any problems arising. When a speed control moves from ahead to astern there is a momentary pause in the minimum current flow with the motor stopped, as either the MSC wipers move over the board or the ESC relay is energised, before the reverse current starts to flow. This explains the apparent anomaly of ESC relay contacts rated at a lower current value than the continuous current rating of the controller. The rating of contacts is the breaking current that they can carry without excessive arcing and surface burning which over time will increase contact resistance to current flow. The ESC designer will have chosen the relay to have contacts which have the necessary physical size to carry the full load current in the same way as the power input/output cable size is chosen.

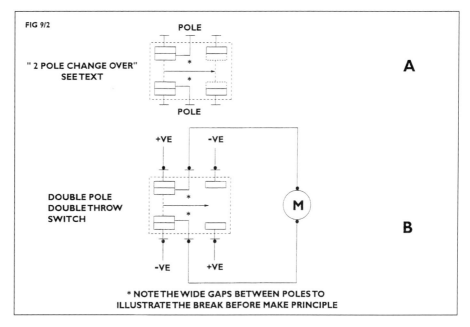

FIG 9/2

POLE

" 2 POLE CHANGE OVER"
SEE TEXT

*

*

POLE

A

+VE   -VE

DOUBLE POLE
DOUBLE THROW
SWITCH

*

*

M

-VE   +VE

B

* NOTE THE WIDE GAPS BETWEEN POLES TO
ILLUSTRATE THE BREAK BEFORE MAKE PRINCIPLE

However, when it is required to reverse a motor on full load, the switching device must be able to 'break' the maximum current flowing at the time of reversal. To reverse a motor the polarity at its terminals is changed within the switching device in a short space of time. This is achieved with a 'changeover' switching action where a double-sided contact will move from a positive contact to a negative contact. A second double-sided contact will move from a negative contact to a positive contact. The 'doubles' are connected to the motor terminals and the 'singles' to the supply and as the two double contacts are physically joined together, but insulated from each other, they move at the same time achieving two pole changeover polarity reversal. Fig. 9/2A illustrates the principle and the interpretation of a catalogue description '2 pole changeover'. Often this is abbreviated, when defining switches, to DPDT, Double-Pole Double-Throw. DPST, Double-Pole Single-Throw, describes an ON-OFF switch where both polarities are controlled. SPST, Single-

Pole Single-Throw, is an ON-OFF switch where one polarity is controlled. Fig. 5/4 in Chapter 5 is an example of a DPDT switch which has a centre off position. The same terminology is sometimes used for relays which are only switches operated electromagnetically instead of manually. However, the more common contact description for relay contacts is: single pole, two pole or 'N' pole changeover. Relays, a very useful tool in the marine worker's armoury, will be discussed in detail in Chapter 15.

One single principle all devices with contacts switching live power supplies must adhere to is 'Break Before Make' (BBM). One thing that must be prevented at all costs is to ensure is the short circuit of live polarities. If this occurs very large currents will flow which could lead to considerable damage to the boat and possible injury to on-lookers as Chapter 8 pointed out. BBM means that the live supply moving contact opens or 'Breaks' one circuit Before 'Making' or closing the alternative circuit. Fig. 9/2B shows a DPDT switch connected to enable motor re-

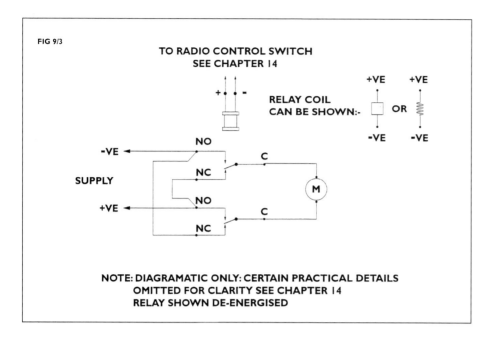

FIG 9/3

TO RADIO CONTROL SWITCH
SEE CHAPTER 14

RELAY COIL
CAN BE SHOWN:-

NOTE: DIAGRAMATIC ONLY: CERTAIN PRACTICAL DETAILS
OMITTED FOR CLARITY SEE CHAPTER 14
RELAY SHOWN DE-ENERGISED

versing. Although the method of illustrating relay contacts differs from switch contacts the principles are the same. However, as relays have two conditions they can be in, energised or de-energised it is necessary on diagrams and on the relay terminals to indicate which condition refers. The de-energised condition of most relays is identified as normal. All the moving contacts are identified by the letter C – common. If the relay is a change-over type each C contact will have two other contacts, one normally open (NO) and one normally closed (NC). Catalogues will usually show a diagram of the relay base where the terminals are numbered and the contacts drawn in the normal or de-energised condition. Care is needed in transferring this onto circuit diagrams as makers differ in their base layouts and numbering. Some makes use C – NC – NO which is clearer as long as the worker relates these to the de-energised condition. A motor reversing relay circuit is shown in Fig. 9/3. The choice of a relay for a particular duty is not complicated but must follow certain principles which will be discussed in detail in Chapter 15.

10

Chargers and Battery Management

By now it will be appreciated that the basis of successful long-term operation of RC equipment is healthy power supplies and to achieve this an understanding of charging principles and correct battery management is vital. Firstly, all dry batteries, either single-use or rechargeable, are chemical in construction and sealed. If the sealing is broken and the contents leak they are corrosive to equipment and extremely hazardous to human beings. Secondly, a high-capacity battery can, if improperly used, be extremely hazardous to human beings, irrespective of its voltage. This applies equally to when it is being charged as to when it is installed in a boat. All through the life of any battery it can be a good and valuable servant but

if the opportunity arises it will become a bad master. Even at the end of its life it has to be disposed of with care to avoid environmental pollution. Workers should contact their local civic authority for guidance and not dispose of batteries in household waste. On no account must any attempt be made to dispose of any battery by burning as this can lead to an explosion with possible disastrous consequences.

Venting

All rechargeable batteries used by marine workers have two common factors. They are sealed and have some form of venting. Nicads not intended for fast charging will vent if they suffer charge abuse. If this happens the cell's future performance is compromised and it should be discarded. However, nicad packs which are constructed from sintered cells and intended for fast charging have an automatic resealing safety venting system which will operate during charge abuse. When fast charging, adequate ventilation must be provided in order to allow gasses to escape in the event of the cells venting. All types of rechargeable cells may be normally charged in any position, either within the boat or removed. However, workers should be aware of the possibility of venting and ideally should install any battery with its vent at the

Two 6V SLAs in a hull. Note the orientation of one positive and one negative terminal of each battery on the right-hand side to the power panel switch to keep the wiring short. The series centre tap connection on the left-hand terminals has still to be made. See Fig 8/1. Note the vents, shown arrowed, with plenty of space around them.

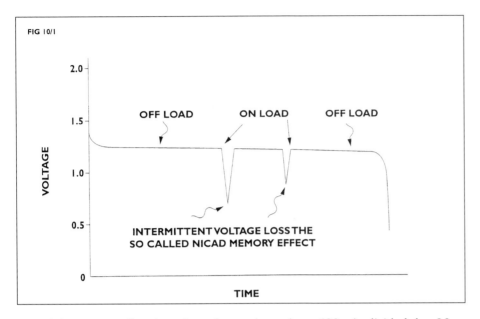

FIG 10/1

OFF LOAD ON LOAD OFF LOAD

VOLTAGE

INTERMITTENT VOLTAGE LOSS THE
SO CALLED NICAD MEMORY EFFECT

TIME

top of the case, to allow it to have free access to the atmosphere. Fast-charging nicads is an abnormal operation and the packs must be removed from the boat and charged with adequate ventilation provided. It is appropriate here to note that because nicads are not environmentally friendly an alternative is slowly becoming available. This is the Nickel Metal Hydride cell (NiMH). These do not contain any hazardous elements and can be disposed of safely. Their capacity is 30 to 50 per cent better than equivalent nicads. However, although it is claimed they do not suffer from the Memory Effect of nicads (see below), which is yet to be conclusively proved, their service life is only a third of that of nicads. At the time of writing they cannot be fast charged and require their own charging regime.

Memory Effect

All standard nicads require charging from a constant current source at a rate determined by their capacity divided by ten. This is known as C/10. For example, a fully discharged 600mAh 4.8V RX pack would normally be charged at 600mA divided by 10 = 60mA, using the trickle charger supplied in the set by the equipment manufacturer. At this charge rate the pack would be fully charged in 14 to 16 hours. This means that the charge equivalent of 160 per cent of the Ah capacity has been returned to the pack. This is fine if the pack is constantly charged from a discharged state, but it is more than likely that only half to two-thirds of its capacity has been used during each sailing session, with the result that repeated charging of a semi-discharged pack creates what has come to be known as Memory Effect.

When a RX supply suffers Memory Effect its voltage under load falls rapidly. It can be intermittent, causing glitching of the servos, or can fail the equipment completely. When the pack is subsequently tested for voltage all seems well and the worker is misled into thinking the failure is something else. Fig. 10/1 above shows the straight-line characteristic of nicads as in Fig. 5/1 but with a voltage dip under load and subsequent return to full voltage – the so-called Memory Effect. Later voltage testing off-load appears to indicate the cell is faultless. What must be fully understood is that workers who repeatedly have long sailing sessions where their packs are almost fully discharged will not suffer this effect but those who have repeated short sessions will. The cure is to completely discharge a pack and then fully charge it at least four times a year. Discharging any battery by shorting its terminals is extremely hazardous and must never be done deliberately. Not only will the worker be exposed to serious injury but the battery will suffer irreparable damage. Discharging nicads requires a controlled regime to ensure the pack is not completely 'emptied' because if this occurs and the load remains connected there is a possibility that polarity reversal will result. Under normal working, where the load demands on a pack are intermittent to the point of exhausting the pack, polarity reversal will not generally occur. It is when a pack is subjected to a continuous high discharge beyond the safe low voltage point that this happens. Although experienced workers can construct their own discharge equipment this is not recommended, and it is far better to invest in equipment designed for the purpose. If the equipment also has multiple cell charge facilities and is capable of capacity analysis the worker has complete control and management of the most vital parts of RC equipment – the RX and TX power supplies.

Battery testing

To ensure a nicad or metal hydride pack is producing power at its full stated capacity it not only has to be charged efficiently but also has to be tested regularly within a system that the worker has confidence in. This can only be done by first charging the pack and then discharging to verify the charge it

has taken, a process known as cycling. No battery pack has an indefinite life. It will only take a number of charging cycles which on average is in excess of 1500 for a nicad pack and in excess of 750 for a NiMH pack. To achieve this requires a number of parameters to be applied so that the whole process can be carried out efficiently. From the previous example it can be seen that a charger rated at 60mA will not efficiently charge a pack with a capacity of 1700mAh, in a reasonable time, when, applying $C/10$, it requires a constant charging current of 170mA. When discharging a pack it is necessary to know the number of cells within a pack to ensure that each cell is not discharged below its safe low-voltage point. The last parameter is charging time which is a product of the C value. The 60mA charge current above is a trickle charge which will not damage the pack if left connected beyond the standard 16 hours. However, nicads can be charged at higher currents as long as the charge time is carefully monitored to ensure the charge is terminated before damage is caused to the pack.

There is no doubt that trickle charging is the safest method but if regularly practised with occasional over-charging the pack life and capacity will be reduced. This slow charging will not show any possible problem within the pack such as a dud cell which will only come to light when the boat is in the middle of the pond and all control suddenly fails. Faster charging is possible as long as the time element is controllable. As a pack absorbs a constant current the pack voltage gradually builds from the minimum safe voltage to its maximum fully-charged voltage and then suddenly exhibits a very small voltage drop. This drop is in the order of 10mV for one 1.2V cell and is known as the Delta Peak. Higher

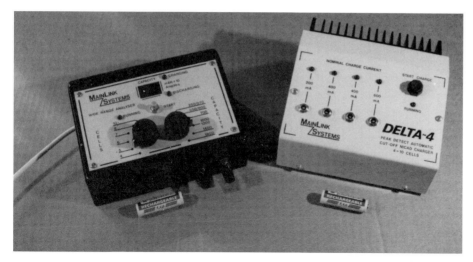

MainLink equipment. The Analyser connections are either 4mm banana plugs or spade terminations. All four inputs on the DELTA-4 (right) can be used at the same time or added to as required.

charging currents will generate heat within the pack so it is important to detect the fully charged state and terminate charging before heat damage can occur. The fully charged state can also be detected by temperature sensing. As each cell reaches its full capacity it cannot absorb any more energy and this is dispersed in the form of heat. If only a single cell is being charged a suitably placed sensor can detect this temperature rise and terminate the charge. With a multi-cell pack one cell may heat up before the majority and be heat-damaged before the sensor operates. Fast charging can also be controlled by a timing system relative to temperature rise within the pack. This calls for experience and knowledge on the part of the operator and is not recommended for the average marine worker. By far the best regime is to use charging equipment which senses Delta Peak over a range of cells and capacities and discharge/ analysis when required enabling the worker to keep test records for each pack. The regular use of discharge/ analysis regime records gives early indication of the end of a pack's life. Experience has shown that this is when the capacity has fallen to 80 per cent of the stated capacity for a RX pack and 70

per cent for a TX pack. But this does not mean that the pack should be discarded. It still has a life either in the workshop or as a power supply for non-safety duties in a boat such as powering auxiliary functions. The logic behind the two different percentages is that a RX pack is subjected to a more onerous life with varying current demands whereas a TX pack has a steady continuous current demand which never alters. It is useful here to note that from new a nominal 4.8V pack, if charged correctly, will operate for long periods at between 5.00V and 5.25V as long as it has the correct capacity for the loads it is expected to drive. The same applies to a TX pack of 9.6V. This will operate for most of its life at between 10.0V and 11.00V.

The author has used a range of equipment from a British Company – Mainlink Systems – for many years (see Appendix 2). The equipment consists of a microprocessor-controlled charger detecting Delta Peak on four outputs charging at 200, 400, 400 and 600mA on packs from 4 to 10 cells. Each output is independent with single start control. It is just a question of plugging in a pack and pressing the 'START CHARGE' button irrespective of whether other packs are being charged.

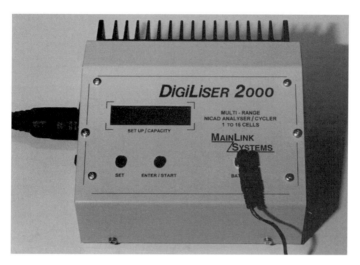

The MainLink DigiLiser 2000. See text.

Delta Peak detection ensures full charge with a visual indication that charging is complete. The unit will handle any pack from 150mAh to 2.2Ah capacity. The charger is complemented with a Wide Range Analyser handling packs containing 4, 5, 6, 7, 8 and 10 cells with capacities ranging from 250mAh to 1.8mAh. The pack is connected via 3.5mm terminals and the cell numbers and capacity set by two switches. Pressing the Start button will commence the discharging cycle down to the safe minimum voltage where the charging will automatically start. The capacity $\times$ 10 of the pack will be shown on the two-digit LED readout. This reads 10mAh for packs up to 990mAh and 100mAh for packs over 1Ah. The first cycle should be repeated twice more to ensure the pack capacity readouts are the best possible obtainable as the act of discharging will rejuvenate a 'tired' pack at the end of a sailing season. It is important to keep records, especially from new, so that a pack nearing the end of its life can be detected. As discussed above this only means pensioning the pack off RX or TX duty and using it on non-safety functions only. What must be appreciated is that cycling alone is of little use and no amount of cycling will revive a worn-out pack. Cycling must be part of an analytical regime supported by accurate records. If practised from new, the marine worker will enjoy total confidence in his equipment knowing that the most vulnerable part of it is as reliable as it is possible make it.

MainLink's DigiLiser 2000 is the latest analyser developed from the Wide Range equipment described above. This is even more flexible and deals with both nicads and metal hydrides packs from 1 to 16 cells and 100mAh to 5Ah capacities, with single cycle, double cycles or discharge-only options available. The machine is very user-friendly both in setting-up and in use, with only two buttons, a liquid crystal display and a 2.5mm DC power connector. It incorporates a 'bleeper' to alert the user to end of discharge and charge periods. It will also draw attention to poor connections which brings the discussion nicely to 'Black Wire' corrosion.

This evil only attacks the negative conductor and it is not the use of nicads or metal hydrides that causes it. It can occur with a simple AC/DC power source and is not confined to RC equipment. It does, however, have one common denominator – moisture. It is an electrolytic reaction which causes corrosion to a negatively-polarised conductor in a moist atmosphere. Of the three RC modelling disciplines, marine conditions are the worst for creating possible equipment failures. The RC system is required to work in humid conditions where ventilation is non-existent because of the need to keep the inside of the hull dry, conditions ideal for breeding 'Black Wire' corrosion and all marine workers must be aware of the danger. Systematic checks of all wiring, especially the negative conductors, to and from the RX power supplies including switch, charging socket and connectors must

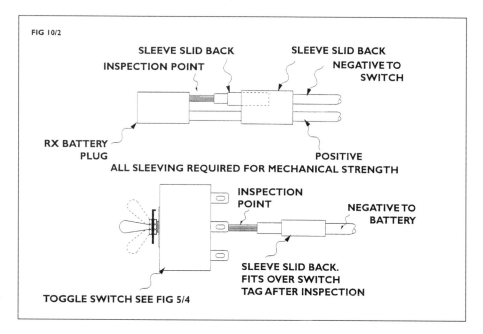

FIG 10/2

SLEEVE SLID BACK
INSPECTION POINT

SLEEVE SLID BACK
NEGATIVE TO
SWITCH

RX BATTERY
PLUG

POSITIVE

ALL SLEEVING REQUIRED FOR MECHANICAL STRENGTH

INSPECTION
POINT

NEGATIVE TO
BATTERY

SLEEVE SLID BACK.
FITS OVER SWITCH
TAG AFTER INSPECTION

TOGGLE SWITCH SEE FIG 5/4

become a regular habit. This is why it is recommended that the wiring harness and switch supplied with the equipment is discarded and replaced with a custom-built system. If the harness is new the leads and connectors can be retrieved and used as described in Chapter 5.

'Black Wire' corrosion is the copper strands making up the conductor literally rotting away under the insulation. As it rots the conductor becomes more and more resistive to the current flow which eventually will prevent the receiver and servos from working. If left unchecked the conductor will completely disappear. In the initial stages the wiring appears dull and will slowly turn black – hence the name. Inspection requires the plastic insulation being peeled back to examine the bare conductor, needing the use of a sharp knife which can easily sever the fragile strands and reducing the current capacity of the conductor. If, however, a custom-built wiring harness is used, inspection points can be built in and this possible future failure avoided. Fig. 10/2 above shows the principles

recommended. Once 'Black Wire' is found the only solution is complete surgery and replacement of the conductor affected. Never attempt to cut back and resolder even faintly tarnished wiring. The solder will not bond and will very quickly become a high-resistance joint leading to inevitable failure.

If using the DigiLiser 2000 there is the added safeguard of an automatic check on the integrity of the harness wiring and connections. If any doubt exists the bleeper will alert the worker to examine the complete system. It will not specifically identify 'Black Wire' but it can cast doubt on the integrity of the charging wiring, the charging switch contacts and the wiring from the switch back to the battery. Note that it will not check the wiring or the switch contacts back to the RX. Equipment storage, with batteries in situ, in damp conditions must never be allowed. If it is necessary to store equipment under such conditions, remove the batteries. If stored in possibly damp conditions the equipment, when required for use, should be left in a warm place for at least 24 hours before the power packs are replaced. Nicads and metal hydrides should always be stored in a cool environment fully charged as both types have poor charge retention in storage. If the storage exceeds 8 weeks they should be re-charged. Before being put back into service they should be subjected to at least two cycles of discharge/charging. Before concluding TX/RX power supply management some workers may find that while attempting to manage their TX packs installed within the transmitter that it is impossible to discharge the pack via the TX charging socket. This is because a diode has been inserted in one lead, from the socket to the pack, to protect the TX circuitry in the event of the wrong polarity being connected. The solution is to remove the pack for cycling which is no bad thing as it gives the opportunity to check for 'Black Wire' within the TX.

Sealed lead acid batteries

The introduction of the sealed lead acid battery solved one of the major problems for the marine worker who needed a propulsion supply with a reasonable power/weight ratio and was completely safe in use. Prior to sealed lead acid batteries the only alternative to large and heavy dry batteries was the rechargeable 12V 'wet' lead acid battery used in motor cars and the 6V version used in motorbikes. Both these types had a poor power/weight ratio and had to be handled very carefully due to their acid content. A high proportion of the 'wet' weight was the outer case material and the large terminal posts. The swiftly-emerging plastics industry solved the case weight problem and the ever-growing use of electronics in industry created a need for a high-capacity, maintenance-free stand-by battery power supply in the

event of mains failure. This was the sealed lead acid battery. One of the most popular SLAs is the Yuasa range where the acid electrolyte is contained within glass fibre wadding which in turn surrounds lead-calcium alloy porous plates. The battery is valve-regulated where virtually all the gasses generated during charging are recombined into the negative plate and returned to the water content of the electrolyte. The outer case is high-impact ABS plastic resin. Each battery has a low pressure auto-reseal venting system in the event of excessive build-up of gasses during charging. The positive and negative moulded-in blade terminals will accept 6.35mm ($\frac{1}{4}$ in) push-on connectors but as discussed in Chapter 8 it is a personal choice whether to use these or soldered connections. However, it should be noted that 'push-ons' may not be able to carry the large currents generated during a short-duration discharge which could result in heat damage to the battery top and surroundings. Appendix 3 lists the size, weight, voltage and capacity of the current Yuasa range.

SLAs must be charged from a constant-voltage supply held within 300mV for 6V batteries and within 600mV for 12V batteries. The battery itself will regulate the current. Generally speaking, when the charge current has fallen to 30mA, the battery can be considered fully charged. *Under no circumstances whatsoever* must a sealed lead acid battery be charged using an automotive battery charger. If this is used it will destroy the SLA in a very short time and could cause an explosion, due to a rapid build-up of internal gas overwhelming the venting system. Constant-voltage chargers are available through most model shops or from specialist suppliers listed in Appendix 2. Some have the facility of 2, 6 and 12V charging via a rotary switch.

If a centre-tapped power supply is installed with two new 6V batteries, as shown in Fig. 8/1 and discussed in Chapter 8, these can be series-charged at 12V. SLAs have a low self-discharge rate which allows them to be left unused for a long time. They should be stored fully charged. The Yuasa range can tolerate a high overdischarge and still recover their full capacity. They must never be left in a fully discharged state for long periods. Marine workers should appreciate that any SLA battery has the potential for serious damage and injury if subjected to short-circuit conditions and this must be born in mind at all times. For those workers who feel they are competent to build a simple constant voltage 6V SLA charger, circuit details can be found in Appendix 3. The charger can be powered from any 12V DC source including an automotive battery charger. It will charge any 6V SLA battery up to 10Ah capacity.

RX switch/charging harnesses

To complete this chapter it is worth looking at the various alternatives available for a custom-built RX switch/ charging harness. One of the benefits of a custom-built harness is the opportunity to equip it with compatible plugs and sockets for the analysing/ cycling/charging equipment. The most useful range are DC power plugs and sockets similar to those used on the Walkman-type personal cassette players. The range differs with the diameter of the centre pin – 1.3mm, 2.1mm and 2.5mm. This enables the worker to construct dedicated leads for different duties. Most, if not all, TX charging sockets use this system. The chassis-type sockets can be mounted behind portholes and other inconspicuous positions in a boat's superstructure. These components are available from Maplins and Tandy Stores in the UK and Tandy Stores and Radio Shack in the USA and Canada. The switch has already been discussed in Chapter 5 and Fig. 5/4 and the three leads can be used from the supplied manu-facturer's harness if they are long enough and new. However, these leads are usually of the same type and physical size used for servos and are vulnerable to damage and a reduction of their current-carrying capacity if any of the strands are broken

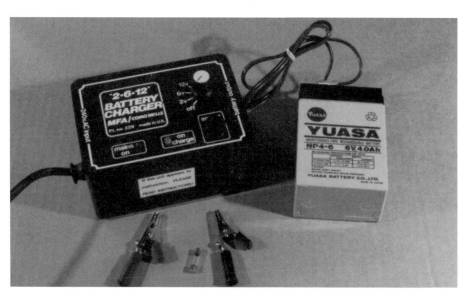

The MFA multi-voltage Sealed Lead Acid charger available from most model shops. The output leads can be terminated with either Lucar connectors or the supplied crocodile clips. A spare fuse is also supplied.

when the insulation is stripped back when looking for 'black wire'. The author has found over the years that using a heavier gauge of wiring is preferable with inspection points built into the harness. This is achieved by leaving at least 15mm of bare battery conductor visible where it is soldered onto the centre tags of the switch and sleeving the leads so that inspection can be carried out when required. The RX battery end is more awkward as each make of equipment will need its own dedicated plug for the RX. This is solved by mounting a small piece of 'Vero' type stripboard (see Chapters 11 and 15) local to the RX and terminating the plug lead and the wiring back to the switch on it. The plug lead is looped through the board for mechanical protection and stripped back about 20mm and sleeved before soldering onto the board. Leave enough space for the inspection sleeve to be slid back. It should only be necessary to do the negative leads but if the worker wants to play ultra-safe there is no reason not to terminate the

11

Tools and Soldering

One of the joys of marine modelling is the ever-increasing level of skill the worker acquires as progress is made within the hobby. The amount of care and patience required to build a complicated superstructure can be used for building and extending RC functions which in turn bring to life working elements either on or in superstructures and hulls.

All marine workers know that certain tools have specific tasks and need care to keep them at the peak of efficiency. No worker would dream of using the back edge of a modelling knife as a screwdriver and the same is true of tools used for electronic work. All ferrous hand tools used on a marine worker's bench will sooner or later become magnetised and if used in the proximity of certain electronic components will at worst destroy them and at best corrupt them enough to cause failure later. For this reason a separate set of tools is required for electronic work, kept only for that purpose and, most importantly, stored separately. There is no doubt that electrostatic damage can occur to present-day electronic circuits once they are removed from equipment and when they are being built. The most vulnerable components are integrated circuits (ICs) which are small blocks of plastic with many pins protruding from the base. These ICs are the heart of the self-build kits discussed in Chapter 13 and need to be handled with great care. When supplied in a kit they are fully protected and it is only when they are removed that damage can be inflicted unless proper procedures, tools and techniques are used. The same care has to be observed if a servo lead is replaced on a servo PCB. The very act of soldering using an inappropriate iron can cause damage to an IC already installed on a PCB through the connecting 'lands'. A dedicated electronics worker will equip his workstation with the maximum facilities, at great cost, to create a totally safe area as he/she will be working on very expensive equipment, but this is not necessary for the marine RC worker so long as basic principles are followed and care at all times is the watchword.

First the workbench. This should be made of wood and if there is any ferrous metal in its construction or on it, such as a metal vice, this should be earthed, not to the mains earth but to a piece of copper pipe driven into the earth outside the workshop. If indoors, try to earth onto the water supply or central heating pipe. An anti-static bench mat is ideal if funds allow although a workable alternative is Maplins' anti-static high density foam sheet – 305mm × 305mm.

Soldering

Soldering is a skill that is easily acquired as long as certain principles are followed. To make a successful soldered joint:

1. The joint must be clean and free from oil or grease before soldering.
2. The correct wattage iron, fitted with the most appropriate 'bit', must quickly raise the temperature so that when the solder is applied it flows freely.
3. Solder must never be carried to the iron on the 'bit'.
4. The joint must remain steady until the solder has 'set'.

This last principle can only be met if the joint is sound mechanically. It is no use just holding two pieces of wire together and hoping that using solder to 'stick' them together will produce a reliable joint that will be failure-free in the long term. What usually happens in this case is that a slight movement before the solder sets creates a 'dry joint' which over a period of time becomes more resistive to current flow and eventually

creates a failure. A sound soldered joint is easily recognisable as it will appear as a shiny pimple of solder whereas a 'dry joint' will have the appearance of a dull crystalline blob made up of individual crystals of solder held together by the flux used when it was made. Over time the flux dissipates, with the joint resistance gradually increasing until it prevents the correct current flow with the resultant failure. Even if a joint is sound mechanically a dry joint can still be created if the soldering heat is insufficient for the mass of metal being heated. Perversely, if there is too much heat it will damage the components, destroy the flux and heat the solder to a point where it will break down and create a dry joint. The solution is the right choice of iron wattage and a selection of 'bits' to fit it.

Any mains-powered soldering iron can exhibit a leakage current into the joint. The way in which this occurs is outside the scope of this Manual, but the reader can be assured that this is typical and is safe for the user. But it is not safe for components such as transistors and ICs which are connected to the joint and can be destroyed or worse still damaged enough to fail at a later date, usually when the boat is in the middle of the pond! Modern soldering irons have been developed to combat leakage current and are double-shafted with a ceramic inner shaft and an outer shaft of stainless steel for strength. As discussed above, too much heat is just as damaging as too little. A reasonable choice for the marine worker is either 18 watts or 25 watts. The 18-watt iron is ideal for electronic kit work but lacks that extra power when soldering large propulsion supply joints. A 25-watt iron can occasionally generate too much heat when soldering on very thin lands (tracks) of PCBs which causes them to lift away from the board. A good compromise is to use a 25-watt iron in

Antex 25watt iron and Regulator which plugs directly into a 13amp UK socket. A harmonised European version is also available.

conjunction with a regulator which enables the worker to select the correct temperature for any soldering task. A recommended combination is the Antex XS 25W iron and the Antex Energy Regulator Part No. UE82060. (Squires – Appendix 2) The iron is double-shafted as above with a very low leakage current of 2μA. It comes with a No 51 bit with a tip diameter of 3.0mm. This will be suitable for most jobs but the worker is advised to supplement it with a No 55 with a tip diameter of 0.5mm for fine work on PCBs such as renewing servo leads and a No 52 with a tip diameter of 4.7mm when maximum heat is required. The modern bit should never be filed as this destroys its self-cleaning properties. In use it is kept clean by wiping it over a damp sponge just prior to heating a joint. The use of a custom-designed stand complete with space for this sponge is highly recommended. The regulator is connected to the iron instead of the mains plug and will regulate the temperature between 100-400°C. It is calibrated for use with the XS 25W iron. Spare heating elements are available and the prudent worker is advised to purchase one at the same time as the iron and regulator. No matter what its size any soldering iron is a valuable servant but a very bad master, capable of inflicting very nasty burns and damage to plastic RC equipment housings etc, if it is not parked in the proper stand discussed above. Bits when not in use must be stored appropriately so that when used they are not contaminated with other workshop substances leading to suspect joints. All the suppliers listed in Appendix 2 offer a choice of stands. The author has found from long experience that a stand with a heavy base, provision for the sponge and storage for bits is ideal.

Prior to any soldering all components should be cleaned with surgical spirit or a proprietary brand of cleaner. Dull

wiring, component leads and PCB lands should be gently burnished with fine grade wire wool prior to using a liquid cleaner. Avoid touching the cleaned areas. All electronic/electrical soldering work should be done using a 60 per cent tin and 40 per cent lead alloy solder containing a non-corrosive flux. The common melting temperature is 188°C. A bit temperature of around 248°C is a good starting point, which experience will soon show whether to increase or decrease according to the size and type of joint being soldered. The iron must be held against the maximum area of the joint with the solder in readiness but not touching. After a few seconds touch the joint, not the bit, with the solder which if the joint is at the right temperature will run easily around it forming the typical shiny pimple which is the hallmark of a sound soldered joint. Remove the iron immediately and wait a few seconds for the solder to set. Remember that excessive heat can do damage so good practice is to use heat shunts where possible on the leads of delicate components. These are in the form of locking metal tweezers which are clipped onto transistor leads etc, preventing heat reaching the device. Another useful tool is a desolder pump which quickly removes molten solder

Heat shunts in use. See Squires – Appendix 2.

A desolder pump and 'helping hands'.

more easily and form a sound joint. The positive and negative tags of a battery are another example. These are usually brass but have been tinned. A good practice exercise for a beginner is to strip stranded cable and twist the strands tightly together and then tin them by heating and judging when to apply the solder in just the right amount. All PCBs have lands of thin copper which have been tinned, giving them a silver appearance. It should be noted that too much abrasive cleaning of any tinned surface can remove the tinning to an extent that if the base material appears it must be re-tinned. If too much solder is applied this is where the desolder pump comes in useful. Soldering irons, stands, spares, solder and soldering aids are available from firms as listed in Appendix 2.

from a joint by suction created when releasing a spring-loaded piston within a cylinder. Most electronic components the marine worker is likely to meet have already been 'tinned', meaning that a thin skin of solder has been deposited onto the wire leads, which are usually copper, during manufacture. When two tinned leads are twisted together and heated the tinning will accept the solder

There are times while soldering when the worker requires three hands to ensure a sound joint! One of the most useful items is a device called 'Helping Hands', comprising a heavy base which carries two crocodile clips on ball-joint arms so that the item held can be angled for the best working position. It is ideal for holding PCBs particularly when kit building (see Chapter 13). Heavier items can be held in a multi-angle vice which can be swivelled through 360° by use of a ball joint. This vice is secured to the bench top with a built-in clamp when required. An excellent example of the type is the MB716 from the MINICRAFT range.

The MINICRAFT Multi-Vice MB716. Note the soft jaws and the ball/socket for unlimited working angles. Can be ordered from any model shop.

Other tools

Probably one of the most used hand tools are pliers. These come in a variety of sizes and shapes and two forms of construction. The best and longest-lasting are box jointed. This means that one half of the pliers is jointed within a 'box' or slot of the other half. Both halves of the joint are machined to a precision fit and with a precision pivot will accurately mate for many years. This type is expensive to produce and this is reflected in the price. For the dedicated electronics worker box-type hand tools are a long term investment which the marine worker cannot justify for occasional electronic projects. Lap-jointed pliers are just that. The two halves are overlapped with each other and held together with a central pivot. If the pivot and the mating holes in each half are machined with reasonable precision the lap joint pliers will retain its mating accuracy for a long period which is more than adequate for the average marine worker. There are a number of jaw shapes and lengths available which can be confusing to the beginner. The most common is the snipe nose which enables working in a confined area common to the majority of electronic work with modern RC equipment. The snipe nose will have flat jaws which ideally should be ground for straightening the pins of ICs. When used for this task the jaws should not be magnetised and ideally made of stainless steel, which is very difficult to magnetise. Other types are round nose, flat nose and bent nose, all extremely useful when working on PCBs. The last hand tool is the side cutter used for trimming the wire ends of components. The handles of tools used for electronic work need to be insulated to prevent electrostatic discharge into components. All the above requirements can be met by a set of five Miniature Precision Pliers at a very economic price in the Squires catalogue listed in Appendix 2 and other retail outlets – Maplins, Tandy and Radio Shack (USA).

Screwdrivers, both flat-blade and cross-point, are also required mainly to gain access to the inside of RC equipment. Available from all those suppliers listed in Appendix 2 are the

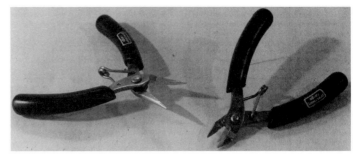

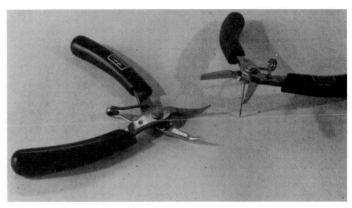

precision range of chrome molyb-denum screwdrivers. The reason for using a precision screwdriver on RC equipment is to ensure that either the cross point or straight slot in the screw head is not damaged by a doubtful driver shape to the extent that the screw becomes irremovable and worse still destroys the plastic thread which holds the two halves of a case together. Access into gear will be required at least once every season to carry out the routine maintenance recommended in Chapter 19. A number of sizes are required of both types to accommodate the variety of screw sizes used. Nothing is worse than attempting to remove a cross-point screw using the incorrect size of screw-driver. Many of the suppliers offer sets and these should be hunted for. Also required are spanner sets both BA (British Association) and Metric. Sets of Hexagon or Allen keys are also a useful addition to the bench. These are avail-able in Metric and Imperial sizes, again from suppliers listed in Appendix 2.

Four stainless steel handtools from Squires, see Appendix 2, which are ideal for electronic kit work. Stainless steel is difficult to magnetise and the insulated handles keep static at bay.

Below: IC pin straightener and insertion and removal tool from Maplins.

Bottom: A Shesto combined headband magnifier and illumination. There is a choice of clip-on magnification lenses. Ideal for small PCB work as well as general marine model building.

Once the marine worker becomes interested in building electronic kits (Chapter 13), the necessity of handling IC components arises. Again for failure reasons the pins have to be protected from electrostatic damage, particularly from fingers, when inserting them into PCBs. Two items are available to assist the worker, an IC insertion tool and an IC extraction tool. Both these tools should be available from the suppliers previously mentioned. When building kits it is often necessary to ensure components are inserted into the PCB at a certain height to fit inside a case. When measuring use either a stainless steel or aluminium rule and once again guard against static pollution. From the previous discussion it can be seen that the success of repeating sound soldered joints depends upon speed with the correct iron temperature and bit, preceded by cleanliness and backed up using practical aids to keep the work steady. Heat-shunt tweezers have already been mentioned and another useful type is the heat-resistant self-grip tweezers. These are either straight or curved for access into tight locations.

Finally, it does occasionally happen that pondside soldering is required. There are a number of portable soldering irons now available which are fuelled by Butane gas. One of the most versatile is the ANTEX GASCAT which can be purchased separately fitted with

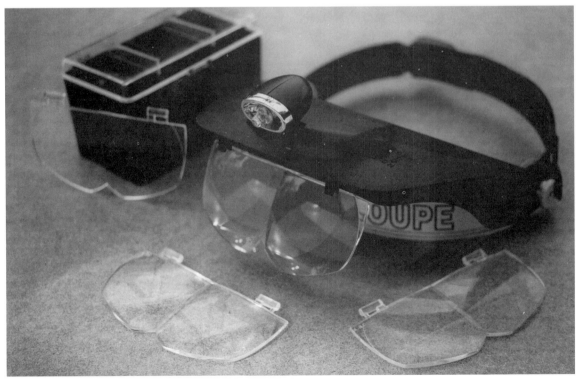

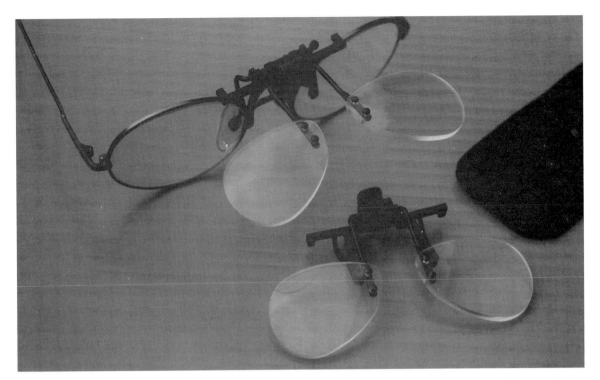

a fine S1 tip or as part of a kit which extends the iron into other very useful areas including silver soldering and hot air for heat-shrinking special sleeving when making up leads etc. It has a clear gas chamber so that fuel usage can be monitored over a period of 55 minutes per charge on setting 1. Workers should, however, be aware that this iron has the equivalent power of a 60-watt iron and a tip temperature of 450°C when soldering. When used for silver soldering and brazing the gas torch tip can reach 1300°C. Great care is needed not only in use but when storing after use. Although the iron has a cover complete with a clip for pocket storage this is not recommended for use as in bright sunlight it is difficult to be sure the flame is entirely extinguished.

For spectacle wearers Shesto 'clip-ons' come with 3 dioptre lenses.

12

Testing

By now the reader will have realised that two electrical parameters keep emerging that tell the worker a lot about the health of his equipment – voltage and current. Both can be read by an instrument called a multimeter. Two types are available, digital and analogue. The difference between the two types can be seen straightaway in the way the readout is presented. A digital voltmeter (DVM) will have a liquid crystal display while an analogue meter will display a pointer moving across an arc with a number of scales. There are two operational differences. The DVM is a much faster instrument and being fully electronic it does not load the circuit as much as the analogue instrument which also takes longer for the pointer to reach its correct position. It is important to keep the meter load on a circuit low because it absorbs power from the circuit which can distort the true reading if the power supply driving the circuit is unable to also provide power for the meter. Meter load is the sensitivity of the meter and for an analogue meter this is stated as ohms per volt. A budget analogue meter will have a low rating of around 2000 ohms, while a higher-quality meter will have a sensitivity of 20,000 ohms per volt on the DC ranges and 8000 ohms on the AC ranges. 'Per volt' refers to the range the meter is set to read, *eg* when set to a 10V range the meter will place 10 × 20,000 = 200,000 ohms across the circuit being tested. The sensitivity of a

DVM is, however, expressed in a different way – input impedance – but it is still the resistance that is offered to the circuit under test. Budget DVMs often do not state their impedance and for this reason should be avoided. Other budget DVMs will offer 1MΩ on DC voltage ranges and 450kΩ on AC voltage ranges. Mid-price meters will offer 10MΩ on DC and 4.5MΩ on AC voltage ranges as well as 10MΩ on both AC and DC voltage ranges. Top DVMs will have impedances of 10MΩ on all voltage ranges.

Although the choice for the first-time marine worker appears to be wide and confusing, the requirement that narrows it down is the ability of the instrument to measure the stall current of DC motors (see Chapter 7). As a long-term investment a DVM reading 20 amps DC with a Data Hold facility (very useful for motor stall readings) would be the recommended choice, an example being the Maplin White Gold WGO22, a laboratory-grade instrument with a price to match. However, two mid-priced meters reading 20 amp DC current can be found in the Maplin Precision Gold range. Both the White and Precision Gold series offer additional facilities throughout both ranges. DVMs are easier to use than analogues, which do need care to ensure the meter lead polarities are correct. If not the moving coil movement to which the pointer is attached will be driven backwards and damage can result. The same thing can happen even driving forward if the range setting is too low for what is being measured, because the pointer will be driven at speed against the end stop and in a severe case actually bent, destroying its accuracy when reading the scale. Most DVMs will indicate + or − in the display according to how it is connected. The above WGO22 has an Autorange selection which protects against incorrect settings. It also has an analogue bar graph below the digital readout which is very useful for sensitive settings.

It is really a question of how far the marine worker wishes to get involved in electronics whether a number of features, such as resistor, transistor and capacitor testing etc, are included which would ultimately be of use as the worker's interest and experience grows. DVMs of course need an internal battery to drive them and this is always supplied. They are also fused internally, usually with two fuses, one for the milliamp range and one for the ampere range. When making the initial purchase it is prudent to also buy spare fuses and at the same time confirm that these will always be available in the future. It is not always appreciated that analogue meters also require an internal battery – sometimes two – to drive the resistance ranges. Again it is prudent to check that these will be freely obtainable for the future. Usually there will be no user-replaceable fuses. Whatever type of meter is used, always fit top-quality leakproof batteries and check for condition at least every 3 months. Once a battery has leaked inside a meter it might just as well be scrapped as its accuracy will always be in question.

All multimeters, regardless of where purchased, should come with test leads and a user manual. Strange as it may seem the test leads are the most important part of a meter because they protect the user. Sooner or later the marine worker will need to use the meter on the domestic mains voltage supply in the workshop. Mains supply voltages whether in the UK or elsewhere are lethal and must be treated with extreme care. What must be appreciated is that these supplies can deliver very large currents which are lethal irrespective of the voltage and the only thing that limits the current flow is the resistance of the human body. This resistance is very high in a young child but slowly reduces with age. When measuring high voltages the user should ensure that only one hand is holding one test lead at any one time. Always attach one lead onto the supply first and then measure with the other. The principle is to ensure that the high voltage current cannot find a path through one arm, across the chest and down the other arm. It is for these reasons that test leads must be of the highest quality and safety possible. This also applies to the design of the meter where these leads are connected.

In the early days of electronics all multimeters were analogue with terminal posts and spade connectors for attachment of the test leads, a design which created live bare metal on the meter top that was potentially dangerous and led to some nasty accidents. All modern meter designs now incorporate sunken sockets with shrouded touch-proof 4mm connecting plugs on the test leads. The other end of the lead is equipped with a test probe. The majority of leads supplied new with meters will have dual-purpose probes with finger safety guards and a crocodile clip which can be screwed off to reveal a slim pointed probe. In use one clip is attached to, say, the negative terminal and the probe can then 'hunt' for a positive to obtain a reading. Alternatively both crocodile clips can be attached, say for a series current reading (see Fig. 7/3). Not all leads supplied with new meters will have fully insulated crocodile clips so the safety-conscious worker may wish for something better. It is easy to make your own meter leads from the large selection of probes and clips available from Maplins and other specialist suppliers. Meter leads come in for a lot of use so mechanical strength is important. The cable should be flexible with thick insulation to take punishment in use and be able to carry large DC currents. Maplins list a Silicon Extra Flexible wire with 0.75mm thickness of insulation and a rated current of 32 amps. Whilst making test leads it is also prudent to make a number of 'jumper' leads of various lengths. A jumper lead has a crocodile clip at either end and is useful for many workshop operations where a temporary connection is required. The rated current can be lower than that for meter leads but extra-flexible wire should be used. Maplins list such a wire rated at 2.5 amps. If a higher current is required in use then two leads can be used in parallel. All leads should be pairs – red and black – and it is a wise habit to always ensure that the correct colour is used to indicate the polarity of the circuit under test or temporarily connected. Occasionally the necessity arises to measure voltages and currents using batteries terminated with makers' connectors. Useful leads can be constructed with the maker's connector on one end and either 4mm plugs to fit the DVM or shrouded crocodile clips on the other. A very useful lead is one that has a connector for the battery on one end and the other end of the negative lead terminated in the plug for the RX. The positive lead is separated with both ends terminated in 4mm meter plugs.

In use the RX is connected up in the usual way without servos to a fully charged and voltage-noted RX battery with the DVM in series to measure milliamps. The system is switched on, TX first then RX. The meter will show the quiescent current which typically will be around 8-10mA of the RX. Switch the RX off. The DVM is now set to read, say, 1 amp and one servo plugged into the RX. Switch the RX back on and note the reading. Subtract the first quiescent current reading and the remainder is the servo quiescent current. Now repeat the exercise operating the TX. Again subtract the RX quiescent current and the remainder is the servo minimum load current. In this way a record can be built up for future reference for all the operational elements within the RX system (see Fig. 5/3). At the end the battery off-load voltage should be checked. It should not have lost any significant voltage. This exercise is very useful to determine which movement of the TX stick causes the ESC reversing relay to pick up and identify the correct polarity connections for astern movement (see Chapter 9 on ESCs). Remember that the servo reverse facility on the TX is available to ensure the ESC relay operates when the stick is pulled back. The exercise also demonstrates the necessity to operate the ESC relay de-energised for forward movement to conserve the RX power supply.

One partner to a DVM which is probably just as important, if not more so, is a Log Book. All testing set-ups should be recorded with a sketch and a list of equipment used. Results should be logged as the tests proceed together with the conclusions drawn at the end. In this way when the next project is started a lot of time is saved by referring to the Log, particularly when calculating the size of power supplies required. Operational notes should also be logged for future reference. Motors should be identified and their stall currents logged. Their operational performance should be noted, particularly if the motor fuses have to be upgraded. Often a change of propeller diameter or pitch will increase current causing the motor fuses to blow, so a record of any upgrading is useful for the future.

There are many other standard features in a good-quality DVM which will come into use particularly when modifying equipment and installing systems into a boat, as will be seen in the following chapters. Therefore the worker is advised to purchase as comprehensive an instrument as the budget allows. If the budget can also stretch to an additional cheap DVM to measure just DC voltage then it is this meter that should accompany the boat to the pondside leaving the other meter in the workshop. The expensive meter is a precision instrument and should be treated with care. Once the marine worker has progressed beyond just steering and propelling a boat across the pond and yearns to inject realistic working functions, a DVM becomes more than just a tool to measure battery volts. It will become a trusted servant and friend and should be treated as such. If it is it will give many years of accurate service and the author never, under any circumstances, allows anybody else to use his workshop DVM! Lastly, always follow the golden rule when using a DVM. Wherever possible always connect a DVM to a dead circuit. When circumstances make this unavoidable double-check and then check again where the probes are to be attached and make the test as short as possible to obtain reliable results. Remember that all mains voltages have the capacity to kill and should be treated with the greatest respect. It is appropriate here to discuss the fusing of mains equipment used in the workshop such as soldering irons, chargers, drills and other mains driven workshop aids. Always without exception fit the appropriately-rated fuse. In the UK there are a number of ratings from 3 to 13 amps that fit the standard '13 amp' plug. Most of the mains equipment used will require a 3-amp fuse. Remember a fuse will not protect you from the lethal consequences of mains contact as it takes too long to rupture. It is there to protect the wiring from the 13-amp socket back to the main fuse box. If the marine worker wishes to ensure additional safety the workshop bench supply can be protected with Residual Current Device (RCD) sockets. In the event of an incident both live and neutral of the supply will be disconnected within 40 milliseconds. In most cases this will provide protection against electrocution. In the UK these safety breaker sockets are available from most electrical supply stores including Maplins.

13

Auxiliary Functions and Electronic Kit Building

All the preceding chapters have gradually led the scale marine worker to a position where the design of his or her project has a hull that can be propelled either forward or astern and steered. There is now a choice of power supplies and auxiliary functions which can bring the project to life on the water which can be added. But crucially the worker now knows that it is not just a case of adding a few additional modules and hoping they will work, and keep on working. Their effect on the prime functions must be taken into account. Firstly, it is necessary to define what is expected of TX and RX auxiliary functions. These are additional functions apart from the two prime functions allocated to driving and steering the boat. They can operate a servo or control the power supply to a working feature. That is the extent of control of the TX on the bank of the pond. However, it is how these two basic control functions can be expanded into interrelationships with additional control circuitry and logic that this and the following chapters will explore.

Working features on a boat can be either visual or audio. Visual features such as masthead and deck lights,

anchors being weighed, fire monitors with working water pumps, tow lines and working cranes, and audio features including engine sounds, sirens, and even music and sounds of parties on the decks of pleasure craft are all possible and have been achieved. The list is almost endless and is only restricted by the worker's imagination and budget! Before discussing the technicalities of fitting working functions it is necessary to ensure that they work in accordance with full-size practice. For example, masthead lights are displayed to a strict code of practice so that other seafarers can make the correct interpretation of what is seen and act accordingly.

There exists an agreement between all seafaring nations to abide by a code of conduct and rules ensuring the safety of crew and vessels at all times, the International Regulations for Preventing Collisions at Sea 1972 (amended in 1989 and 1991). Fortunately for the marine worker an inexpensive publication exists to teach seagoing personnel sufficient knowledge of these Regulations so that they can meet the needs of being an Officer of the Watch, entitled *A Seaman's Guide to the RULE OF THE ROAD*. This book contains a mine of information essential to the correct display and use of all safety elements on board any type of vessel the worker is likely to model. As a teaching guide it contains many coloured examples of lights and shapes of visual symbols plus dimensions of the placing of equipment enabling the worker to obtain the correct scale effect on the model. Details of this publication can be found in Appendix 3. The discussion so far might appear to be out of place in this chapter but as it will become clear, before the worker gets down to building any electronic kits, essential planning has to take place so that a broad picture of voltage and current requirements can be made to satisfy the principles already discussed in Chapter 8. This can only be done once the numbers of, for example, lights to be lit in certain circumstances are known for the correct scale appearance. What is the point of creating a miniature replica of a full-size vessel if it cannot be operated correctly? Many marine modellers go to extraordinary lengths to ensure scale fidelity so there is no reason why the correct working practice cannot be followed if at all possible. This is where model research and electronic planning must go hand in hand.

Sounds

The first effects to be discussed are those which the onlooker would expect to see and hear when a vessel is under way. The most obvious is the sound of the vessel's engine which will immediately concentrate the onlooker's attention. Many of the vessels modelled are representative of diesel-powered boats, from a simple fishing boat to a merchant vessel and fast patrol boats. A fishing-boat diesel sound will be that of a single-cylinder engine whilst other vessels require a multi-cylinder sound. These sounds or frequencies can be created electronically and there is a wide choice of modules available either ready built or in kit form (see Appendix 2). The main problem, however, is getting the sound out of the hull whilst at the same time keeping it waterproof! A loudspeaker is obviously needed and this has to be chosen and sited with care so that the sound is truly representative of the prototype and the loudspeaker will not be compromised by the damp atmosphere it is working in. These problems and solutions will be fully discussed in Chapters 15 and 17. The majority of diesel sound units available will work either on 6 or 12V which is selected either when the unit is built or when a ready-built unit is modified following the manufacturer's instructions. Because of the problems with getting the sound out of the boat, a 12V unit is preferred as this increases the speaker output in terms of wattage and ability to faithfully reproduce the characteristic low-frequency 'thump-thump' of a diesel engine's low revolutions. This is particularly true of the single-cylinder engine. With the boat at rest and the engine ticking over, what happens as the boat starts to move? The engine revolutions increase and ideally the sound should indicate this is happening. This is achieved by feeding the increasing voltage appearing at the motor terminals from the speed controller into the sound unit which responds by speeding up the mixture of frequencies and creating a sound illusion of a diesel engine's revolutions increasing. All engine sound units with this facility will have six leads, two for the positive and negative supply, two output leads for the loudspeaker and two leads for connection to the drive motor. These two leads are not polarity-conscious as the unit's electronics will respond whether the boat is going forward or astern.

All sound units will consume a high current, more when the supply is 12V

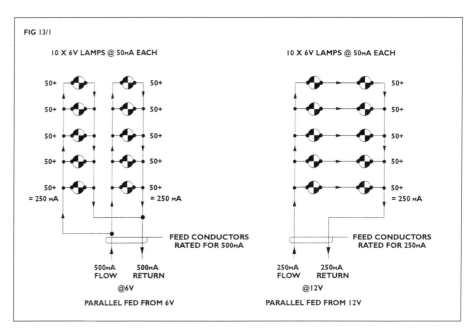

FIG 13/1

10 X 6V LAMPS @ 50mA EACH

50+   50+
50+   50+
50+   50+
50+   50+
50+   50+
= 250 mA   = 250 mA

FEED CONDUCTORS
RATED FOR 500mA

500mA   500mA
FLOW   RETURN

@6V

PARALLEL FED FROM 6V

10 X 6V LAMPS @ 50mA EACH

50+
50+
50+
50+
50+
= 250 mA

FEED CONDUCTORS
RATED FOR 250mA

250mA   250mA
FLOW   RETURN

@12V

PARALLEL FED FROM 12V

rather than 6V. As more units are added to a project it is essential that a schedule of supply volts and estimated current requirements is created, together with a record of whether the unit current is continuous or intermittent. For example, a diesel sound module would be continuous while a siren would be intermittent. Some commercially-available modules such as the 'robbe Modellsport' range from Germany list current consumption as well as the voltage requirement. If current data is unavailable a reasonable assumption for planning purposes can be made. For a single-cylinder module allow 100mA, for a large or multi-cylinder module 200mA, and a destroyer siren 300mA, while a adjustable pitch and sound sequence siren such as on a police boat would sink 500mA. These current figures can be confirmed once the modules are either purchased ready-built or kit-built, using the series current measuring technique discussed in Chapters 5 and 12. Once known, they are totalled into a final figure to determine the supply load and fuse capacity (see Chapter 8). These last two

figures can be reduced by applying a diversity factor by reaching a conclusion as to usage. This will differ from one project to another. A fishing boat will only sound its horn or siren occasionally with a single-cylinder diesel sound continuous whereas a fast police launch will have long periods of a high-current siren sounding with a continuous multi-cylinder diesel sound. Where possible it is prudent to err on the generous side when determining the power supply capacity, echoing the recommendation made in Chapter 8 of fitting the largest-capacity power supply the hull will hold. However, with rating fuses it is more prudent to be conservative. Experience will soon show whether the rating requires up-grading.

Lights

Lighting is another area where thought is needed and as a result considerable savings in power supply capacity can be achieved. Many workers may not realise that wiring two 6V lamps in series and feeding the pair with 12V will halve the current compared with feeding the two in parallel. The light output of either system will be the same. Two examples illustrate the point. All vessels are required to exhibit port and starboard sidelights – red and green respectively. Two 6V 50mA lamps, wired in parallel and each fed 6V, will consume a total of 100mA. The same rated lamps wired in series and fed 12V will consume 50mA, a saving of 50mA. It is quite common for working boats such as tugs to have as many as eight or ten deck lights. These can be wired in series pairs fed in parallel. Assuming each consumes 50mA at 6V the total current for ten lamps would be 250mA at 12V series/parallel fed. If all ten were fed in parallel the current at 6v would be 500mA or ½ Amp (see Fig. 13/1 opposite). A spin-off of this is the reduction in wiring of series-fed functions compared with parallel-fed ones. To use these techniques the worker must remember that with series-fed equipment all the voltages must add up to the supply voltage and all the individual currents must be the same. With parallel feeding the supply voltage remains the same but each individual item's current can be different. In both cases the total current will determine the rating of the feed conductors (see Fig. 13/1). The reduction in conductor size can be quite significant when wiring mast lighting and other restricted areas. This is where planning pays off before construction has started.

Dual functions

Another area where initial planning can solve a problem before it appears is identifying the operation of dual functions full-size practice requires. One example is the operational require-ments of a vessel, when under way, to indicate when manoeuvring. This is done by a blasts on the siren – one short blast means 'I am altering my

course to starboard' – two short blasts 'I am altering my course to port' and so on for a variety of manoeuvres. These siren signals may be supplemented by a masthead white light which will flash as appropriate – one short flash or two short flashes etc. There is no problem in operating a model siren other than that of creating a realistic volume of sound which will be covered in later chapters. The problem here is operating both siren and light at the same time. The easiest way is to parallel-feed both the lamp and the siren module from the same switched voltage. If, however, the only white lamp available is 6V consuming 50mA but the siren module needs 12V to get the right volume, a problem now exists. This is solved by still feeding both items 12V but inserting a dropping resistor in series with the lamp feed to reduce the voltage down to 6V at the lamp terminals. This technique requires a small calculation using Ohm's Law (see Appendix 3). The series circuit still requires 50mA to flow but 6V has to be lost across the resistor, hence the description 'dropping'. The calculation is R = E1 – E2 divided by I where E1 = 12 (the supply voltage), E2 = 6 (the voltage to be dropped) and I = 0.050A (the series current). Note that the current is expressed in amperes. Working the calculation, $12 - 6/0.050 = 6/0.050 = 120$ ohms or 120Ω. Resistors will generate heat so the correct wattage value has to be chosen to ensure they do not burn out. The wattage is calculated using $W = E^2/R$. Substituting the above values, $W = 6 \times 6/120 = 36/120 = 0.3W$. Note that Appendix 3 gives two other ways of calculating wattage which will produce the same answer. When using Ohm's Law care must be taken to ensure I, E and R are in amperes, volts and ohms if errors resulting in a value several orders too large or too small are to be avoided.

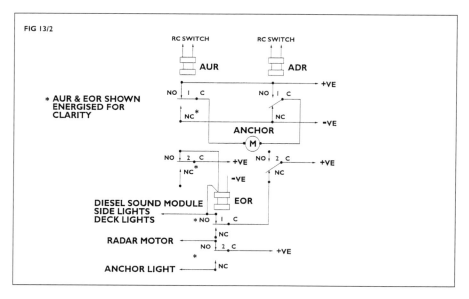

Looking in a supplier's catalogue the nearest wattage value to the value above is 0.4W. This will be adequate if the resistor is located in an open space. Often the worker has need to enclose components within confined spaces, for example a mast, and in these circumstances it is prudent to double the calculated wattage, in this case to 0.6W. Note that there is an internationally-accepted code for identifying resistors by colour and expressing their values in print (see Appendix 3).

These dual sound or visual functions can occur more often than one would think and at this stage in the planning it is a wise policy to write down all the functions required and then study this list for possible combinations. One such combination is what happens as a vessel prepares to weigh anchor and gets under way. Generally speaking, when anchored a vessel is required to exhibit a white light, usually at the top of the foremast. This light is extinguished before getting under way. Prior to this the engines have to be started and the anchor weighed. This adds up to four operations the remote control circuitry has to switch. The easiest way is to switch each function separately but this option eats into the limited number of switching options available. However, a little thought will reveal that all four can be linked together and controlled by two switching functions. The immediate question is why four? One is the anchor light. Two – engines 'ON' – Three and Four – raising and lowering the anchor (this requires two switching functions to change the anchor motor polarity). These last two functions hold the solution.

Fig. 9/3 illustrated the principle of switching motor polarity using a relay. This method of polarity reversal is a combination of active and passive switching, active when the relay is energised and passive when de-energised. Either way the motor always has power at its terminals. Remember that this example illustrates the polarity change-over required within an ESC which has circuitry to control the flow of power regardless of polarity. Anchors or cranes or any other function which requires a motor to run either way needs two relays to operate the polarity changeover by active control switching of the relay coil. If these relays control the 'Up' and 'Down' of the anchor they can be designated Anchor Up Relay

(AUR) and Anchor Down Relay (ADR) – the two top relays in Fig. 13/2 opposite.

Further study of this circuit reveals that NC (Normally Closed) contacts as well as NO (Normally Open) contacts indicate the state of the circuits at any one time. If the NO contacts are 'made' this indicates that the circuits are live. The NC contacts indicate a relay is de-energised and if both relays are, then the anchor is at rest. This is very useful as it can be used to 'prove' the state of a circuit and therefore a function in relationship to other functions. The AUR and ADR in Fig. 13/2 have two sets of changeover contacts each. The anchor motor is wired so that the polarity will change when either relay is switched on using the RC switching discussed in Chapters 14 and 15. Note that for clarity one relay, the AUR, is shown energised as this makes the understanding of what follows easier. The third relay, Engines On Relay (EOR), has its coil positive switched by a NO contact of the AUR. However, to maintain its energised state, when the anchor is fully up and the motor switched off, the de-energised condition of the ADR feeds the EOR coil positive over its own NO contact 1 and NC contact 2 of the ADR. This is a 'stick' feed circuit and is very useful in maintaining function feeds without continuous RC system control. The 'stick' circuit is broken when the ADR is energised, lowering the anchor, de-energising the EOR when the vessel returns to port. The 'stick' circuit also feeds the diesel generator module and the port and starboard lights. A second set of contacts feeds the rotating radar motor when the EOR is energised and when it is de-energised it feeds the anchor light. With this circuit six functions are controlled by two RC switching options – raising and lowering the anchor. What the onlooker sees and hears is: the vessel anchored and a white light lit up confirming this. The anchor is weighed, the anchor light is extinguished, the engines start up at tick-over speed, the sidelights switch on and the radar starts to rotate. The engines speed up as the vessel man-oeuvres out of port. Upon return, as soon as the anchor starts to drop everything is switched off as the circuit resets itself, with the anchor light confirming the vessel is now at anchor.

Particularly note this symbol * on Fig. 13/2 as it refers to relays AUR and EOR shown energised for clarity and understanding on how the circuit works. Also omitted for clarity are anti-interference diodes usually fitted across the relay coils. These will be discussed in Chapter 15.

Electronic kit building

So far the discussion has demonstrated that if a marine worker desires to ultimately produce a fully-operational reproduction of a full-size prototype, he or she must adopt exactly the same disciplined approach to building, with planning taking the lead before 'any wood is cut or soldered joint made'. It must be a stage-by-stage process to keep interest alive and to enable appreciation of how many of the functions interrelate. All working functions require wiring and conn-ections of some order. Far better to design for this than endeavour to install them into a finely finished and painted piece of superstructure. This means that decisions have to be made as to what electronic modules are required to achieve certain effects. These can be either ready-built or self-built. Either way voltages and currents must be known for planning decisions regarding wiring and power supplies. What type of RC switching is going to be used and what space will be required

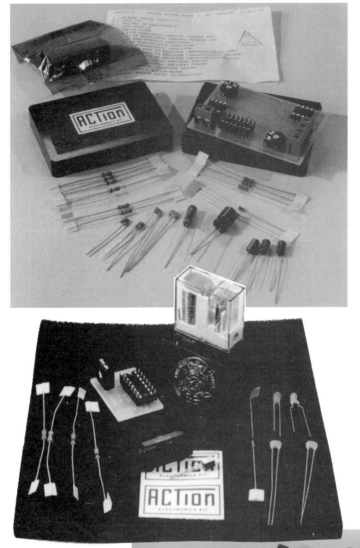

for modules, loudspeakers and other equipment are questions which also need to be settled. All of these points will be discussed in later chapters but the foregoing illustrates that the model shipyard can produce an exciting variety of ongoing work not only of ship-building but of electrical, electronic, systems engineering and planning!

One UK supplier, ACTion, offers a comprehensive range of sound units ranging from diesel and steam to sirens and hooters and warship sounds. Light modules include a beacon flasher and a morse/aldis unit. Those workers who find considerable satisfaction in electronic kit building can move onto kits of electronic speed controllers, switchers (Chapter 15), and a host of other support modules (see Appendix 2). Most kit manufacturers also offer ready-built modules and a service for when things go wrong. This last is usually most unlikely if the worker has adopted a disciplined approach to kit building. The first prerequisite is the mastery of soldering small printed circuit boards (PCBs). This is not difficult as long as the worker follows the principles set out in Chapter 11. Secondly, always read the kit instructions thoroughly before unpack-

Three ACTion kits laid out. Note the three different means of protecting ICs. A plastic bag, a foam strip and a hard plastic container. The photograph on the right shows the header pins and socket, bottom right, discussed in Chapter 14 and Fig 14/1.

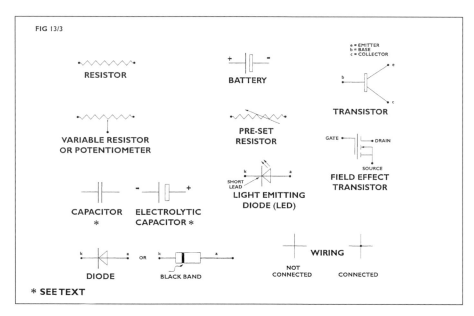

FIG 13/3

RESISTOR

VARIABLE RESISTOR
OR POTENTIOMETER

CAPACITOR
*

ELECTROLYTIC
CAPACITOR *

DIODE

BATTERY

PRE-SET
RESISTOR

LIGHT EMITTING
DIODE (LED)

SHORT LEAD

BLACK BAND

OR

e = EMITTER
b = BASE
c = COLLECTOR

TRANSISTOR

GATE — DRAIN

SOURCE

FIELD EFFECT
TRANSISTOR

WIRING

NOT
CONNECTED

CONNECTED

* SEE TEXT

ing the components, which will be small and can easily roll off the bench and be lost. The author has found from experience that the best safeguard against this happening is to construct a tray approximately. 200mm × 200mm with 20mm lips all round and subdivided to form two partitions 60mm × 100mm. The inside should be given two coats of matt white emulsion paint. In use the large area is for working on the PCB and the two small areas for storing the components as the building progresses. Generally speaking any kit will consist of resistors, capacitors, diodes, transistors, integrated circuits (ICs), solder and hardware and will usually include a case for the completed module. ICs are the heart of most kits and require handling with extreme care to avoid static pollution from any magnetic source or human contact with the base pins. Transistors can also be polluted but are not as sensitive as ICs. Many kits require all components to be soldered directly onto the PCB including ICs. ACTion, however provides IC sockets which are soldered onto the PCB and the IC is left until last, after the work has been thoroughly

checked, to be plugged into the socket, which minimises the possibility of pollution.

Components should only be unpacked as required as construction proceeds. Identification is made easy as all manufacturers include comprehensive information in the building instructions. Resistors have a colour code, details of which can be found in Appendix 3. Capacitors will carry either a manufacturer's code which the kit supplier will provide or the capacity value (again see Appendix 3). Some capacitors will be polarised – these are electrolytic and each end will be marked either positive or negative, positive with a red end or negative with a minus sign and arrows pointing to that end. Extreme care must be taken to ensure electrolytic capacitors are inserted into the PCB correctly. The board holes should be identified with + and – symbols. Occasionally workers may have the need to 'read' an electronic circuit and here a knowledge of component symbols is invaluable. Fig. 13/3 above shows the most common symbols likely to be met. Most kit PCBs are high-quality glass

The incorrect way to 'load' a PCB (left). The example on the right shows how heavy items fitted first can support the PCB as work progresses.

fibre with all the components' physical appearance printed on one side which makes identification very simple. Where each component fits there are holes drilled exactly at the correct pitch for it to literally just drop in. As mentioned above, electrolytic capacitors are shown with the correct polarity holes marked and other items such as diodes will be similarly treated. Note that ICs and sockets, if used, have an identification slot at one end to ensure correct fitting. Some PCB circuits require wire links to be fitted. Always check before construction begins if these are required and fit them first. Leave any external wiring connections until last after the work has been checked. Each component should lie as

flat to the board as possible without strain and sometimes the designer will require the height to be within certain limits.

Work in a disciplined manner, fitting and soldering several components at a time in groups – resistors then capacitors etc, leaving the semi-conductors until last. If the design includes relays and terminal blocks fit these early on as they will provide 'legs' to the board when turned over. These large items will often cover up their identification printed on the board so it is wise to make a note prior to fitting if the designer has omitted to do so on the supplied paperwork. Often the wire links mentioned above are under the relays which is why they should be fitted first. As each wire-ended component is fitted splay out the wire(s) to prevent it dropping out as the board is turned over. Do not press the wires flat onto the board. Examination of a typical kit PCB will reveal that the underside comprises the circuit made up of thin pre-tinned copper lands connecting the components together. Around each hole will be a small tinned area with a silver shine to it. The rest of each land will be of a

One of the author's development boards using 'helping hands'. Note the servo-type lead on the right-hand side is anchored through three additional strain relief holes.

colour which is a protective lacquer to prevent liquid solder from flowing down the land. Some lands will appear wider than others. This is to ensure the copper can carry the circuit current. Occasionally the designer will require the worker to build up these heavy current lands with solder to increase the current capacity. The protective lacquer will be missing in these areas. Construction and soldering should follow the techniques given in Chapter 11 using the recommended tools. Solder as fast as practical using the minimum of heat to ensure a perfect joint. Use the correct bit for each task and do not be afraid of changing bits whilst the iron is energised. It is designed for short periods for this purpose. Remember to park the hot bit safely. Always use a pencil bit for the small land joints changing to a larger bit for the wide land relay/terminals/heavy duty wiring joints. Where a servo type lead is required, for connection to the RX, always use the pencil bit. Stranded conductors should be tightly twisted together and very lightly tinned to prevent individual strands from shorting out adjacent tracks. Too much and the conductor will not pass through the PCB. Check each component that its value/polarity is correct for that place on the board before and after soldering. Trimming the scrap wires is recommended in two stages. As construction proceeds trim each wire back to within approximately 15mm of the PCB. If an error is discovered in the final checking this 15mm will prove invaluable in salvaging the component for re-use. Remember that when all components are fitted if one is found to be in the wrong place there will be the correct one somewhere incorrectly fitted!

When all the components are fitted and the first stage trimming is complete, carefully examine each joint to check the following:

1. Has it been soldered?
2. Is the joint sound?
3. Is there any joint where the use of too much solder has resulted in it flowing where it should not have done onto an adjacent joint?

In the last instance a good magnifying glass helps. If there is any doubt the use of the desolder pump will swiftly confirm suspicions. There is no fail-safe method of either preventing this from happening or indeed checking it has happened other than extreme care in construction. However, when the initial joint is about to be soldered the author has found it helpful to make a sketch of any areas where, even with care, a short could occur. This comes in useful during the checking process. Once the worker is completely satisfied, the ICs, if any, are inserted, and the board checked to see that none of the first-stage wires are in contact with each other, testing to the maker's instructions can be done. If all is well, and only then, each component wire is clipped off just proud of its joint. Do not under any circumstances cut into the solder as this has the effect of lifting the joint and its land away from the board and building in a future failure.

The majority of kits will include an enclosure for the unit and instructions for fitting. It is unwise to thread external leads through holes in one half of the casing as this makes it difficult to assemble and disassemble in the future. Better to file slots with rounded ends. Any delicate conductors such as servo type leads should be provided with strain relief to prevent them being fractured at the PCB surface. This can be achieved by sliding a reasonably tight 25mm length of sleeving over the lead prior to soldering to the board. When assembling into the case a

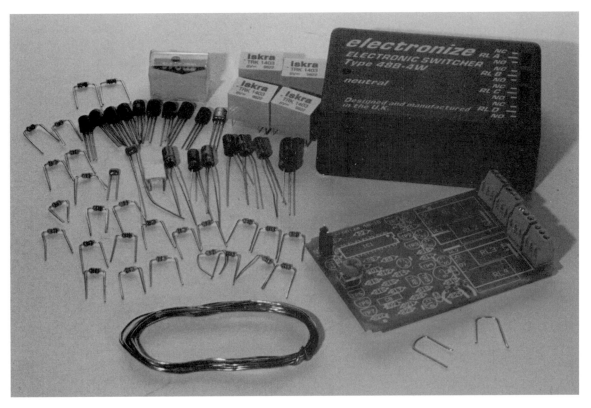

The 'electronize' four-way Switcher kit laid out. Note the large number of resistors which require careful identification before work commences. The two components to the left of the IC container on the top row are diodes which can be easily mistaken for resistors with one black band. Again note the use of a header pin on the PCB alongside the variable resistance. This kit supplier pre-forms components and shorting links as shown.

miniature nylon cable tie (see Chapter 16 or 17) is secured over the sleeve end close to the board and adjusted, before being fully tightened, so that there is a loop of lead inside the case with the tie preventing the lead from being pulled out of its exit slot. Do not forget to fully tighten once satisfied that any strain on the lead is taken by the casing and not the board. The sleeving prevents chafing of the lead and adds mechanical strength within the exit slot.

Planning integrated working functions, building the modules and finally seeing the vessel perform as its full-size prototype is very rewarding especially when the RC gear has been improved to a performance beyond its designer's expectations. It would not be out of place therefore to finish this chapter with a summary of the key elements of electronic kit building. Always read and study the kit instruction manual

before unpacking a single component, other than the PCB, again and again until there is no doubt as to the identity of all the parts and where they fit. Ensure there is a complete understanding as to the polarity of every component affected. Keep all ICs in their protective wrapping until the last minute. Avoid all human contact with IC pins. The IC insertion and extraction tools mentioned in Chapter 11 are a wise investment. Only have those components required for any particular stage in the construction loose on the bench at any one time. Use only dedicated tools and never ever carry solder to the joint on the bit. Heat the joint for a second or two and place the solder on it. When the solder runs freely quickly remove the iron and wait – a perfect joint! Check and double check each stage before going on to the next. Before applying power, double check that all ICs are inserted

A completed 'electronize' ESC shown on the comprehensive 'paper-work' supplied. Note the clear placement schematic alongside the circuit diagram. This ESC has a metal base which doubles as a heatsink for the power MOSFET.

This dredger is not only 'scratch-built' but can carry out fully-controlled dredging operations – all by remote control. Planning the control of the auxiliary working functions in the design stage is essential for a successful end result.

the correct way round. If the average marine worker applies the same dedication and care to building electronic kits as is applied to building complicated superstructures, the author cannot see any reason why the outcome cannot be anything other than complete success.

14
Extending Functions including Transmitter Modifications

The opening discussion in Chapter 13 drew attention to the basic operational mode of any RC system, *ie* that the basic control a TX has over its RX is limited to moving a servo arm through an arc or controlling an electric motor via some form of speed control. As the aero hobby developed, a need arose to provide a servo which would run from one end of its arc to the other, switching off when both extreme points were reached. This is used to retract aircraft undercarriages. It is controlled on the TX by a switch which is designated, as one would expect, 'Up-Down'. The need now is to expand this and the basic theory of how the servo system works so that a better understanding of how it can be modified to operate the additional functions the marine worker requires can be achieved.

Chapter 2 described how each function is a pulse whose width is varied between 1.0 and 2.0 milliseconds. Each TX function either has a potentiometer which is connected to a stick, a turning knob attached to a 'pot' shaft, a sliding action known as a linear pot or a switch

as above. If each function output from the RX is connected to a servo, the pot inside the servo will mimic the corresponding pot within the TX. Fig. 13/3 introduced the symbol of a variable potentiometer. Studying this will show a resistance between two points with a third point or wiper able to travel along the whole, selecting a different resistance either side of it relevant to each end. There are two types of tracks within pots, linear and logarithmic. Linear means that when the wiper has travelled 50 per cent along the track the shaft or external slider has also moved 50 per cent of its total travel. Linear pots are the ones used in RC equipment. In the TX the pot has its three connections linked into a circuit which can detect the value of resistance from each end to the wiper. One end of the pot will always be at minimum resistance when the wiper is at that end. In effect one end and the wiper are connected together. Using a switch instead of a pot 'fools' the circuit into believing that one end is connected with the wiper and transmits this fact to the RX, which responds by driving the servo motor to its maximum position.

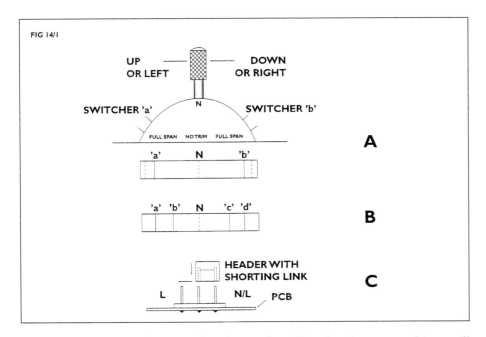

FIG 14/1

UP OR LEFT — DOWN OR RIGHT

SWITCHER 'a'   N   SWITCHER 'b'

FULL SPAN   NO TRIM   FULL SPAN

'a'   N   'b'   **A**

'a' 'b'   N   'c' 'd'   **B**

HEADER WITH SHORTING LINK   **C**

L   N/L   PCB

Because this is a special servo, when its pot position agrees with the TX position the motor is switched off. If the switch makes a separate contact either way it is thrown, then either end will be detected and the servo will move accordingly. Although developed for aero use, these special servos play a useful role in marine work which will be returned to later. It should be noted that these servos cannot be used as normal servos and workers should be aware that they exist and sometimes are offered at bargain prices. One manufacturer labels them in red to identify them. Always check the identity code.

What is evident in a switched function is that the RX output can be one of two pulse widths. If an electronic module is plugged into this output and can detect which pulse is received and react accordingly by energising a relevant relay, then a two-way switcher has been created. In this case, however, what is required on the TX is a switch with a centre 'Off' so that one 'On' position will transmit a narrow-width pulse and the other 'On' position will transmit the full-width

pulse. Exactly the same thing will happen if the two-way switcher is connected to a stick outlet. Pushing the stick fully forward will operate one switcher relay and pulling it back will operate the second. In Fig. 13/2 the two relays, ADR and AUR, can now be controlled by the switcher relays. Now if the TX switch or the stick is labelled 'Anchor Up – Anchor Down', operating 'Anchor Up' will start the anchor motor and the relay sequence as described in the previous chapter. With the anchor up, the TX control is moved to 'Off' or stick-centre position and the anchor motor stops. In the meantime the other functions, diesel engine, radar scanner etc, are now operating by the EOR 'stick' circuit and will only cease when the 'Anchor Down' is signalled and the circuit resets.

At this point it is prudent to recap basic switching theory before discussing more complicated circuits. A TX has N functions which range from a basic two-function to eight functions. Each function transmits a pulse whose width can be varied by either a rotary potentiometer attached to a 'stick' or a

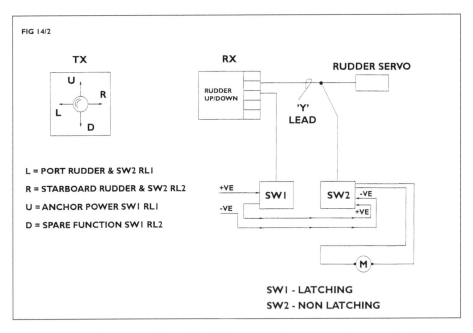

FIG 14/2

TX

U

R

L

D

RX

RUDDER UP/DOWN

'Y' LEAD

RUDDER SERVO

L = PORT RUDDER & SW2 RLI

R = STARBOARD RUDDER & SW2 RL2

U = ANCHOR POWER SWI RLI

D = SPARE FUNCTION SWI RL2

+VE

-VE

SWI

SW2

-VE

+VE

M

SWI - LATCHING

SW2 - NON LATCHING

linear pot attached to a slider. The RX processes the pulse and either drives a servo to a position which 'mimics' the TX control position or uses the pulse to energise a relay after determining where the TX control position is. This last statement is fundamental in understanding the variety of switchers available to the marine worker and how they work. On a four-plus function TX there are two sticks controlling four functions, two of which are already dedicated to rudder and propulsion. This leaves two stick functions available for switching modules. One will be up and down where the rudder is left and right and the other will be left and right where the speed control is up and down. Fig. 14/1A illustrates how stick movement operates the basic switcher sequence. The stick can be moved anywhere on its arc up to two points 'a' and 'b' just off full span without trim with the switcher remaining dormant. Once the stick reaches either point the switcher will detect these points and energise one of the two switcher relays. In its simplest form this is a momentary operation because when the stick

moves back towards neutral whichever switcher relay is energised will be de-energised. Another way of describing this simple action is non-latching. This can be used to sound a whistle or siren or to operate a motor which raises or lowers an anchor. If the two relays only have one set of changeover contacts each and no other circuitry is required, the anchor motor circuit shown in Fig. 13/2 can be used. If, however, the rest of the Fig. 13/2 circuit is required then the switcher relays can be used to energise the AUR and ADR relays. A more complicated switcher is available which has four switch points shown as 'a', 'b', 'c' and 'd' on Fig. 14/1B – the 'electronize' type 48B-4W. Although very useful this type has to used extremely carefully in allocating function duties, because as the stick is stroked through its arc it will momentarily energise at relays 'b' and 'c' to get to either 'a' or 'd'. If, for example, the anchor motor is connected to 'b' and 'c' this will rotate when not required. The solution is to use the two outer points for the anchor motor and the two inner points for two

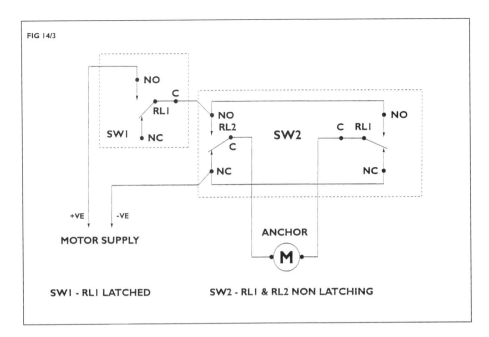

FIG 14/3

NO
C
RLI
SWI NC

NO
RL2
C
NC

SW2

C RLI NO

NC

+VE -VE

MOTOR SUPPLY

ANCHOR
M

SWI - RLI LATCHED   SW2 - RLI & RL2 NON LATCHING

other functions used during a sailing period – the siren etc. Another more sophisticated switcher is the latching type. The switcher relay energises in the normal way but remains energised as the stick is moved off the switch point. To switch the relay off the stick is moved back to the switch point and it is this second 'pulse' which de-energises the relay. One kit supplier, ACTion, offers a 'Universal' Two Function Switcher the worker can custom set up with 3 pin headers which are plugged into the PCB to select either latching or non-latching operation on each relay (see Fig. 14/1C).

So far the discussion has shown that the two remaining stick functions on a four-function TX with two already allocated to steering and propulsion can be used to extend control to another four functions which can be a mix of latched and non-latched or to eight functions which will be all be non-latched. This is achieved without any modification of the TX and using either kit-built or ready-built switcher units. However, it does require dexterity on the part of the operator and it is slow in operating the sticks to find the switching points. Incidentally there is no reason why the output from the RX cannot be split with a Y lead and a servo connected in parallel with the switcher unit.

It is obvious that the functions that could be servo operated in this way are extremely limited and great care is needed to ensure the switcher points are not reached and initiated when not required. One way in which this option is viable is to include the anchor motor control as part of the steering stick function, remembering that when anchor operation is required the vessel is at rest and steering is not required. However, this creates a problem in operating the rudder when 'at sea'. What is not required is to inadvertently operate the anchor motor, particularly the raise rotation, which could very easily stall the motor. The solution is to use an additional switcher on the 'Up' half of the stick to control the power to the motor switcher. Fig. 14/2 schematic shows the principle and Fig. 14/3 the circuit detail. The rudder servo works in the normal way with

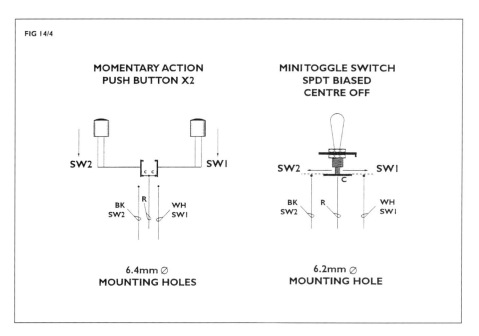

FIG 14/4

MOMENTARY ACTION
PUSH BUTTON X2

MINI TOGGLE SWITCH
SPDT BIASED
CENTRE OFF

6.4mm ⌀
MOUNTING HOLES

6.2mm ⌀
MOUNTING HOLE

Switcher 2 operating at extreme turns. No power is switched to the anchor motor until the 'Up' stick Switcher 1 latches the anchor motor supply into Switcher 2. With the vessel at rest rudder movement is inconsequential and unseen as the anchor motor is operated by the non-latching Switcher 2.

A neater and more elegant way of operating switchers at the TX is by switch or push-button, rather than hunting for the switching point on a stick arc, as was discussed above. There is no problem in converting a TX to switch operation. It just needs care and an accurate written record kept as the work proceeds. The worker by now knows that any TX function is controlled with the aid of a variable potentiometer or pot. Some makes use linear pots on functions other than those on the sticks. Whatever the type they all share a common wiring layout. There is a connection at each end of the track and one connection to the slider. However, before any attempt is made to open a TX and commence work inside the worker is well advised

to check on the warranty conditions with the importer/manufacturer of the equipment. If this is in order a start can be made by first assembling the RX, switchers and power supply and checking that each switcher is working correctly using the function it is intended to convert. If all is well, start by removing the telescopic aerial and, where fitted, the separate RF module. Now equip the working area with a piece of thick, soft, polystyrene foam to protect the TX front panel for the next stages. The retaining screws holding the back in place can be released but be careful when unscrewing so as not to damage the plastic threads within the case. Make notes where short and long screws are located as severe and irreparable damage can be caused to the case on re-assembly if a long screw is forced into a short screw location. Ease the back slowly away as sometimes there are internal items secured to it. Next the TX power supply is removed. Most modern TXs have nicad packs which are plugged in so removal is relatively easy, but be aware that the pack could be retained by sticky pads which will need careful use of force to release. All the removed components should be accounted for, listed, and carefully stored away, particularly the retaining screws not only to ensure the complete case security at the end but if left rolling about on the bench they can badly score and damage the TX front panel and if by chance one gets inside and is not noticed can cause serious damage when the TX is reassembled and switched on for testing. The pot wiring can now be identified and recorded with a sketch and wire colours. Each conductor is then carefully un-soldered from the pot.

The author always 'marks' each conductor with a plastic cable marker as each becomes free. These markers carry a number 0 to 9 in black on an orange background. They are available from one of the specialist suppliers, Squires, listed in Appendix 2. The important conductor is the one soldered to the centre tag on the pot. In many TXs it will be red and it is the conductor that will be connected to the C – Common – tag and switched either to one or the other remaining conductors. Fig. 14/4 shows two alternative switch options – either push button or a 'Off 'toggle switch biased to the centre. Note that each option is related to Fig. 14/3 to clarify switcher control. Select a convenient location on the TX to mount either option, repeatedly checking that the space is adequate internally and neither switch option is foul of other components. Either option requires a mounting hole approximately 6mm in diameter. The toggle switch also requires an additional hole for the anti-turn washer tag. Before drilling this hole, make certain that the orientation is correct as this determines which way the switch dolly operates. The termination of the conductors is best done outside the TX

using the 'helping hands' accessory described in Chapter 11. Each wire should be sleeved prior to soldering and then the sleeve pushed over each tag. Either switch option can be installed into the TX from the inside, the push button switch having a removable cap, and locked with the mounting nuts. The pot wiring is usually long enough to be relocated but if this is not the case the additional length can be added by jointing, using the same colour wiring. Do not forget to sleeve the joints. Double-check all the wiring, making notes and a sketch of the modified internal wiring for future reference. Before replacing the back temporarily connect the power supply and fit the RF module if required. Switch on the TX and then the RX with the switchers still connected. Using either the switch or pushbuttons the system should now work as before. If not, switch off and remove the TX power supply. Carefully check all the work against the notes and sketches made during conversion to locate the fault. Re-test and if all is well, tidy all the wiring using miniature nylon cable ties. Reassemble the power supply, fixing it with double-sided adhesive pads if required. Fit the back with care using the correct length screws in their correct positions. Fit the RF module if required and the aerial. Switch on and re-test. The switch or pushbuttons can now be labelled to identify which switcher is controlled by each switch/button operation.

The modifications discussed so far have been modest extensions of TX functions using either self-build or ready-built equipment available on the UK market. For those workers whose budgets will allow there is an integrated system available that offers a four-function system capable of being expanded into seven basic functions by adding switched and proportional

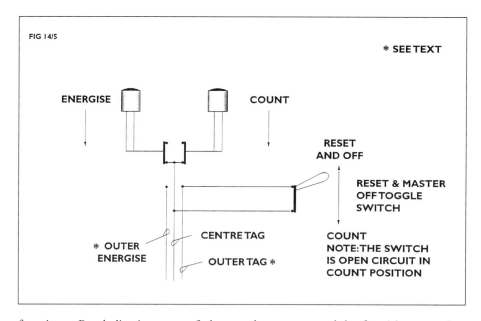

FIG 14/5

* SEE TEXT

ENERGISE

COUNT

RESET
AND OFF

RESET & MASTER
OFF TOGGLE
SWITCH

* OUTER
ENERGISE

CENTRE TAG

OUTER TAG *

COUNT
NOTE: THE SWITCH
IS OPEN CIRCUIT IN
COUNT POSITION

functions. By dedicating any of these functions the system is further expanded into a maximum of 104 individual functions which are a mix of switch and servo operations! This is the 'robbe' Futaba F-14 Expandible RC System marketed in the UK by Robbe Schluter UK (see Appendix 2). Of even greater marine interest is the F14 Navy version, mentioned in Chapter 9, which has a twin stick unit fitted on the left-hand side of the TX. The F14 Navy can be expanded in the same way as the standard F14. Investing in such a system also brings all the advantages for servo operation such as Dual Rates, ATV, servo reverse, and other features discussed in Chapter 4. A programmable sequence function is also part of the system. The major advantage of the F14 series is that it can be expanded from a very basic system to a system tailored to individual requirements as funds become available. This is important as it allows the worker to build the system on paper first using the maker's comprehensive mini booklet 9871/0001 describing the options and modules available. This ensures that funds are economically directed into

the correct modules for either a modest or a complicated multi-function system.

For those workers with limited budgets there is a seven auxiliary function switching system available on the UK market which requires just two prime functions on the TX to operate. It is the Gemini GES-7W Multi Memory and works on the same basic principle as switchers operate in as much it can differentiate between the two signals generated at the extreme ends of a prime function movement at the TX. With the control module connected to the appropriate RX output if the TX stick is moved from centre to end 'a', the unit will count one function. Every time the stick repeats this movement the counter 'steps' sequentially up to seven and with the next 'step' back to one. If the count is left indefinitely on any number that function can be energised by moving the stick in the opposite direction to end 'd'. This is a latched 'switch on' and can be 'switched off' by repeating the 'd' movement. So any or all of seven functions can be located and switched as required. These functions have physical outputs similar

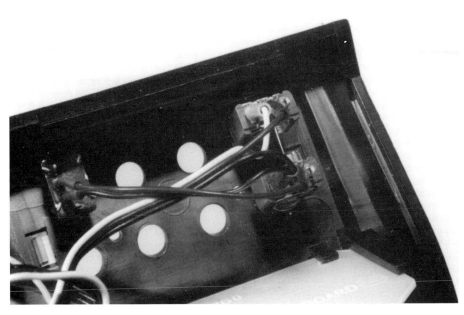

The conversion of Fig 14/5. Note the three 'pot' wires from bottom left now connected to the two right-hand push buttons.

in appearance to a RX except these have a red LED opposite each one and there is an additional eighth output. Each LED will light when the function is energised. However, the user needs to know where the counter is at any one time to activate any of the functions. This is where output eight is activated by holding the 'a' position, for approximately 5 seconds. This illumin-ates LED No.8 for this period and resets the count back to one enabling the user to start again from a known position. The 'a' position has a third operation. Hold 'a' for reset and then wait an additional five seconds and all the energised functions will be switched off.

There is an option of either 6 or 12V at 1 ampere to supply all of the

The two pushbuttons and toggle switch of Fig 14/5 installed on a robbe Futaba F16 transmitter.

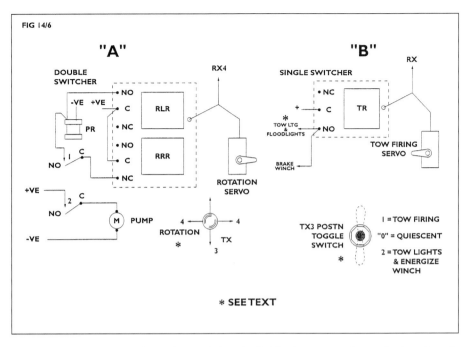

FIG 14/6

"A"

DOUBLE SWITCHER

RX4

"B"

SINGLE SWITCHER

RX

* SEE TEXT

switched outputs including the eighth one. Whichever voltage is chosen, it is separately fused internally with fuse integrity indicated by green LEDs. Gemini offer two types of ready-built units to plug into the outputs. One is a terminal board and the other is a relay which upgrades the 1 amp switching to 10 amps. The facility of an output from reset eight can be used to power either an aural or visual indication that reset has been activated. Although the system can be used without TX modification Fig. 14/5 shows the additional wiring and a 'Reset' and 'Master Off' toggle switch which the author has found to be more convenient in using the system. The TX conversion follows the same procedure as discussed with Fig. 14/4 except that prior to starting the system is operated to identify the individual 'Count' and 'Energise' connections on the existing function being converted. It is important to double-check these connections and as before to label them clearly. The positioning of the pushbuttons and the switch needs careful consideration to suit

individual ergonomics and when installed and tested labelled clearly.

By now the worker will have realised that there is a choice of switcher operation at the TX either using a stick or linear slider or a switch. Fig. 14/6 shows both types and emphasises the need to plan which type is required prior to any TX modification. The 'A' circuit is primarily to operate a servo – function 4 – which rotates a water cannon. Although not shown for clarity function 3 also operates a servo which raises or lowers the cannon. The double switcher with two relays, Rotation Left Relay and Rotation Right Relay, is connected into RX output 4 using a Y lead. The switcher, a Fleet FPS 10B2, has an adjustment facility to move the switch point of both relays. This is used to adjust the switching point of either relay at the extreme end of the stick movement using the stick trims. When water is required the trim is moved for extreme left-hand movement. With the stick hard over, RLR picks up and in turn picks up the Pump Relay PR which is stuck up over RRR NC contact. With

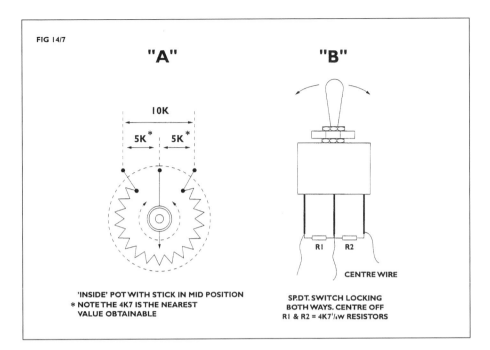

FIG 14/7

"A"

10K

5K* 5K*

'INSIDE' POT WITH STICK IN MID POSITION
* NOTE THE 4K7 IS THE NEAREST
VALUE OBTAINABLE

"B"

R1 R2

CENTRE WIRE

SP.D.T. SWITCH LOCKING
BOTH WAYS. CENTRE OFF
R1 & R2 = 4K7 ¼w RESISTORS

water on, the cannon can be trained to direct it and when required the water is switched off by moving the trim and the stick to the right which breaks the stick circuit of the PR as the RRR picks up.

Fig. 14/6B shows another version of a dual-function servo/switcher circuit. This time, however, a single switcher is used to switch on lights which indicate that a tug is towing and floodlights to illuminate the towing winch area at the same time the tow winch is energised. The function is controlled at the TX using a three-position toggle switch. The centre position '0' is quiescent. Moving the switch to 1 causes the servo to move one way to trip the tow line firing mechanism. If the tow line is successful in attaching itself to the stricken vessel, the switch is moved to position 2 when the lights will illuminate and the tow winch is energised. This enables the operator to take up the tow line slack and proceed with the tow. At the end of the tow Fig. 14/8 is operated but before that the three-position switch needs ex-planation.

Already discussed is how any TX function has either a pot or a switch for operation. A two-way switch connects the centre tag conductor to either end conductor so that the internal TX circuit is always under control. However, fitting a three-way switch will mean that in the quiescent position the centre conductor will effectively be an open circuit which is undesirable. What is required are additional components to 'fool' the circuit into believing that the function is in the centre of the pot

An internal view of a transmitter stick showing the potentiometer wiring. See text and Fig 14/7A.

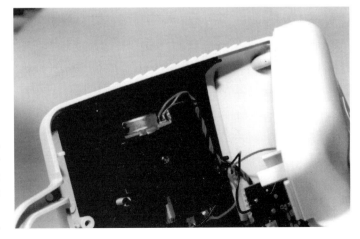

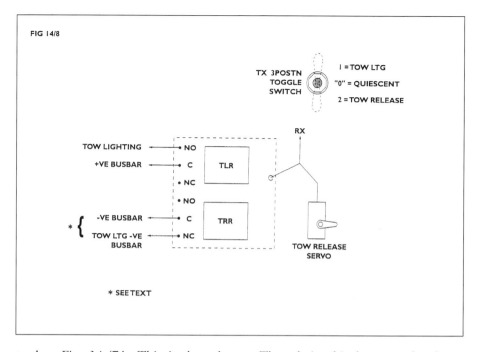

FIG 14/8

TX 3POSTN
TOGGLE
SWITCH

I = TOW LTG

"0" = QUIESCENT

2 = TOW RELEASE

RX

TOW LIGHTING → NO

+VE BUSBAR → C   TLR

NC

NO

-VE BUSBAR → C   TRR

* { TOW LTG -VE → NC
     BUSBAR

TOW RELEASE
SERVO

* SEE TEXT

Compared with the top ESC the bottom one has two additional wires below the power wiring on the left. These are connected to a switch to use the internal BEC circuit when required. See Chapter 5. The use of the two- and four-way switchers is discussed fully in Chapter 14. Note the 'neutral' adjustment facility and the clear identification of the relay contacts.

track – Fig. 14/7A. This is done by wiring two resistances R1 and R2 across the switch in Fig. 14/7B. The problem the worker now faces is what value resistances to use. The total value can be within a range of 3000 to 10,000 ohms depending on the make of the TX and is usually printed on the back of the pot. If forced to measure using a DVM disconnect as if it is left in the circuit an incorrect reading could occur. Fig. 14/7B assumes the pot value is 10k ohms.

The relationship between the three-sequence towing switcher relays deserves further expansion to show how de-energised relay NC contacts can be used to make life easier when operating a system. Position 2 of the toggle switch in Fig. 14/6B lit the floodlights and the basic tow lights if the tow line firing sequence was successful. These basic tow lights are lit when towing a vessel up to a certain length. Beyond that additional lights are required. These are lit using Position 1 of the switch in Fig. 14/8. As both switchers are unlatched they are left energised indicating the lighting is 'on' by the switch positions on the TX. Note that the tow firing switching sequence, Fig. 14/6B, is 0-1-0-2. When the tow is completed the tow line is released with the switch sequence in Fig. 14/8 of 0-2. This not only releases the tow but also energises the TRR which breaks the NC contact negative feed to the tow lighting busbar and switches off all the tow lighting and the floodlights. As the tow firing mechanism and the towing hook release

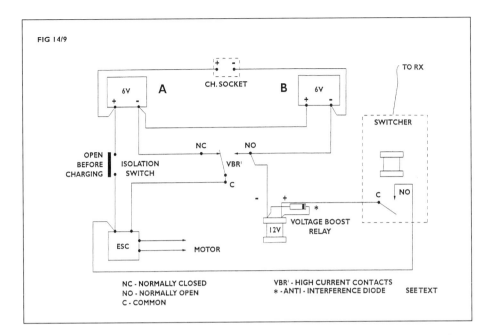

FIG 14/9

CH. SOCKET

TO RX

A   B

6V   6V

SWITCHER

OPEN
BEFORE
CHARGING

ISOLATION
SWITCH

NC   NO

VBR'

C

NO

C

VOLTAGE BOOST
RELAY

12V

ESC   MOTOR

NC - NORMALLY CLOSED
NO - NORMALLY OPEN
C - COMMON

VBR' - HIGH CURRENT CONTACTS
* - ANTI - INTERFERENCE DIODE   SEE TEXT

system all have to be reset 'in port', the switches can be left until the tug 'docks'. What this demonstrates is that the marine worker should always be aware of the possibilities of using NC contacts in this way to create automatic switching sequences.

Fig. 14/9 shows another use for a single switcher – Propulsion Motor Boost. It needs to be a non-latching type controlled by a switch on the TX for speed of operation and safety. There are many motors that will quite happily run on 4.5V to 15V. This circuit is for a propulsion system designed for 6V but also requires extra speed quickly. Two 6V batteries are wired in series with battery A normally feeding

The voltage boost equipment of Fig 14/9. The middle top is the VBR. To its right is the ACTion non-latching switcher. Note the empty left-hand IC socket which creates a latched unit when used.

the ESC with 6V via the isolation switch and the VBR[1] NC contact. When the switcher relay is energised the VBR breaks the 6V negative feed and replaces it with a 12V negative from battery B over VBR[1] NO contact. If the propeller diameter and pitch produce a more than satisfactory performance on 6V, the boost on 12V will be outstanding and it is for this reason and for the safety of the worker and onlookers that the circuit must non-latching. Fig. 14/9 has for the first time shown a diode fitted across the VBR coil. This is a precaution against the old enemy interference and is an introduction to the next chapter which amongst other things will discuss relays. So far in this chapter no mention has been made regarding the rating of relay contacts which again Fig. 14/9 draws attention to. This too will be discussed in the next chapter.

15

Relays, Switches and Sound Units

Preceding chapters have shown how relays are used as an interface with electronic control circuits to switch functions, handle high DC currents and change the polarity of motors. So far most of the relays have been part of purchased equipment where the selection of the relay for a particular purpose has been done by the designer of that equipment. All the user needs to know is how much current these relays will switch and, in the case of the Gemini system in Chapter 14, what voltage is required for the relay coils. All this information is supplied with the units when purchased, but when the worker decides to extend his or her control with further relay logic as in Fig. 13/2, in-depth knowledge is required to make the correct choice of relay for a particular purpose. For that to happen, fundamental principles must be followed to achieve a reliable system.

Relays

A relay is an electromagnetic device that attracts an armature to a core face when a voltage is applied to a coil wound around the core. A relay can be either DC or AC and only DC relays are used in RC work. This is mentioned as there are often AC relays available cheaply in surplus stores and these should be avoided. The coil voltage is usually a guide and if this is 120 or 240V they will be AC. However, the author has also seen 24V AC relays on sale. The moving armature is mechanically attached to either a single NO contact or to a bank or banks of NO and NC contacts. The electro power required to move these contacts is dependent upon the number of contacts and their physical size which in turn is governed by the current the contact is required to carry. For example, a four-pole changeover contact relay will require double the coil current compared with a single-pole make- or break-contact relay. Both sets of contacts are rated the same for current. All relay coil voltages quoted are nominal – 6, 12 or 24V. These voltages fit nicely into the range of battery voltages used in marine work.

A heavy-duty relay shows the contacts on the right attached to the armature which pivots on the left. The return spring keeps the armature away from the pole face in the middle and keeps the common centre contact C against the top NC contact above it. When energised this contact is broken and the bottom NO contact made. This is a 2-pole changeover relay. See text.

The relay module described in the text and Fig 15/1. Note the angled terminal blocks and the cutouts for access to the terminal screws and the test points.

disperse safely. A diode is a 'gate' which allows a voltage only to flow in one direction. A diode symbol is shown in Fig. 13/3 and in use across the VBR in Fig. 14/9. Note the identification band which must be the connection to the positive relay coil terminal. The last coil parameter is the operate/release time usually quoted in milliseconds (mS). A lightly-loaded armature will operate and release in approximately the same time. However, a large heavy bank of contacts will require a longer operating time but will release quickly due to the weight of the contact bank. These operate and release times only become important in relay logic if there is a possibility of relays racing each other and is something that the designer should be aware of.

Each nominal voltage has an upper and lower limit usually described as 'operating voltage range', eg a nominal 6V relay will operate between 4.5V and 7.8V. This information is vital as it indicates that the relay could be used on a RX 4.8V supply but would be close to failing to pick up if the coil voltage dropped to below 4.5V. Often the relay specification will quote the 'must release voltage'. This tells the user that the coil voltage must fall to below the figure quoted for the relay to release. This does not usually concern the marine worker but it is useful if it is intended to use the relay coil in a solid-state circuit where the coil is energised using a transistorised switching circuit. When a relay is energised a magnetic field is created which exists all the time the coil voltage is applied. When this voltage is switched off the magnetic field collapses and in doing so creates a voltage at the coil terminals – the back Electro Motive Force (EMF). This voltage is opposite in polarity to the energising voltage and is considerably higher in value. If left alone, this voltage spike will flow into other circuits causing damage and inter-ference. To contain these spikes a diode is fitted across the relay coil making the spike circulate back into the coil and

Relay contacts are possibly the most misunderstood components in RC. One misunderstanding has already been touched upon in Chapter 9, that is, ESC relay contacts which are rated far lower than the continuous current rating of the ESC. The reason is that the relay contact rating is the breaking current that each contact can carry without the contacts welding together. The moment of relay operation in an ESC is when the motor current is zero and therefore there is no arc between the contacts. It is the arc across two contact faces that, if it is excessive over a long period, will ultimately weld the two faces together. When current is flowing across two closed contacts there is a resistance at the point of con-tact. If this contact resistance is large then there will be a voltage drop across the contacts. All modern relay contacts are designed to ensure as low as pos-sible contact resistance with the contact material playing a leading role to achieve this. There can up to ten different contact materials ranging from silver tin oxide to gold/silver and gold plating used for differing duties. It is unnecessary for the marine worker to get involved in choosing the appropriate contact material other than to know that these do exist. Generally speaking a contact with a silver content is suitable for marine work. A relay should be selected for the duties the contacts are required for. It is obvious that if large currents are to be switched then the appropriate current-rated contacts are chosen. However, it is often not appreciated that using the same heavy-duty contacts to switch low currents are inappropriate as unnecessary power is being used to switch the relay and strangely, for reasons outside the scope of this discussion, that a heavy duty contact used for switching light loads will exhibit a greater voltage drop than when it is used for the load it is designed for.

The majority of relays available are designed for installation into PCs or a form of stripboard generally used for circuit development. One very useful stripboard is type 1919 by Vero, stocked by Maplins in the UK. Tandy Stores also have a range of small circuit

boards by Radio Shack which will accommodate one relay and a bank of small screw terminals such as the Camden range of PCB Screw Terminal Blocks in the Maplin catalogue. This range available interlockable in two and three ways to provide larger multiples. These blocks have the 'rising clamp' type of cable connection which protects the stranded wiring from the screw terminal. Production of relay modules is an easy task after laying out the design and identifying all the connections on paper first. Fig. 15/1 overleaf shows a typical layout based upon a Radio Shack board DIP1. Note the use of wire loops and terminal pins which are test points for circuit checking. The anti-interference diode is soldered directly across the relay pick-up pins on the copper side of the board so as to be as close as possible to the coil. Check and double-check that the identity band end is connected to the land going to the positive terminal which is identified immediately with a spot of red lacquer. The author uses redundant nail varnish surplus from the female side

The anti-interference diode soldered across every relay coil of the modules.

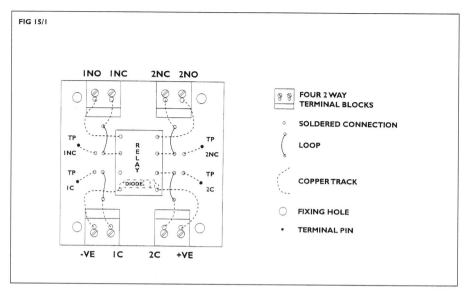

FIG 15/1

INO INC   2NC 2NO

FOUR 2 WAY TERMINAL BLOCKS

SOLDERED CONNECTION

LOOP

COPPER TRACK

FIXING HOLE

TERMINAL PIN

TP INC   RELAY   TP 2NC

TP IC   DIODE   TP 2C

-VE IC   2C +VE

of his establishment! Failure to mark this terminal followed by an incorrect polarity connection to test the module will result in a burnt-out diode. When using heavy-duty contacts, the copper lands to and from the contact pins should have their current-carrying capacity increased by soldering lengths of tinned copper wire to them. These particular Radio Shack boards are sold as a pair joined together which enables a number of modules to be stacked, forming space-saving relay banks. The separation pillars are available from Maplins in various lengths. Note in the photo that the bottom board terminal blocks are angled outwards for access to the terminal screw heads, further enhanced by the cutouts in the top boards. Note the contact nomenclature used in Fig. 15/1 is in agreement with relays AUR, AOR, EOR and the PR in Figs. 13/2 and 14/6A and are the relay modules shown in the photo.

Currently available modern relays have coils requiring either 5 or 12V. The older 6V relay is becoming scarce, and although the modern 5V coil can be used on a 6V supply it should only be for a short duration. This is because these relays are usually fully sealed and

are in a very confined environment which leads to an unwelcome rise in coil temperature. In the initial design stage the worker is advised to contemplate a 12V system using the centre tap supply discussed in Chapter 8 and Fig. 8/1. The other advantage of using 12V relays is the lower coil current, compared with a lower coil voltage and higher current, which reduces the required power supply capacity. A worker using relays for the first time is well advised to try to standardise on two types. Both should be with coil voltage as above and one fitted with 2-amp 2-pole changeover contacts. The relay pinning connections should be on a 0.1in grid as this is the standard stripboard size. This 'standard' relay is used for relay logic and light switching duties such as small motors and lighting etc. For heavier duties such as water pumps and bow thruster motors the Automotive range is worth looking at with contact ratings of 16 amps for the second 'standard'. These relays have 12V coils. Both types can be found in the catalogues of the two specialist suppliers, Maplins and RS Components (see Appendix 2). In designing relay circuits the coil resistance is a very useful figure as the coil current can be calculated using Ohm's Law (see Appendix 3). This result is used to ensure the correctly rated contacts are used when switching relays as well as calculating power supply loads and fuse ratings. Always bear in mind the diversity factor that not all relays are energised at the same time.

Switches

Towards the end of Chapter 4 mention was made of micro switches operated by a servo disc with either a detent or a hump in its circumference. For their size and simplistic operation micro switches offer very high current switching in a small package. The most common switching is SPDT although DPDT versions are available. Switching currents can be as high as 15 amps. By far the biggest range is by RS Components which includes a fully sealed sub-miniature SPDT switch rated at 2 amps and incorporating flying lead terminations, ideal for marine work in deck-mounted structures such as gun turrets. Micro switches are extremely reliable as long as care is used in their mounting and setting up. The mounting must be substantial enough to ensure that there is no movement between the switch and the operating cam other than that intended for operation. Radial adjustment must be provided so that the switch body can be moved and the operating button accurately set. A micro switch comprises of a rectangular body with a button on the top at one end. Depressing the button results in a 'snap' action which brings the contacts together extremely quickly to reduce arcing. Although the button can be operated by a variety of actuators its movement to the 'snap' position, pre-travel, is around 1mm. The 'snap' or differential

can be as low as 0.1mm with an over-travel of between 0.1mm and 1mm. These small limits can multiplied by using a lever pivoted behind the button and fitted with a roller which travels over the cam surface. The majority of micro switches are side-mounted with either solder terminals in the base or blades which will accept push-on Lucar connectors. Switches available are basic, button-only operation or with a chosen type of actuator. Some types of micro switches come with a kit of actuator hardware. The important dimension in setting up a switch is the overtravel. If this is exceeded the whole assembly is under strain as the cam tries to force the button into the switch. Conversely, if there is no overtravel the contacts will have insufficient pressure on them and a high resistance contact will result. However, once set up and the switch is securely locked in position, fault-free operation can be expected for a long period. Of the two specialist suppliers RS Components have the more comprehensive range to offer.

Reed switches operated by a magnet offer a clean way to detect movement without putting any mechanical load on a system. They can be used as rotary limit switches on gun turrets, cranes, water cannon etc. When linear

Servo-operated micro switches. A standard plastic disc is used carrying a substantial pin which 'strokes' either switch button as it passes. This picks up the relay below the aluminium channel which is stuck up over its own contact and the other micro switch NC contact. The reverse movement drops out the relay. The method ensures an easy setup without servo overrun problems. A metal clevis is used due to restricted space. Note the essential locking nut.

A servo connecting rod operated micro switch. These are available from model shops.

operating they can be used on crane hoists to prevent overrun. A reed switch is hermetically sealed within a glass capsule with the reed in two halves to form the contact. It operates when the long face of the magnet is parallel to the wide face of the reed, inducing magnetism into both halves so that one half becomes a north pole and the other half a south pole. The attraction of the poles causes the switch to close. When the magnetism is removed the springiness of the reed enables the switch to open. They are available either plain or capsulated in a plastic block. The reed can be a single NO contact or a Change Over (CO). For their size the current rating is surprisingly high – 1 amp is not uncommon with 3 amps being available. Installation is not difficult as long as one principle is followed: the connecting lengths of reed must be kept in line with the glass body. They can be shortened but remember that reducing the length also reduces the magnetic force available to close the switch. Any of the adhesives such as thick cyanacrylate and polyester resins will bond the switch in position as long as the worker recognises the need to ensure the switch cannot turn on its axis. Most reed switches have flats on the reeds where they exit from the capsule which can be used as anchoring points for the adhesive. Do not use any form of metal clamp for obvious reasons. The capsulated reed switch is better for marine use, making installation that much easier.

To round off switches, the need to replace the supplied RX switch can be met by a variety of types as well as the toggle switch discussed in Chapter 5 and Fig. 5/4. Nothing destroys the illusion of a scale vessel more than an obvious switch located on the face of a detailed superstructure. The toggle switch can be hidden beneath a hatch cover, while a capstan can be used to turn the spindle of a rotary switch. Where space is limited a miniature locking push button can be located behind a porthole and operated through it. If there are adjacent portholes one can be used to access the RX charging socket already discussed towards the end of Chapter 10. Two more alternative switching circuits are shown in Fig. 15/2. Both include an LED indication when power is switched to the RX. This could be a yellow LED and sited behind a porthole. Alternatively a green or red LED could be one of the vessel's sidelights. There is no reason why both sidelights cannot be wired in parallel off either switch. Remember each LED needs its own current-limiting resistor (see Appendix 3).

Sound units

Producing authentic sound from a scale vessel on the water is one of the most challenging projects a marine modeller faces. Its volume has to be many times greater than the scale to overcome the background noise around the listeners and it needs depth and ambience to be authentic. Sound is produced by moving air at different frequencies causing pressure changes which the human ear detects and translates into 'sound'. Pure or prime frequencies can be generated electronically with little trouble. It is the harmonics of these prime frequencies that separates them into the recognisable sounds that the

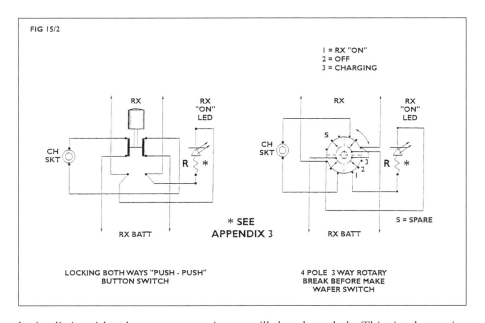

FIG 15/2

1 = RX "ON"
2 = OFF
3 = CHARGING

RX

RX "ON" LED

CH SKT

R ⧸ *

RX

RX "ON" LED

CH SKT

S

3
2
1

R ⧸ *

S = SPARE

RX BATT

* SEE APPENDIX 3

RX BATT

LOCKING BOTH WAYS "PUSH - PUSH" BUTTON SWITCH

4 POLE 3 WAY ROTARY BREAK BEFORE MAKE WAFER SWITCH

brain distinguishes between say a siren or a high-pitch whistle. All workers are no doubt familiar with hi-fi systems in their homes and will know that the loudspeaker and its placement is the key to quality listening. Also known is that many loudspeaker enclosures contain two speakers, one to handle the base frequencies and the other for the mid to high frequencies – the tweeter. Two speakers are used because a single speaker designed for all frequencies is a compromise, whereas a speaker designed for base frequencies is far more efficient. It is also larger as lower frequencies need more power to 'pump' the air. Mid to high frequencies need less power and this is why tweeters are small. From this the marine worker can conclude that choice of the right speaker for marine sounds is one of the crucial steps to obtaining authenticity. Just in the same way as the hi-fi system requires its speakers to be housed in enclosures and placed in the room for the best possible results, the housing and placement of loudspeakers in boats require careful thought and installation. If any obstruction is placed in front of the hi-fi speaker the sound performance will be degraded. This is the major problem with boats. The speaker needs total freedom in front of it whilst the last thing a boat needs is a large gaping hole in either the hull or the super-structure! So a compromise has to be made. Before that, speaker size and type has to be married to the sound it will radiate. A diesel generator sound needs low frequencies to create the illusion of powerful engines moving the vessel to sea or the 'putt-putt' of a fishing boat slowly moving along the

A prototype smoke unit by Tomahawk Products – see Appendix 2. Electronically controlled with safety features, it can be manually or remotely switched. The four LEDs in the centre indicate the unit status during operation.

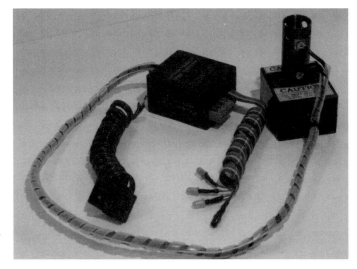

Top: Two sound units, siren and horn, mounted on top of a loudspeaker firing downwards using the whole hull as a sound box.

Above: A Mylar cone loudspeaker. Note the bayonet fixing ensuring the LS is always locked into the correct position.

whistles, while the square range of 77mm and 87mm with a lower frequency range of 75Hz and 150Hz are suited for the deeper stronger siren and diesel generator sound.

There is no reason why the hull cannot be used as an enclosure with the loudspeaker mounted under the deck and 'firing' upwards. The obvious problems are disguising the loudspeaker grill and stopping any water from entering. The author solved this in two ways on a model of a fast off-shore drilling rig supply boat. These boats have a large deck area from the forward-mounted superstructure right to the stern, used in the full-size original to carry oil rig replacement parts. A plastic coupling collar used for rainwater downpipes was fitted over a modified plastic lid with its centre removed. A hole was cut in the decking and the lid, after being sprayed matt black, was glued to it upside down so that it formed a coaming on the top surface. A 77mm-square 5-watt Mylar loudspeaker was fitted underneath. A plastic housing from a failed washing machine pump was glued into the top of the coupling and the whole sprayed matt black. When fitted to the coaming and suitably secured with scale roping the unit looked like oil rig maintenance parts. On the undersurface the two diesel generator units are fitted alongside the speaker. The boat has twin motors which are individually controlled on the turns by mixing so that with the outer motor speeding up and the inner slowing down the two generators produce an authentic sound. In the photo, note the two plugs for connection to the power supply and the motor connections. These are required to automatically increase the generators' speed as each motor accelerates. They are common connections on all generators. With this system the assembly can be bench-

coast. Either way the speaker needs to be as large as possible and sited nearer the stern than the bow. It also needs to be installed 'firing' upwards so that the sound does not become directional. Ideally it should be waterproof as a paper-based loudspeaker cone does not live well with any form of moisture and will certainly be completely ruined if it becomes thoroughly wet. Fortunately there is the Mylar range of loudspeakers stocked by Maplin available which are 'fully weather and splashproof' and have a frequency range ideally suited for marine sounds. The small round range of 49mm and 56mm diameters have a frequency range of 200Hz to 20kHz which is ideal for high-pitch sirens and

tested and the generators adjusted to obtain the correct mix of sounds. In use, the sound appears to surround the boat and at speed, even with the after deck awash, no water has penetrated the coaming.

This boat also requires an emergency siren sound and a hooter. This system is located within the superstructure in the bows. A series of ¼ in-diameter holes were drilled in the horizontal-sloping fore part to form a circular matrix the diameter of the Mylar loudspeaker fitted underneath. The outside part of the matrix was covered by the boat's plastic identity decal. Again the electronic sound units are installed local to the loudspeaker. In use, although the decal reduces the sound output this is compensated by running the units at 12V to increase the output. Both of these methods use the whole hull as a loudspeaker enclosure and with the inevitable vibration from the assemblies seems to add a depth of aural realism. Both these systems use double sound units feeding one loudspeaker. To do this certain additional components are needed to ensure the system will work efficiently. The ACTion range of sound units include a mixer which is fed by up to four units whose volume controls become pre-amplifier controls. The loudspeaker is connected to the mixer output. Adjusting the 'slave' pre-amplifiers enables a balance of sound to be achieved. The system also increases the audio power output. From experience the author has found that a two-speaker system, when more than two audio sounds are required, creates a more authentic result. Using the complete hull as an enclosure works on the principle of preventing the sound waves from the back of a loudspeaker cone from reaching the front. It is when these two waves meet out of phase that distortion occurs degrading the overall sound. Although not as

efficient, installing a loudspeaker upside down so that it 'fires' into the hull is feasible if no other alternative exists. Large plastic containers fitted over loudspeakers can be used to 'feed' the sound out through gratings in superstructures. Whatever system is used, always ensure the loudspeaker is firmly bolted to a substantial base to keep vibration down. As discussed above, vibration can help in sound distribution but it must be controlled. The major problem is getting the sound out. If a vessel has a number of portholes in its superstructure do not glaze them on the basis that every little helps! Bear in mind also that loudspeakers contain large and very

Top: Diesel sound generator and loudspeaker mounted underneath the after deck, described in the text, of *Orkney Express.*

Above: A RX rotary switch operated by a capstan. The ribbon cable also switched other static functions which would normally be required before the vessel left port. The RX supply wiring is separate from the ribbon cable.

A cable form carrying masthead functions. Note the use of cable markers. The separate cable on the left is the screened aerial cable. The screening is removed once the cable is clear of the main form.

efficient magnets which should be kept away from sensitive RF equipment and aerials. Furthermore loudspeakers are heavy and should be installed as low as possible within a superstructure to prevent the vessel becoming 'tender'.

The above once again demonstrates that the informed marine worker needs to plan carefully the implications of extending working features before any construction of a boat project commences. Certainly from the RC side any additional working features will affect the capacity required both in the RC power pack and the propulsion supply which will be used to feed the auxiliary functions. This main power supply voltage has to designed carefully to meet all the requirements expected of it. This is why a centre-tapped supply is strongly recommended as it opens up all the options. Fortunately for the scale worker the subjects modelled usually have plenty of room to accommodate large batteries which can also double up as ballast. Fitting as large a capacity supply as is practical insures the project against possible problems and failures in the future.

16

Installing RC Equipment

It is understandable that when a beginner experiences an unexplained event when using RC equipment the blame is nearly always placed on the radio link. Either someone else is transmitting on the user's channel or 'Those useless nicads' – again or 'I should never have bought that make anyway – Fred says it's never reliable!'. The real truth is that modern RC gear is extremely reliable and any failure to operate consistently is nearly always the result of a number of fundamental mistakes made back in the workshop during construction. If a basic set of gear is installed according to the maker's instructions within a sailing boat, with the possible addition of a sail winch, and the system's batteries are fully charged the whole will perform reliably time and time again as long as the batteries are charged correctly and the gear properly maintained. It is only when the worker deviates from the basics that possible failures can be unwittingly built in.

Clean and dirty wiring

Chapter 6 and Fig. 6/1 introduced the principle of clean and dirty wiring. The basic installation above is the basic clean wiring. Any other wiring introduced into the hull other than further connections to the RX must be

considered dirty. As Fig. 6/1 showed, all the clean wiring is kept to one side of the hull with the dirty wiring on the other. A tidy installation will contribute much to keeping failures at bay. Early in hull construction the two wiring runs should be established by using self-adhesive pads stuck about halfway down inside the hull. Eventually these will enable miniature nylon cable ties to secure the wiring runs. Both of these items are available from specialist suppliers listed in Appendix 2.

Which side of the hull is 'clean' and which is 'dirty' is usually decided by the position of the rudder servo, which is in turn decided by the hull construction. Where possible, the servo should be installed along the length of the hull and not across it. This spreads the

The author's ESC test boat, *Orkney Express*, with ESCs mounted for ease of removal. Note the 'clean' wiring top left separated from the 'dirty' wiring bottom left. The RX aerial connection can be seen mounted on the vertical upstand top left. Two motor fuses are also on test - 'in line' and blade type.

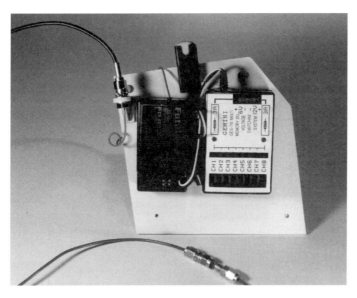

RX panel and aerial connection. The optional 'in line' connectors are shown at the bottom of the photo. These are Vitelec components available both in UK and USA. For details, including the GEMINI GES-7W module shown and discussed in Chapter 14, see Appendix 2.

bility of severe damage to the RX plastic case when attempting to remove the RX when they are used, as the author knows to his cost. Velcro pads are in two halves. One half has small hooks and the other has small loops. When pressed together these lock into each other and hold the RX firmly. Velcro mounts also offer a small degree of vibration reduction as well. When it is necessary to remove the RX it comes away cleanly, and the mount can also be removed from the equipment without causing damage. When positioning the RX, do it in conjunction with positioning the RX battery and whatever switching system is used. Bear in mind battery access and its weight in regard to the final trim of the vessel. Light items such as RXs and control modules such as Gemini can be mounted on wing panels as shown in the photo. This leaves the depth of the hull interior clear for the more heavier items.

Access to the RX for crystal changing can be made easier by housing the crystal external to the RX. The author knows of only one RC manufacturer who produces a Crystal Extension Lead, Futaba, but as crystal pin centres are standard irrespective of manufacture this accessory can be used with any make of RX. The part number is P-RB8088. It can be ordered in the UK from any retailer who deals with Ripmax plc. Outside the UK workers should contact Futaba in their own country. Generally speaking the RX aerial can be terminated within a few inches of the RX and replaced with a plug/socket system. However, there are some RXs whose aerials are part of the RF circuitry and should never be interfered with. The makers usually bring this to the attention of the user. Because all RC systems are designed firstly for aero use and have long range, when they are employed for marine use with its short range requirements,

rudder forces being imposed on the servo along its length. Generally speaking, rudder servos will be installed offset from the hull centreline due to the geometry of the rudder tiller and the servo horn. Whichever half the servo is in will decide the 'clean' side. Rudder servos should be firmly screwed down without the anti-vibration inserts. Ch.Hd or Rd.Hd with washers under the head screws must be used, not C.Sk as these will split the slotted lugs on the servo. It is a wise precaution to double-nut the screws. If possible access to the servo should be built-in.

The RX

The RX position should be determined with care, bearing in mind future crystal changing and the exit for its aerial. RXs do not have any fixing lugs, a feature inherited from the aero days as when fitted in an aeroplane the RX is wrapped in anti-shock material and enclosed in a box. The author has tried many types of fixings over the years and has standardised on using Velcro mounts available from Maplin's. On no account use double-sided self-adhesive pads, because there is a strong possi-

liberties can be taken with the reception architecture in the boat – the aerial. Unless the scale worker is prepared to accept a whip aerial or a length of stranded wire draped across the superstructure a problem exists with the RX in the hull separated from any aerial arrangements in the superstructure. This separation can only be solved by providing a connection between the two halves unless the worker is prepared to always install the aerial back into the superstructure every time access is required – not a practical option. Inserting an aerial connection is a perfectly sound solution as long as it is suited for its purpose. Having digested the previous chapters the worker will know that the transmitted signal is not only complicated but is also very low in power. The 'front end' RF circuitry of any RX is very sensitive and very selective so as to only receive the signal intended for it. The RX aerial is part of this 'front end' and its job is to ensure that the maximum signal possible exists for a successful instruction to arrive at the servo. As previously discussed, marine workers can take advantage of the reduced range required but there is a limit to this and any action to extend this advantage beyond safe operational limits must be carefully thought through before doing it. The author is certain that interfering with the 'front end' circuitry of a RX, by for example introducing an aerial connection, must be beyond reproach and of a fail-safe nature. In the past other authorities have suggested that a simple plug and socket 4mm banana-type connector is more than adequate. This solution is totally rejected for two reasons. Firstly, the aerial circuit is working at mega frequencies and technically the connector should be designed for this (the details are outside the scope of this manual). Secondly, the connection must be fully mechanically

sound to ensure 100 per cent connection at all times.

To achieve these two objectives will be costly compared with a banana plug or any other option, but bear in mind that there is a considerable monetary investment being pushed away from the bank every time the marine worker goes sailing and he is relying on the equipment consistently working safely. Listed in Appendix 2 is Vitelec Electronics Ltd, which can supply a range of suitable SMA connectors. The jack connector can either be cable mounted or bulkhead mounted. Part numbers for either option are listed. The coaxial

The RX aerial plug connection socket (bottom left) is wired to the outer railings on both port and starboard sides. Note the two servos at the top of the photo. These rotate the water cannons via the chain drive. Note that the bottom right cable form is terminated as recommended on p.159.

A moulded 'Yot Pot' used to waterproof a yacht RX. (Photo Chris Jackson)

cable designed for use with these connectors is Type RG174. The cable is just under 3mm overall diameter – ideal for marine purposes. The connector is designed for RF working with a threaded coupling. The total cost is only a few pounds/dollars and well worth it for peace of mind. The chassis-type socket requires a 6.5mm fixing hole reducing to 6.1mm from the inside surface to an opposite anti-rotation flat. The photo shows the connector mounted on a wing RX installation alongside a crystal extension lead unit. This installation, with the RX connected to a fixed socket, is not so convenient as the plug terminated onto the RX aerial and the socket located within the superstructure. This last method is all right as long as the user can see to connect it up without turning the superstructure upside down with consequential damage to it. Whichever method is adopted, a coaxial cable is recommended which means it has a screen mesh underneath the outer plastic covering. This is useful and should be left on where the cable is run or passes near 'dirty' wiring. Once clear, the outer covering and the screen can be removed leaving the inner insulated conductor to act as the aerial. On scale

models there are many options for the aerial position. Obvious ones are inside or outside masts. Where there are twin masts there is often a scale aerial between them and there is no reason why this should not be the working aerial. Scale liberties should be taken to increase the scale diameter to approach that of the original as it is the surface area of an aerial that is important to its efficiency. One of the author's tugs has a scale dipole aerial on the foremast and this is used for the RX aerial with the inner conductor running down the inside of the mast. On another boat the metal hand railings either side of the superstructure are connected in parallel to the RX aerial, forming a grid-like system. In approaching solutions like these, measure the aerial length prior to cutting and ensure the alternative system approximately equals this figure. It is not vital to be absolutely exact.

Previous chapters have dealt at length with alternative RX-battery switching systems. Installation of whatever is chosen will be entirely dependent upon the boat design and availability of locations. Nearly all scale subjects will have some part of the superstructure fixed and these locations are preferable. Endeavour to locate both battery and switching as close to the RX as possible to keep voltage losses through the wiring as low as possible. At one point the wiring changes to a plug for connection into the RX. Keep this lead as short as possible as although the rest of the wiring can be adjusted in size for minimum volt drop, this part is the maker's standard and cannot be modified. Remember to leave access for the 'black wire' inspection points (see Chapter 10, Fig. 10/2). Once the battery and custom-built switching system has been installed do not connect to the RX but check for polarity at the output plug. Switch over for charging and again check for polarity. If the maker's harness is used then these checks are not necessary.

Whatever type of speed control is preferred it should be installed as close to the motor as is practical to keep the power wiring short. If the unit is mounted across the hull the wiring will naturally separate itself into 'clean' and 'dirty'. This area is the most vulnerable for induced interference so make sure the RX wiring is kept well clear of the power wiring and both sets are firmly secured into their respective cable runs. The battery positive to the speed controller should be fused using an 'in-line' fuseholder of good quality close to the speed controller. The Bulgin range is highly recommended, and this also includes a sealed version. Before installation make sure there is adequate slack in the motor wiring so that the fuseholder is easily accessible for fuse changing. It is important to get the assembly sequence of these fuseholders right. First thread each half of the outer casing onto the wiring, followed on one half only by the spring and either the solder thimble or collar with screw terminal. Bare the stranded conductor for $\frac{1}{8}$ in for the thimble and $\frac{1}{4}$ in for the collar. For the thimble splay out the strands and solder carefully to leave a 'domed' appearance. With a fine file clean off the flux and excessive solder to produce a flat surface. Use the No.52 bit on the iron and work quickly to avoid overheating the assembly. Remember to keep the plastic casing halves away from the work area. For the collar termination leave the conductor as stripped and *do not* solder. Insert the stripped end into the collar and tighten the screw so that it bites into the bare strands. In-line fuseholders should always have the spring under the thimble or collar, never between them and the fuse. Assemble the fuse-holder/s, twin speed controllers, but *do not* fuse. Terminate the wiring onto the

motor, which should already have been suppressed (see Chapter 7, Fig. 7/1), by soldering. Again work quickly to avoid damage to the suppressors. Never use push-on connectors to an electric motor – they will eventually work loose.

Run the power supply conductors, together with the earth wiring to the earth busbar (see Chapter 6), back to the main power supply battery which ideally should be located amidships. This part of the installation should have been planned within the length of the power wiring of the speed controller. Avoid intermediate disconnection points if possible unless as in the author's case it is required to test and evaluate a selection of speed controllers. Before terminating on the battery check and double-check the wiring for polarity as a mistake can be costly. When satisfied solder the connections. At the same time as the wiring is proceeding a record should be made of cable colours back to a wiring diagram. Accurate records will make fault-finding much easier plus being a useful tool for future projects. Again identifying each cable with plastic markers (see Chapter 14), will save valuable time when fault-finding in the future. After a final check on all the connections so far, preparations can be

For quick crystal-change yachts use a 'Pot' for the RX. This can be a discarded screw-top container or a purchased 'Pot' as shown opposite. (Photo Chris Jackson)

A neat yacht installation module. Note the breadth of hull required for a sail arm servo. (Photo Chris Jackson)

made for the first testing of the system from the TX. The boat should be secure in its cradle and the rudder/propeller clear of any obstructions. At this stage the motor fuse should still be out. Make sure both RX and TX batteries are fully charged. Leave the TX aerial collapsed and plug in a temporary RX aerial if it has been decided to modify it. Switch on the TX and then the RX. Operate the rudder control and check the response of the rudder for left-port, right-starboard. Reverse the servo on the TX as required. Now check the throttle for correct response. With a servo-operated MSC this will be obvious. With an ESC listen for the relay to pick up. If the relay picks up for forward movement on the TX, reverse the function to pick up when going astern. Switch off the RX and insert the motor fuse. Switch the TX back on and test for correct motor rotation and any glitching of the other servo. If all is well, repeat the range check described at the end of Chapter 3. The same result should occur. If glitching occurs at any point

in these initial tests, disconnect the speed control from the RX and re-test. With fully-charged batteries the glitching will disappear. If using a servo MSC, disconnect the servo from the motor control board and reconnect the servo to the RX. If using an ESC, plug a spare servo into the RX. Re-test. All should be well. In the very unlikely event of faulty operation something has occurred to the equipment between that initial first test and now. The only option is to return the gear to the manufacturer with details of the fault.

If, however, the gear with two servos operates satisfactory it is more than likely that the initial problem came from the speed control circuitry, particularly if the unit is not of the same manufacture as the rest of the gear. Not all ESCs are compatible with all RXs. If kit or ready-built ESCs are used always check with the kit supplier as to compatibility before purchase. Motors can also create problems particularly those 'bargains' salvaged from domestic consumer equipment. Usually the culprit is quickly identified, with replacement being the only cure. It just requires a logical, disciplined elimination of possible causes. The wipers on MSC control boards often cause serious arcing which can be reduced or eliminated by ensuring that each moving wiper is in correct contact with the board over its entire travel and increasing the wiper pressure for better contact. The foregoing has discussed the worst possible outcome of these initial tests, so that the worker is aware of what could happen and how to deal with it. It is more than likely that all will be well, establishing that the basic safety functions, steering and propulsion are correctly installed and creating a benchmark to which further work can be measured. The worker now knows that if the installation of further more complicated functions creates operating problems, then that additional work must be the cause. Installation must be a stage-by-stage process, testing after each stage. Installing a complete system which fails when tested leads to total chaos with the worker not knowing where to start looking for the cause.

In Chapter 14 the use of a Y lead to split a function output to drive a servo and a switcher was described. All equipment manufacturers can supply Y leads and a prudent worker will have several of these very useful accessories in stock. Some makers offer 'Boosted' or 'Filter' Y leads and most offer various lengths. Extension leads are also in every RC catalogue and are also in various lengths and again 'Filter' or 'Boosted' leads are available from some makers. Normally it should not be necessary to use these leads in marine work unless the run from RX to servo is in excess of 1 metre or if severe interference is proved to be external to the equipment. There is, however, one exception. Some high-frequency ESCs have been known to cause interference which these leads will usually cure. The custom-built RX switching system discussed earlier presents a problem with the final lead and plug into the RX. Again most makers can supply a short lead with the correct power plug and one end bare for connection into the custom unit.

Yacht rudder servo and sail winch. Note the deck fitting to ease the sheet exit. (Photo Chris Jackson)

Once the marine worker has decided to extend the equipment into areas which require modification, and the carefully designed fail-safe polarised system of connection is broken, extreme care is needed to ensure that whatever replaces it also replaces the integrity of the original system. To this end a stock of the maker's type plugs and female sockets are a useful addition to the stock cupboard. A stock of the servo type three-core flat cable is also useful. Bear in mind that there are differences between makers of the positive/signal/negative relationship of the cores. At least one specialist supplier, Amerang, lists a 15-metre coil of servo cable which will be in the 'hitec' equipment servo colours. Often at the UK shows spare items as above can be found on traders' stalls. Universal servo plugs and female sockets to make up leads are also available, although workers should note that these are not polarised and must be used with extreme care.

Once the safety elements, steering and propulsion, of the RC system are in place and tested the remaining management items, charging sockets and switches of the RX and main power supply can be installed. Again double-check for correct polarity on both systems. Test the charging regime as if preparing for a normal sailing session. When completed there is no reason why the vessel cannot be launched for its first water trials even with a partially completed superstructure. This will enable a check to be made on ballast which in turn will determine the amount of hull space left for installing any additional equipment. Any modifications required to correct normal running problems can also be addressed whilst the hull interior is clear. When checking the ballast, make allowance for the weight of additional equipment that will be added for the non-safety functions.

17

Installing Auxiliary Equipment

The auxiliary functions within a RC system are non-safety inasmuch as if they fail the ability of the system to return the vessel to the pondside is not compromised. However, if these functions are installed in a haphazard way, they can materially affect the safety functions to an extent that these will fail and in the worst case with catastrophic consequences. Even the addition of one auxiliary function, such as a diesel generator, could cause the main power supply to fail if the generator supply is not fused correctly.

Fusing

It is a myth that the purpose of a fuse is to protect the equipment. The principle role of a fuse is to protect the wiring back to the supply and the supply itself. Its secondary role is to protect the equipment from further damage if has developed the ability to sink a current greater than the rated fuse and the fuse ruptures. For example, if the above generator is not fused and suddenly creates a complete short-circuit across the main power supply, many hundreds of amperes would flow through the wiring from the generator back to the SLA battery. This wiring would quickly become like the element of an electric fire setting alight its surroundings. The SLA volts would

quickly fall leaving the boat without power. Impossible? The author has seen it happen and it was not a pretty sight for the builder to see months of work destroyed for the want of a fuse costing a few pennies.

The first task before installing the auxiliary functions is to plan all the fusing arrangements likely to be required using Fig. 8/1 and the principles set out in Chapter 8 as a general guide. From experience the author has found the 20mm chassis-mounting fuseholder is the best for this type of work. It is an open fuseholder with a solder tag at each end. There is a PCB version with a separately-available cover which will also fit the tagged type. Maplin's stock both types. Miniature tag strips are used to form a positive busbar fed from the fuse. The opposite row of tags are also formed into a busbar for the negative return wiring. Note that the 6 and 12V negatives are common. The other row of tags is the Earth busbar referred to in Chapter 7 and Fig. 7/2. In the author's fusing design an electronic fuse, F2, is used for the anchor and tow winch motors as these are particularly vulnerable to stalling. An electronic fuse will automatically trip on short-circuits and reset after a period of time. If the fault is not cleared it will go on tripping until it is. F3 feeds EOR contacts 1 and 2 functions and F4 alone feeds the water

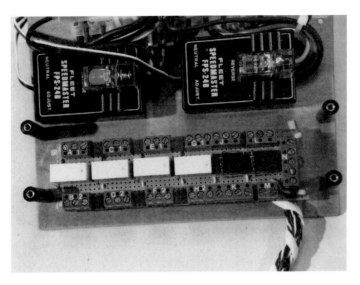

A relay module with terminal blocks. Note the block identities and the two diodes fitted across the relay tops due to space limitations underneath. The two ESC RX connections on the left would normally be run clear of the power 'dirty' wiring.

pumps. One pump is the water cannon and the other is the bilge pump which will automatically pump out when water is detected in the bilges.

Where possible all terminations should be soldered. However, with a modular system as discussed in Chapter 13 terminal blocks are used. These should be of good quality and employ a clamping system that secures the conductor between two flat surfaces. Terminal blocks with the terminal screw bearing down on the conductor should be avoided. Technically speaking, a stranded conductor should never have the bare end twisted together and soldered before being clamped into the terminal. The reason for this is the phenomenon of cold flow of solder which in time loosens the grip of the terminal clamp. This has been known amongst professional engineers for a long time and time is the key to whether this is applicable to marine modelling. It takes a long time for cold flow to occur and create a failure and certainly this time element is far beyond a sailing season. Non-soldered twisted ends can cause failures when rogue strands short between the miniature terminal blocks used in marine modelling, and these can be

difficult to locate. The so-called 'correct' way to terminate is to solder a thimble onto the stranded end and terminate onto the thimble. Unfortunately there is no ready supply of these various-sized thimbles in the UK so this solution cannot be recommended. On balance, the author recommends stripping the conductor for twice the length required, twisting the strands together and then folding the length back on itself to form a flat end. The rounded end is squeezed tight and then very lightly soldered. Being flat, the recommended clamping action will hold the conductor firmly and being lightly soldered the end will spread under pressure. In the maintenance programme (see Chapter 20), all terminal screws are inspected and tightened annually which will guard against cold flow of solder.

Relays

Chapter 15 dealt with the more commonly available relays that are intended for either PCB or Vero stripboard mounting. However, the worker should be aware that the older type of relays with screw connections are still available. These are all power relays capable of switching 10 amps with 12V coils. The relays plug into bases with the screw terminals. The Omron MK Series has a manual test button and an indicator to show the relay status. Also discussed in Chapter 15 were reed switches operated by magnets. A reed switch can also be operated by a coil wound around the glass envelope. When sealed into a block it becomes an extremely useful relay, mainly because it will operate on a very low coil current switching a respectable 1 amp. Available with either single- or double-pole contacts at coil voltages of 5V and 12V needing only 10 to 11.4mA to operate, these relays can be used as part of a solid state circuit. The 5V coil will operate over a range of 3.8V to 11V. For those workers who like to experiment, the simple solid state circuit in Appendix 3 should be of interest, as an ideal introduction to experimental work. The author designed it many years ago as a switcher working direct from a RX output. This switcher uses a reed relay with 1-amp contacts which can switch either low-current auxiliary functions or a relay such as the EOR in Fig. 13/2. The circuit can be built onto Vero stripboard with 0.1in matrix. The component placing is not critical but the CMOS IC needs to be handled carefully to avoid magnetic contamination. An IC 14-pin socket is recommended. The 47k pre-set is used to adjust the switching point on the TX.

Chapter 15 and Fig. 15/1 discussed the production of relay modules. These can be mounted either by bolting them down or using the Velcro pad system. Of the two it is better to bolt them down firmly so that the blocks cannot move when tightening the terminals. They should be mounted on a sub-base rather than directly into the hull so that a group can be lifted clear when fault-finding. Arrange the sub-base layout so that 'clean and dirty' wiring is kept apart. This will occur with switchers. Where the 'dirty' wiring is required to run down the hull, keep it in a separate run to the existing one as this helps when fault tracing. Stranded wiring is preferred to solid conductors for its flexibility and a variety of colours should be used for identification. It is a good idea to compile a wiring schedule before work commences showing the wire function, destination and colour. In this way the worker has complete control and reduces the possibility of errors occurring. However, when errors do occur, and they will, finding the

fault and correcting it is that much easier.

Wiring between hull and superstructure

The most difficult problem to solve is inter-wiring between hull and superstructure. There are three areas to consider: the aerial, connections to RX outputs, and function wiring. The aerial problem has already been addressed in Chapter 16 by the use of a high-quality RF connector. Connections to RX outputs can be the individual servo leads but using these is messy and time-consuming when having to part hull and superstructure. A little thought will show that, for example, for two servos the number of conductors required between the two halves is four not six; two signal, one positive, and one negative. The more RX functions there are between hull and superstructure the more economic the wiring becomes as long as it is recognised that both DC supply conductors must be adequate to carry the current required. This way will require gear-type female sockets

A 'piggy-back' arrangement with two 'clean' modules mounted above the relay module shown opposite. Note the RH module wiring to the relay coils running down to the circuit board opposite where they are soldered direct. The other end of this loom can be seen bottom right in the photo opposite. All the 'dirty' terminal block wiring will exit from the middle right.

to accept the servo plugs. These sockets are then connected into whatever choice is made for the interconnecting system. At the hull end, servo plugs convert back for connection into the RX. Over the years the author has experimented with a number of interconnection systems and has established a number of principles.

1. The number of conductors must be the minimum that can be achieved by analysing the circuits and identifying the commonality as in the example above.

2. Within this minimum, allowance should be made for at least three or four spares for conductor failure and future development.

3. The resulting cable form must be as flexible as possible to avoid strain on the superstructure, which can at worse push it out of alignment.

4. The actual parting connectors must not be so stiff to separate that damage occurs when undue force is used to part them.

5. The cable form at the opposite ends of the connectors must be firmly fixed and mechanically strengthened by sleeving to prevent internal fracture of the individual conductors due to movement of the cable form.

6. The 'clean and dirty' principle must be observed by having a separate cable form and connectors.

Before discussing recommended connectors it is worth while to discuss what types are not recommended and why. Any form of spring 'touch' contacts, whether commercial or home-made, will eventually fail mainly due to the lack of pressure present at the point of contact. Superstructures by their nature are light in weight and have to be easily removable. Audio and Video connectors – DIN Series and SCART are space-greedy and both have high-grab contacts which can be hard to part. However, the Miniature DIN series from Maplin are worth considering if not more than nine ways are required. At first sight PCB Edge Connectors appear ideal. They are very efficient in space/ways but have high grab and require substantial precision mating which most superstructures would be incapable of. The D Series of connectors are borderline. They can be considered where space is not a problem either for installation or in use. Although the range can go as high as

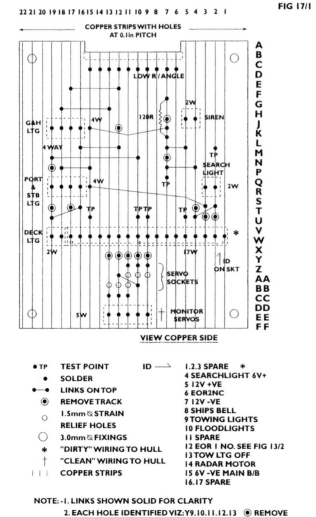

FIG 17/1

22 21 20 19 18 17 16 15 14 13 12 11 10 9 8 7 6 5 4 3 2 1

COPPER STRIPS WITH HOLES AT 0.1in PITCH

A B C D E F G H J K L M N P Q R S T U V W X Y Z AA BB CC DD EE FF

LOW R / ANGLE

G&H LTG   4W   120R   SIREN

4 WAY

2W

PORT & STB LTG   4W

TP   SEARCH LIGHT   2W

TP   TP TP   TP

DECK LTG   *

2W   17W   ID ON SKT

SERVO SOCKETS

5W   †   MONITOR SERVOS

VIEW COPPER SIDE

● TP	TEST POINT	ID →	1.2.3 SPARE *
●	SOLDER		4 SEARCHLIGHT 6V+
●—●	LINKS ON TOP		5 12V +VE
◉	REMOVE TRACK		6 EOR2NC
○	1.5mm ⌀ STRAIN		7 12V -VE
	RELIEF HOLES		8 SHIPS BELL
◯	3.0mm ⌀ FIXINGS		9 TOWING LIGHTS
*	"DIRTY" WIRING TO HULL		10 FLOODLIGHTS
†	"CLEAN" WIRING TO HULL		11 SPARE
¦¦¦	COPPER STRIPS		12 EOR 1 NO. SEE FIG 13/2
			13 TOW LTG OFF
			14 RADAR MOTOR
			15 6V -VE MAIN B/B
			16.17 SPARE

NOTE:-1. LINKS SHOWN SOLID FOR CLARITY

       2. EACH HOLE IDENTIFIED VIZ:Y9.10.11.12.13 ◉ REMOVE

50 ways the maximum for marine work should be restricted to 19 ways due to the high retention force needed to part the higher values. D Series should only be used with plastic covers to prevent accidental short-circuits with metal covers. All these options have the same rationale. All the function wiring is terminated within one half of a plug/socket mating system. Should, say, a power failure occur this necessitates a difficult and long testing procedure which inevitably leads to opening up the plug/socket assembly to identify which function is at fault. What is required is a system which enables each function to be quickly isolated and if at fault removed for repair. One or two functions can be directly wired into a plug/socket system but functions beyond that require a more manageable arrangement.

This brings the discussion to the system the author has developed over a number of boats. It is based upon a range of PCB connectors with a pitch of 0.1in (2.54mm), suitable for mounting on Vero stripboard with the same pitch. The nylon plugs are straight, polarised and sit flat on the stripboard with square pins protruding into the copper strips and soldered. The back wafer shields the connecting pins and provides the locking and polarising. The socket housing accepts a tin-plated phosphor bronze terminal to which a conductor is either soldered or crimped. Once pushed into the housing it locks. Each terminal is rated for 2.5amps. The system is known as plate racking and consists of each function wiring being terminated into sockets which plug onto a board permanently fixed within the superstructure. The board distributes and sorts out the functions into a multi-way plug on the board to which the hull cable form socket mates. Also terminated on the board are the female equipment sockets

for servo transfer into the hull cable form discussed above and the dropping resistor in series to the siren masthead lamp discussed in Chapter 13. The 'Straight' series of board plugs range from 2-way up to 17-way in nine values with corresponding sockets. If space is at a premium a right-angle 10-way plug and a 12-way socket are available. These will mate with the appropriate 'Straight' components. Fig. 17/1 illustrates how ten functions and forty-three conductors are terminated on a 60mm × 75mm board which sorts them into groups for transfer via a 17-way plug/socket into the hull. The two servos are transferred via a 6-way plug/socket. The major functions, masthead lights, siren and searchlight etc, can all be isolated by separation of their individual plug/ sockets. Note the dropping resistor, test points, links connecting copper tracks and removal of portion of tracks to isolate circuits. The test points are PCB pins available from most specialist suppliers. Note the staggered separation of the negative and positive TPs to avoid accidental shorting when using test prods and crocodile clips. An unfortunate short will quickly burn out the copper track on the board and worse the conductor back to the supply, ruining hours of

A 'clean' wiring run in the course of installation. Note the two extension lead connections held clear of the bilges (top left). These will finally be wrapped in polythene and sealed for further protection. The Earth connection to the prop shaft casing can be seen bottom left.

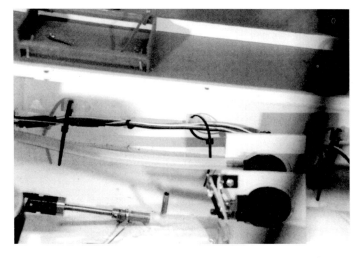

An automatic Bilge Pump Switcher is a wise investment. The two probes on the right will operate the unit once water is detected. The switcher can also operate the ship's siren as well as the pump to alert the skipper before he abandons ship!

work. All parts for the system are available from Maplin's. Care is needed to ensure the copper tracks are not overloaded especially the DC positive and negative tracks. Any track likely to carry more than 1 ampere should be thickened by soldering a solid conductor along its length or built up with solder. As an alternative to one set of connectors with the cable form terminated in the hull as discussed at the beginning of this chapter the hull end of the 17-way cable form can be dealt with identically to the superstructure, giving an option of unplugging either end whichever is the more convenient. This also creates the possibility of using a secondary, much longer, cable form for testing the system with the hull and superstructure more accessible internally. All wiring should be stranded using a size compatible with the current the function is sinking. Unless unusually high currents are involved, 7/0.2mm equipment wire capable of carrying 1.4A is more than sufficient. Use solid colours and bi-colours and create a

wiring schedule showing origin and destination of each end, wire colour and plug/socket terminal number. This discipline will reduce, if not eliminate, installation errors.

Installation of auxiliary features

Sound modules should be located close to the loudspeaker to keep the LS wiring as short as possible. Velcro is recommended for fixing. Remember that the positive supply is usually used to switch these units so that a common negative can be used. Do not forget to check the total current as above. Those units that have adjustment facilities to alter the sound character and volume need to be located where they can be reached easily at the pondside. No matter how good the sound seems in the workshop, when on the water a totally different impression is created which can only be improved by fine tuning there and then. Rotating radar units are a common sight on most scale models and are easy to create using miniature motors and gearboxes. It is just as important to suppress these motors in the same way as the drive motors. Use the same values recommended in Chapter 7 and Fig. 7/1 but reduce the working voltage to 100V and use a resin-dipped ceramic capacitor. These are small and perfectly adequate for these miniature motors. All auxiliary function motors for cranes, pumps etc, must be suppressed using the appropriate-sized capacitors that can be fitted easily across the motor terminals. The capacitor values are as above except adjust the working voltage range to as high a value as is consistent with the physical size. Auxiliary motors should be used with care in multi-function systems where their control wiring can be in close proximity to wiring sensitive to interference. Motors specifically designed for model use will not normally cause any problems. It is only when the budget-conscious worker uses other motors that interference problems can arise.

Water pumps are a favourite feature and create much interest and amusement amongst spectators. The author has found the most efficient are those designed and supplied by the specialist suppliers. It is not generally appreciated that to pump and lift water to a height and then discharge it to a distance of 2 metres requires an efficient motor to keep the current down to a reasonable level. This in turn keeps motor interference to a minimum and reduces the possibility of creating failures elsewhere in the system. Bilge pumps are also available and are an insurance against losing a large investment of not only money but time and effort. Bilge pumps are entirely automatic and work following detection of water by probes installed at the lowest point of the hull. It is recommended that two sets of probes are installed, one set in the stern and one set in the bows, wired in parallel at the control module. The subject of this chapter can never be bought to a satisfactory conclusion because there will always be another new challenge to successfully create yet a different realistic function. As RC gear becomes more and more sophisticated, with programmable memories, it opens up possibilities for control of complicated functions working as a series of events, just like the full-size prototypes, at the touch of a button.

18

Operation and Insurance

All the building of the model is completed and the RC gear installed. Everything has tested OK and the minor problems which were detected quickly and sorted because you had kept accurate records. All the power supplies have been charged, the capacity of the nicads is known and a range check has been carried out. The weather is reasonable, so what is stopping you from heading out with model and cradle? Reading this chapter, the author hopes.

Operational requirements

Before setting out thought has to be given to what the sailing toolbox is to contain and what is the programme of sailing for that most important first sea trial? Pondside tools should kept to a minimum, because the fewer tools available the less chance there is of

carrying out a repair or modification that will end in disaster. Keep the tools to a selection for tightening screws and nuts, a portable soldering iron, a length of cored solder and a basic DVM. The toolbox should also include spare fuses and crystals in a crystal tidy. Over a period of time, experience will show what additional items need to be added to cover the individual model's requirements. Unless the worker is fortunate in getting it right first time, propellers will also be required in alternative diameters and pitch. Make sure you are fully conversant with how to hand a propeller (see Chapter 7). The only point of the first sea trial is to enjoy that feeling of satisfaction as months of effort moves away from the quay under full control of you – The Master. The second point is to check the basic performance and to fine-tune all the adjustments both on the TX and in the model. To do this effectively all non-safety functions should be disabled by not fusing them, leaving only steering and propulsion working. A final check and you can head for the pond.

Each time a TX is picked up and switched on it becomes an object that can cause serious injury itself and at worst a fatality in conjunction with the model. Before a TX is switched on the telescopic aerial must be extended at least halfway before the RX is switched on. This ensures the TX assumes total

It is essential at all times when sailing to indicate to others the frequency channel your transmitter is using. The aerial eye protector ball is also a wise investment against injury to others and possible litigation. Available from K-Bits - see Appendix 2.

control of the system when the vessel is out of the water and nearby onlookers are at their most vulnerable to possible injury from spinning propellers etc. All TX aerials when extended have the potential to cause serious damage to eyes of humans and animals. They should always carry an identification in the form of a 'flag' of the channel the system is using (see Appendix 1), and the extreme end should be equipped with an aerial protector as shown in the photo. Prior to launching the safety side of the system, rudder and propulsion, should be checked for correct operation after warning all onlookers, especially small children and their parents, to keep fingers well away from the stern and propeller. Now check that the non-safety functions are 'dead' and not responding to the TX. If possible allow an assistant to place the vessel on the water whilst you retain control of the TX. Never ask a stranger to hold the TX whilst you deal with the model. This is a sure recipe for inadvertent operation and possible disaster. If the size, weight or delicacy of the model prevent launching whilst retaining control of the TX this can be solved by either using a launching trolley, where there is a ramp, or by using two slings and lowering the

model into the water. Once the vessel is afloat, extend the TX aerial to its full length and apply a very small amount of power to check the direction of movement is what is expected. According to which way the vessel is facing, either slowly drive forward or astern checking the rudder response agrees with the orientation of the TX. Remember that with the vessel moving forward port-left, and starboard-right will agree. If coming towards the operator it will be the reverse.

At a reasonable speed with the rudder amidships and 'hands off' the TX is the vessel moving in a straight line or turning port or starboard? Whichever way it is, correct it using the TX stick trim only still with rudder amidships and 'hands off'. The ideal conditions for this adjustment is a flat calm. Any swell or chop on the water will confuse the test. Repeat this check at speeds below and above the initial throttle setting and adjust the rudder trim for a compromise setting. Return to harbour and retrieve the model remembering that this is the most vulnerable time for accidents to yourself and onlookers. Switch off the RX then the TX. With the model safe in its cradle and with access to the rudder linkage, switch on

Funnel smoke adds just that bit of realism that awakens spectators' interest.

Unusual subjects all with additional working functions call for ingenuity and imagination when designing and implementing such as this fighting galley with working oars, and a Noah's Ark with moving animals.

the TX and then the RX. Move the rudder several times and note its position relative to the model's centreline with the TX stick amidships. It could be a few degrees offset either to port or starboard. Now centre the trim lever on the TX which will cause the rudder to move back to its original setting. With the mechanical linkage adjust the rudder back to the few

degrees position found with the rudder trim. Lock the setting. Switch off RX first then TX, reassemble and return the model to water following what should now be an automatic procedure.

Repeat the first straight-line exercise. The vessel should now sail in a straight line with full trim possible on the rudder for different water conditions in the future. Now get to know its performance under all settings of the throttle. Practice moving astern and docking. A vessel under way has no brakes, but a short burst of reverse engines can do wonders when manoeuvring in harbour. If time and power supply capacity is available return to port, retrieve the model and fuse the non-safety functions and return to the water following all the previous safety procedures. All should work without difficulty. There is no reason why, if care is taken and faults eliminated during building and installation, any

Although apparently small when afloat, large models such as this battleship with tall masts present hazards to onlookers when being launched and retrieved. Public Liability Insurance is essential.

RC system should not work reliably first time. The only reason for adopting a stage-by-stage approach to first-time testing is to eliminate the possibility of interference between safety and non-safety systems when the model is on the water and in an environment not previously encountered. If problems do emerge it is easier to identify and cure them. One area where a problem may occur is the motor fuses blowing when under load. The author has experienced this only twice with ESCs, but never with MSCs. Exhaustive investigation and testing did not reveal anything untoward. Uprating the fuse type cured the problem and the only conclusion drawn that it was an idiosyncrasy of that particular make of ESC.

Insurance

Whatever your interest, scale modelling, yachts, fast electrics etc, the operation of a radio-controlled vessel in a public place carries a heavy responsibility which if not recognised could have serious financial consequences not only for the operator but his/her family. Operation and insurance of a RC vessel go hand-in-hand. If an accident occurs and the operator has acted responsibly and can show all reasonable steps had been taken to operate the system safely the insurance company will support him/her in the event of a Public Liability claim. That is of course if he/she is insured! The easiest and quickest way to obtain cover is to join the local sailing club. For those who have no local club it is worthwhile to check their Household Insurance Policy – Liabilities. Bear in mind however that basic cover is for the policyholder named in the policy schedule. Any extension of cover, say to include a minor, will be detailed in the section paragraphs. In any case it is prudent to check exactly what cover is available with the insurance company, to what amount and does cover extend to 'model watercraft'. This should be done in writing to avoid future misunderstandings. Lone UK marine workers can also apply to join their respective national body as individual members. For contact information see Appendix 3.

19

Maintenance

The greatest threat to equipment reliability is complacency. Today's consumer electronics are taken for granted to such an extent that when they do fail the user immediately cries 'foul' and blames everyone and everything except him- or herself. A little thought will show that an hour or two spent in maintaining equipment will more than repay the effort involved. Just because a modern TV does not need maintenance and appears to operate without failure for months or even years is not an excuse for thinking that RC equipment can do the same. The difference is that RC equipment is a mixture of electronics and mechanical workhorses with an interface that both require occasional attention, *ie* annual maintenance. If the recommended hand tools, test and battery charging/cycling equipment discussed in previous chapters has been acquired there is very little else that the marine worker needs to carry out the Maintenance Programme listed in the table on p168. These additional items are a large good quality soft bristle brush which can be obtained from most model or art shops, a mini vacuum cleaner from Squires and two Electrolube products available from Maplin (see Appendix 2).

Accidental submersion

Before the maintenance programme is discussed in detail, however, it is useful to look at ways and means to ensure no lasting damage is caused following accidental contact with the medium our vessels are designed for – water. No matter how careful the user is, sooner or later part of a RC system is going to be totally submerged. Usually when this happens it is only for a relatively short period of 20 or 30 minutes. It could be the accidental dropping of the TX into the pond or a collision between vessels resulting in hull flooding. Once the TX/vessel has been recovered, the first thing to do is to switch off the power and, if it can be done quickly and easily remove, the batteries. Any water that can be drained off do so. If a TX is involved, remove the aerial as this instantly provides a convenient drain hole. It is prudent to have a roll of kitchen towel available in the toolbox to mop off the excess water on the equipment casings. Endeavour to return to the workshop as soon as possible. With a TX, remove the crystal and dry with kitchen paper towel and spray the pins with Electrolube EML200 required for the maintenance programme. Crystals are sealed so there is no more to be done. Never on any account use WD40 or any other water inhibitors. If not already done, remove the aerial and batteries. Dry with kitchen towel and spray the aerial with EML200. Put to one side. Do the same with the batteries or pack, not forgetting any lead connectors. Put to one side. Do not attempt to clean externally. Instead carefully dismantle the TX but do not attempt to mop up any water with towelling as this action could disturb pre-set pots. Instead gently shake out any water. Now arrange all the parts, including those put to one side, on a tray lined with kitchen towel and place in an airing cupboard or some other place where there is a circulation of warm air. Leave for at least three to four days. *Never, never* use a hair dryer or any other form of hot-air drying. Not all PCBs are impervious to absorbing water and if subjected to a high temperature change will warp and lift the delicate copper tracks or lands, building-in a future failure. Once thoroughly dry, operations 1 to 8 of the Maintenance Programme are implemented.

The boat equipment is treated in the same way for minor water contamination. The majority of RXs, ESCs and auxiliary modules can be disassembled. Those with sealed casings are sometimes possible to part using a sharp modelling knife. But be careful – fingers are precious! Most makers will service these items for a modest charge. If sealed servos are in use, a mild soaking will not affect their performance. If unsealed, replace them for they will need a complete strip-down and service, which will be discussed later on. If the boat has been involved in submersion for a period of time there is no other option than to strip all the equipment out including the wiring looms and dry it out using the techniques already discussed. If this happens the worker will be thankful for making detailed records of the installation. Once the equipment is out the hull should have any water mopped up and be left to dry naturally in a temperate atmosphere – not the airing cupboard. SLA batteries will need several charge/discharge cycles after a prolonged submersion. Discharge them using a medium-wattage auto lamp of the appropriate voltage. The rest of the

The result of a loose terminal screw caused by vibration due to a motor mounting failure. The high motor current through the terminal block created arcing under the loose screw. Arcing creates heat hence the melting nylon. VET should help to prevent this type of failure. See text.

equipment is assembled in conjunction with operations 9-16 of the Maintenance Programme.

The Maintenance Programme

This brings the discussion neatly to how the Programme is designed around two acronyms – VET and TART. Before interfering with what appears to be perfectly working equipment it is wise to establish a benchmark. The Vessel Equipment Test (VET) regime emerged following an almost disastrous failure the author experienced some years ago. A screw in a power terminal, the nylon type where the screw is in direct contact with the stranded wire end, was loosened by vibration from one of the drive motors whose mounting screws had also worked loose. The vessel is a fireboat (appropriately!), with twin motors normally working at 6V but with a motor boost circuit increasing the drive to 12V at the touch of a switch on the TX. The result on the performance is spectacular externally and in this instance would have been even more spectacular internally. With the increased current flowing through the loose terminal arcing heat occurred

MAINTENANCE PROGRAMME

MATERIAL
Large Soft Bristle Brush
Mini Vacuum Cleaner
Contact Cleaner Lubricant – Electrolube EML200
Contract Treatment Grease – Electrolube SGB200

PROGRAMME
Charge all power supplies and then VET *

TRANSMITTER (TX)
1   Check for damage and clean externally
2   Remove aerial, back (and RF module if applicable) and dust out
3   Corrosion check. (Contact clean RF module sockets – EML200)
4   Crystal check – for damage and identity
5   Crystal pins lubrication – SGB200. (Module pins – EML200)
6   Cycle TX battery and check capacity
7   Check and tighten all internal screws
8   Replace back, aerial (and RF module if applicable) and tighten aerial

RECEIVER (RX)
9   Remove all plugs and switch assembly. Check for corrosion
    Contact clean RX sockets using EML200
10 Check switch assembly for 'black wire' corrosion
    (see Chapter 10 and Fig. 10/2)
11 Check RX aerial for physical damage
12 Cycle RX battery and check capacity

SERVOS & SAIL WINCHES
13 Check for corrosion. Clean servo/winch sockets – EML200
14 Check all servo linkages and Sail Winch Sheet runs

SPEED CONTROLLERS
15 Servo Type – see text
16 Electronic Type. Check Power Input/Output connections.
    Contact clean both types RX sockets using EML200

17 TART[1]

GENERAL
18 Check motor fuseholder and renew fuse/s
19 Check all auxiliary fuseholders and renew fuses
20 Reassemble whole system and charge
21 Test as an 'on water' system including range check

* VET – Vessel Equipment Test
[1] TART – Transmitter And Receiver Tests

enough to melt the nylon and the cable insulation and if left would undoubtedly have caused a fire. VET is designed to annually check for the root cause of these type of failures. For vibration to become apparent, the system must be fully charged in your normal way prior to VET. Now start checking all terminal blocks for tightness and possible corrosion. Check the propellers are clear of obstruction then run the drive system at full power for a minute or two. Switch off and check all the motor mountings, prop shaft connections, rudder connections and top up the prop shaft lubrication. Any undue vibration should be investigated and corrected. Check the prop(s) for tightness and any lateral movement of the shaft in its casing. Now carry out a full functional test of the whole RC system. This will establish the benchmark against any possible failure introduced during the rest of the programme. Now to the detail. Each operation is numbered and can be ticked off as it is completed.

Transmitter

1. Clean the outside of the case with surgical spirit and check for damage. Minor cracks can be repaired with thick cyanoacrylate adhesive used sparingly (never use the thin variety as this can run inside and cause a major problem). Spray a soft fluffless cloth with furniture polish and rub the case all over. If this is done several times throughout the sailing season it keeps the TX looking good and gives the opportunity to check for damage.

2. Before removing the back check you are not in violation of the maker's guarantee with the model shop/importer/manufacturer. Use the brush to dislodge debris and the vacuum cleaner to remove it.

3. Check for corrosion, particularly of the battery compartment contacts if using dry cells or separate nicads. Any corrosion should be carefully scraped off using a non-metallic scraper if possible. Very bad cases of corrosion may need the use of a metal scraper. This should be used with extreme care to prevent shards of metal penetrating and covering the electronics causing possible future failures. Grease the cleaned surfaces with SGB200. If supplied spray the RF module socket with EML200.

4&5. The crystal casing should be free of dents and the pins tight. If there is damage, however slight, discard it. It is not worth the risk of failure in using a suspect crystal. Grease the pins, SGB200, and spray the socket with EML200.

6. Cycle the TX battery and check capacity (see Chapter 10).

7. Include the lubrication of the stick pivots in this operation. The tube supplied with the aerosol cans which fits the spray heads is useful here if access is difficult. The EML200 is the best one to use as it will clean as well as lubricate.

8. When re-assembling, make sure the screws are used in the correct holes – short and long. Do not overtighten and if one seizes up remove and clear the thread. These fastenings can very easily be destroyed if care is not exercised.

Receiver

9&10. If there is corrosion this is, probably, where it will be. Examine the servo lead contact pins through a magnifying glass for signs of 'black wire' corrosion particularly the battery input. In very bad cases of neglect it will have spread to the pins. In these cases there is no other option than to scrap the RX. For mild cases, spray the pins with EML200 and using a new servo plug, kept for the purpose, keep mating plug to socket, alternating with

EML200, until the corrosion is cleared. Check elsewhere for 'black wire' (see Chapter 10 and Fig. 10/2).

11. If the aerial is original check for any cracks in the insulation and if found replace with the same length and gauge of stranded wire. This is a simple task which can done in two ways. If the worker does not feel confident enough to part the RX case and replace the aerial on the PCB, a satisfactory job can be done by measuring the exact length of the old and then cutting it off leaving an inch (25mm). Measure the replacement less 1in and strip one end and the old stub about half an inch (12mm). Slip a piece of sleeving that is not too loose over the new aerial. Twist the stripped ends together not too tightly and solder. Bend the joint flat away from the sleeve side and ease the sleeving over it. Use two miniature nylon cable ties (Chapter 16), to secure the sleeving and strengthen the repair. To replace at the PCB measure the length when the board is free of its case. Remove the old with the minimum of heat using the desoldering pump (Chapter 11). The aerial might be threaded through a hole in the PCB to anchor it. Use this for the replacement. There should be a protective grommet as part of the case. Thread the replacement through it. Strip the end the minimum for the board connection and solder on quickly. It is prudent to leave a small loop above the joint to ensure there is no strain on the track or the pin if there is one. Assemble carefully, ensuring the grommet is in the correct place.

12. If after several cycles the capacity cannot be raised above 80 per cent the pack should be retired – Chapter 10. Bear in mind that if individual cells are in use (not recommended due to the unreliability of the spring-loaded holders), it may only be several of the cells that are incapable of reaching 81

per cent capacity. If using the MainLink DigiLiser 2000 individual cells can be cycled and their capacity checked.

13. Check for corrosion and spray the lead plug with EML200. Every three years strip each servo down and regrease the gear train with servo grease obtainable from your model shop. Use only grease recommended by the manufacturer. Replace waterproof gaskets and the servo lead obtainable from your model shop as most manufacturers supply these as spares. If the servo has been immersed in water for a period, carry out the three-year replacement regime immediately.

14. To keep RX current to a minimum check all servo linkages and lubricate. Check all winch sheet runs for smooth working.

15. Servo type speed controllers – MSCs – need the servo treated as in 13 above. Check the resistance board for warping and current burns. If warped mount it on a thicker foundation plate (see Chapter 9). The copper lands can be cleaned with very fine wet-and-dry abrasive paper, cleaned off with surgical spirit and then well greased with SGB200.

16. ESCs can only be checked for connections and spraying the servo type lead with EML200. The motor fuses are dealt with under 18 below.

17. TART. This acronym, Transmitter And Receiver Tests, is designed to establish the stability of the RX supply without the boat's RX switch harness in circuit but using the operational battery supply. From Chapter 10 and Fig. 10/1 and the discussion on the 'black wire' problem the most common equipment failure is an unstable RX power supply when under load. Chapter 5 and Fig. 5/1 established that nicads and NiMH cells exhibit a steady voltage under load right up to the point of their capacity being exhausted. This voltage should not fluctuate under load by more than

a few milli-Volts. The purpose behind TART is to monitor the actual voltage as close as possible to the RX input when load is applied by the servos as they operate in response to commands from the TX. The current flowing in the circuit is unimportant because of the straight-line characteristic of the supply. Even if the supply capacity is below that required by the system it will not affect the result of the tests. All that will do is to shorten the time scale the supply is capable of sustaining. To set TART up a modified Y lead is required. This must be a true Y lead with one plug and two sockets. The later type with two moulded integral sockets is not suitable. To modify, cut off one socket and terminate the three conductors in a suitable terminal block. The signal conductor is terminated for safety. The two supply conductors, positive and negative, are connected to a DVM set to read at least 10V DC. From Fig. 10/1 if the voltage at the input to the RX falls significantly when the supply is asked to supply load current then there is resistance somewhere in the supply circuit. It could be a high resistance cell in the battery or resistance in the supply conductors – 'black wire' – or a suspect switch or dry joint.

The first task is to establish a benchmark. A known good-supply pack is plugged into the other Y lead socket. Switch on the TX and plug the Y lead into the RX. The DVM will read a voltage somewhere around 5V – the precise value does not matter. What is important that it does not fluctuate when the TX is operated and the servos respond. Operate the TX several times and record the results. Leave it on for a good 10 minutes, operating the system as if sailing, with the motor running and making several alterations of course. The RX voltage should not vary

by more than 300 to 500mV, if at all. Switch off and change the battery supply to the installed battery, once again using the Y lead. Switch on and repeat the test as before. The result should agree with the first test. The voltage level is not important. It is the stability under load that the test is looking for. Switch off and connect the battery to the internal switching system and the system into the Y lead. Switch on and repeat the test again. If all is well all three results will be compatible. If there is high resistance anywhere in the supply circuit TART will find it. Having read the Manual this far the marine worker will know how to eradicate the problem.

18 to 21. These items are self-explanatory. Fuses age over a period and if left in service will eventually blow for no apparent reason – nuisance blowing – so it is a prudent precaution to renew them annually.

The additional requirement of controlling functions under water, in this model submarine, underlines the need for regular disciplined maintenance and equipment of the highest quality.

20

Computer RC Equipment

This Manual would not be complete without a discussion of the latest computer systems and their suitability for the marine modeller. Before getting into the details of these sophisticated systems, one things needs to be made clear. This equipment does not do anything more than a basic system – it just does it better, with more precision and offers more sophisticated mixing of servo functions and settings, coupled with the ability to store individual model settings. The gear is targeted towards the competitive side

of marine modelling and offers a competitor a system which once set up for a particular model/course/weather condition can be retrieved from a memory. The relationship or mixing of rudder and throttle can be programmed to suit a boat's performance at any rudder position and can be switched in or out to suit course and weather conditions. Sail control can be more accurate and again more sophisticated. The precision is obtained by employing upgraded servos which come at a price. It will not on its own

Left: A two-function two-memory Computer Steerwheel 27MHzTX which programs the servos to a limited degree of sophistication and then stores the data for each individual model to be called up when required.

Right: A three-function ten-memory Computer Steerwheel TX which programs the servos to a high degree of sophistication. Digital trim and exponential steering are two of the many features. PPFM or PCM on 40MHz with fail-safe on PCM which returns throttle and rudder to pre-programmed safe settings in the event of loss of signal.

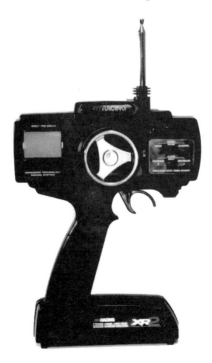

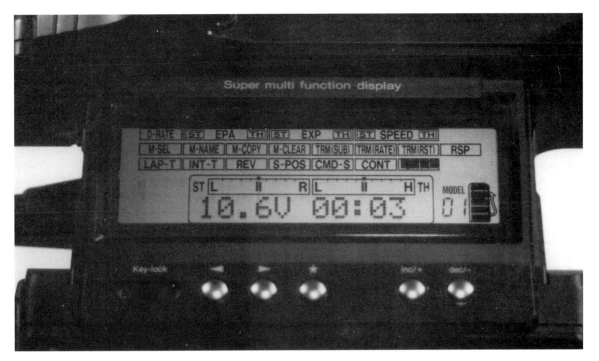

win races! It just makes the application of driving and sailing skill more effective.

The majority of computer TXs are of the three-function steerwheel design and come as TX and RX only with nicad pack for the TX, charger and switch harness. There are no servos provided and these must be purchased separately. It is a waste of money to use Standard-type servos if the user is to gain the maximum result from the gear. Upgraded servos are a must. These have metal gears double ball-raced and, at the top of the range, coreless motors. The resolution is remarkable with the centring extremely accurate either way. Trims are digital at the press of a button and very accurate. One TX requires seven presses to move the trim 1 degree. Most designs are easy to program with large displays. Ten model memories are not unusual. A typical specification includes Twin Rate and Exponential steering curves, multi-point throttle curves with exponential option, pro-grammable steering response, servo

reverse on all three functions with graphic display of servo and trim positions, option of PCM or PPFM with appropriate RX, lap timer and counter, and copying of data between memories. A back-up battery is built into the TX to protect the memories when the main nicad pack is empty. Most employ a comprehensive warning system for the nicad. both visual and audio, and a black non-reflective aerial. Those marine workers interested in computer gear should appreciate that to get the most from these systems the servo linkages and winch sheet runs must be of the highest quality without any slack which will destroy the precision which the system and high-quality servos are capable of delivering.

These steerwheel sets are of pistol-grip design with an enclosed trigger. There is a steering wheel for one function with the trigger for the second function – throttle. Squeezing the enclosed trigger produces forward movement and pushing it forward creates astern movement. The third

A typical TX Computer display. Note the accurate state of the battery voltage indication and the precise position of each servo setting. Most computer TXs allow the modification of settings during racing to suit weather conditions etc.

function is usually programmable into whatever use is required. In the author's view these computer designs are of little use to the multi-working function scale modeller. There is, however, a computer system available in the 'robbe' Futaba range. This is the F16 which is an uprated version of the F14 Navy mentioned in Chapter 9. The inclusion of a computer allows the expansion of up to 76 functions, memory for up to 102 models with ability to expand further, PCM/FM switchable, extensive trim options, exponential and dual rate, twin-stick dual control option, two supplementary freely programmable mixers, comprehensive timer system and a genuine 12-hour operational capability. The key advantage of the F16 is that it starts as a basic two-stick four-function system which can be expanded in steps as the budget allows or as the worker's current project requires.

The present design of RC equipment has probably reached a point where very little further development will be made other than to fine-tune the very comprehensive specifications now available except in one area – crystals. These have been at the heart of the radio frequency circuits in RC gear for well over four decades. The system of having to physically change a channel is time consuming and clumsy. Technically, using crystals also limits the number of channels it is possible to arrange within an authorised band. With modern TX designs changing the crystal is quick and easy. With any of the boat disciplines it means removing the superstructure or deck panel or waterproof pot in a yacht, before removing the RX to change the crystal. If, however, a RX was permanently fitted with a standard reference crystal then frequency synthesis techniques could be used to change channels when required. In very broad terms, it works by the RX 'listening' to the TX transmission and automatically locking itself onto the TX frequency. By changing the TX crystal and re-transmitting, the RX changes onto the required channel.

At the present time there is very little incentive to change the present technology for surface users. If any

A modern RX showing the extensive use of Surface Mounted Technology where components are mounted direct onto the copper side of a PCB. This is a two-function RX. For size comparison the top two sockets are for the crystal and are 5mm apart! Note that this design is also used for a three-function RX. The unused third output can be seen at bottom right.

change does come it will be in the aircraft band of 35MHz where quite serious difficulties have arisen where a number of separate transmissions on legal channels have caused RX 'blocking' leading to loss of control. Ironically, if technological change does come in the 35MHz band then possibly 40MHz will follow as it has in the past! In the authors view any meaningful advancement of radio control for surface users must come in the UHF band, for several reasons. Firstly, UHF does not require a long and dangerous telescopic aerial which in the heat of competition can cause serious injury to other users. There is minimal likelihood of interference to or from other users. The official recognition of the use of model telemetry means that it could be integrated into a UHF control system using techniques and economic frequency synthesiser and micro-controller chips already available and used in other consumer equipment.

This leaves one area where change could occur in the immediate future. Appendix 1 has noted that the official regulatory authority in the UK, the RA, has never adopted the mandatory requirement of FM modulation for 40MHz. This means that Amplitude Modulation equipment can be used legally in the UK. Economically such equipment should be cheaper than comparable FM equipment which should encourage marine workers with tight budgets to change to 40MHz if and when AM equipment appears. There is no reason why existing servos, ESCs, switchers and other auxiliary items will not work on AM equipment. It remains to be seen what if any interference problems arise with AM compared with FM.

This chapter concludes the manual with the author's one last piece of advice. Be sure to fail safe, happy boating and May Your RC Force Never Leave You.

Appendix 1
Radio Control Model Frequency Bands

The radio control of models is a world-wide leisure activity recognised by many countries, with regulatory agencies ensuring the harmonisation and correct use of the radio control bands. In Europe the radio frequency spectrum is regulated by the Conference of European Posts and Telecommunications Administrations (CEPT) of which the UK Radiocommunications Agency (RA), an Executive Agency of the Department of Trade and Industry, is a member. So that all aspects of model radio control use in the UK can be safeguarded a committee, the Joint Radio Control Users Committee, liaises with the RA. The JRCUC has amongst its members national association representatives of the three modelling disciplines – aircraft, boats and cars. The majority of individual clubs are affiliated to these associations so any major problems of interference etc, may be channelled upwards through to the JRCUC for advice and where appropriate consultation with the RA. Individual workers who are not members of a club may contact the JRCUC through:

Mr D W McQue, The Secretary, Joint Radio Control Users Committee,
6, Laburnum Grove,
Bletchley,
Milton Keynes MK2 2JW

Tel: 01908 378277.
E-Mail: g4nju@compuserve.com

Of the four bands listed at the beginning of Chapter 3, three are the legal UK bands for surface use including water. Marine workers should appreciate that surface use includes other radio control models, such as cars etc, which may be operating legitimately in their vicinity. It is in the interests of all radio control users to practice safe operating procedures at all times by checking that their channel is free from other users before switching their transmitter on and operating a regime of switching on the TX first followed by the RX. Always check the correct operation of rudder and propulsion system before placing the vessel in the water. Switch the RX off first then the TX after sailing. Always fly the correct indication for the channel in use and remember that the TX aerial has the potential of causing injury to humans and animals. If any malfunction or doubt of the integrity of the radio control link occurs the operator should endeavour to retrieve the vessel as soon as is practical.

27MHz Band (UK) 26.96 MHz to 27.28MHz General Use

This is the original model control band and it is shared with other legal users, mainly CB radio. It should be used by marine workers with care after studying tables A to E. In reading these tables it should be noted that over the years the band channels have been expanded from the original six solid colours of Brown, Red, Orange, Yellow, Green, and Blue by 'splits' identified by dual colours. Tables B and C illustrate that one dual colour can be two different frequencies. Also two other solid colours have 'appeared', Black and Purple, in Table D together with the first split colour in Table E – Grey/Brown. Table E shows the availability of one manufacturer's crystals in the UK. These are for sets employing AM modulation which is the preferred mode, being less susceptible to CB interference. Note that the above Grey/Brown conflicts with one of the two Blacks in Table D, emphasising the point of not taking colours for granted. Other manufacturers supply crystals but always ensure they match your equipment. Users are strongly advised to check crystal frequencies against the tables before purchase and use. Beware of using second-hand crystals of doubtful origin and note that 27MHz FM modulation crystals are virtually unobtainable in the UK.

TABLE A

Five spot frequencies used for low power telemetry and telecommand devices which are not operational channels for CB Radio.

TX (MHz)	Colour	
26.995	Brown	Whilst it is possible that these five channels may suffer from interference they should provide the best operating frequencies in the band.
27.045	Red	
27.095	Orange	
27.145	Yellow	
27.195	Green	

Note: Any other 'solid' colour frequency within the radio-controlled model band 26.96 to 27.28 MHz is also allocated to CB Radio with two exceptions – Black and Purple. See Table D.

TABLE B

Five split frequencies which are not operational channels for CB radio

TX (MHz)	Colour
27.020	Brown/Red
27.070	Red/Orange
27.120	Orange/Yellow
27.170	Yellow/Green
27.220	Green/Blue

TABLE C
Five split frequencies which are also allocated to CB radio and operational.

TX (MHz)	Colour
27.025	Brown/Red
27.075	Red/Orange
27.125	Orange/Yellow
27.175	Yellow/Green
27.225	Green/Blue

TABLE D
Two 'bastard' colours plus the 'old and new' Blue colour.

TX (MHz)	Colour	Use Status
26.970	Black	CB clear
26.975	Black	Also allocated to CB
27.245	Blue (old)	Also allocated to CB
27.255	Blue	Also allocated to CB
27.270	Purple	CB clear
27.275	Purple	Also allocated to CB

The channel colour/s in use identity must be flown from the TX aerial at all times. An aerial tip protector is optional but strongly recommended. For suppliers see Appendix 2.

TABLE E
Currently available Futaba crystals. Check other manufacturers for the availability of their crystals for their equipment. Do not use this table in isolation. Read in conjunction with Tables A to D. * See text.

Colour	Channel (MHz)	Use Status
Grey/Brown	26.975	Also CB *
Brown	26.995	Clear of CB
Brown/Red	27.025	Also CB
Red	27.045	Clear of CB
Red/Orange	27.075	Also CB
Orange	27.095	Clear of CB
Orange/Yellow	27.125	Also CB
Yellow	27.145	Clear of CB
Yellow/Green	27.175	Also CB
Green	27.195	Clear of CB
Green/Blue	27.225	Also CB
Blue	27.255	Also CB

Harmonised frequencies throughout CEPT are: 26.995, 27.045, 27.095, 27.195 MHz, using 10KHz gaps in the CB band.

40MHz Band (UK) 40.66MHz to 41.00MHz Surface Use only

The band consists of 34 channels at 10kHz channel spacing with the centre frequency of the first channel being 40.665MHz and then 40.675MHz, 40.685MHz 40.695MHz etc. The channel identification flag in the UK is the three last digits, *ie* 685, in white on a green background. An aerial tip protector is optional but strongly recommended. See Appendix 2 for suppliers. Also note that manufacturers do not necessarily produce crystals to cover the complete 40 meg band. Check prior to ordering.

In Chapter 2 it is stated that all 40MHz equipment in the UK using the band is FM. Although this is not a mandatory requirement, a historical note is required to justify why this is so. In the early life of the band a specification MPT 1354 was produced to which the early and subsequent equipment has complied to. It has been the understanding over the years of both manufacturers and the JRCUC that FM was a mandatory requirement. In early 1999 the UK regulatory authority, the RA, acknowledged that MPT 1354 had never been incorporated in UK legislation and therefore there is no restriction on the type of modulation used for model control equipment as long as it complies with the standards laid down in European Technical Specification ETS 300 220-1 and -2.

Workers intending to compete outside the UK should note that the following channels are harmonised with Europe: 40.665MHz, 40.675MHz, 40.685MHz and 40.695MHz.

458/459MHz Band (UK) 458.5MHz to 459.5MHz General use

As Chapter 3 noted, equipment for working this band is very scarce in the UK (see Appendix 2). Potential users should note that the band is also allocated for general telemetry and telecommand devices between 458.5MHz – 458.95MHz and specialised telemetry between 458.95MHz – 459.1MHz. Whilst the potential for mutual interference is minimal the RA advises radio control users to avoid the specialised part of the band. At the present time, because of lack of interest in the band, there is no agreed format for a channel identity flag.

Whichever band is favoured marine workers will find it prudent to acquire several sets of crystals to have available at the pondside whether sailing socially or competing, where crystals can be changed to obtain a sailing channel. Remember it is important to operate your equipment and vessel safely at all times, not only in your interest, but to avoid accidents to third parties. The need to adhere to safe practice and proper standards of radio control cannot be overemphasised.

433/434MHz Band (UK) 433.05MHz to 434.79MHz Model Telemetry General Use

Following representations from the JRCUC this band may be used for Model Telemetry, *ie* data signals from model to operator. This includes aeronautical use and 'lost model' transmissions. The maximum permitted Effected Radiated Power is 10mW. Channel spacing 25kHz.

The band is harmonised within Europe and as there are other users who can radiate on a higher power, care is needed in selecting a channel in a given locality. The JRCUC recommends 434.025 to 434.775MHz for aero use. Marine workers would be prudent to avoid these channels. There are British manufacturers of approved RF modules listed in *The*

Yearbook & Buyers Guide from the Low Power Radio Association. See Appendix 2.

Surface Use Radio Control Frequencies outside Europe

United States of America

Two bands are allocated and must be used in accordance with FCC regulations. Both AM and FM modulation is permitted on each band. These bands are not exclusive and users are considered secondary by the FCC. Users are required to fly a channel number flag.

27MHz Band (USA) 26.995MHz to 27.255MHz Surface Use only. Six channels numbered 1 to 6 at 50kHz channel spacing.

75MHz Band (USA) 75.410MHz to 75.990MHz Surface Use only. Thirty channels numbered 61 to 90 at 20kHz channel spacing.

Addendum

Chapter 2 and Appendix 1 discussed the modulation requirements of the 40MHz band where it appeared that FM was mandatory but it is now established that both FM and AM are legal. Costwise AM should be cheaper than FM and on a par with the 27meg alternative. The availability of 40meg AM gear would be a major consideration for many aspiring marine workers' budgets. Too late to be included in Chapter 2 is the arrival of two Basic Twin Stick - Two Function budget sets of 40meg AM gear from two RC manufacturers – the Futaba Attack 2DR P-FP2DR/40A and the hitec Ranger 2Z AM(131).

Both sets are two function and 'dry' but with optional nicad conversion. Both come complete with receiver, two servos and switch harness. Both have battery condition LED's and servo reverse. Both are under £50 (1999 price), with the hitec having an advantage of being £10 cheaper. At these price levels there is no reason why beginners cannot enter marine modelling in the 40meg band with all its advantage of 34 channels interference free from other users. There should be no technical reason why AM cannot live alongside FM and if this proves the case it should not be long before multi-function AM sets become available.

Radio Control Equipment Suppliers

Note: All major RC equipment manufacturers have divisions in most European countries, the USA and Canada.

Futaba   Ripmax plc, Ripmax Corner, Green Street, Enfield, London. EN3 7SJ
Tel: +44(0) 181 804 8272.
Fax: +44(0) 181 804 1217.
Email:
ripmax@compuserve.com/
http://ourworld.compuserve.com/
homepages/ripmax
Systems, spares, service.
Marine modelling items incl. kits and yachts via retailers.

hitec   Amerang Ltd, Commerce Way, Lancing, West Sussex. BN15 8TE.
Tel: +44(0) 1903 765496.
Fax: +44(0) 1903 753643.
Systems, spares, service.
Marine modelling items including kits and yachts via retailers.

JR   MacGregor Industries Ltd., Canal Estate, Langley, Slough. SL3 6EQ.
Tel: +44(0) 1753 54911.
Fax: +44(0) 1753 546983.
Systems, spares, service.

SANWA   IRVINE LTD, Unit 2, Brunswick Industrial Park, Brunswick Way, New Southgate, London.
Tel: +44(0) 181 361 1123.
Fax: +44(0) 181 361 8684.
Systems, spares, service.

robbe   robbe Schlüter UK. 51 Sapcote Road, Burbage, Hinckley, Leicestershire, LE10 2AS.
Futaba
Tel: +44(0) 1455 637151.
Fax: +44(0) 1455 635151
Systems, spares, service.
Marine modelling items including kits and yachts via Retailers
ripmax@compuserve.com/
http://ourworld.compuserve.com/ homepages/ripmax
Systems, spares, service.
Marine modelling items incl. kits and yachts via retailers.

Appendix 2
Specialist Suppliers

On 22 April 2000 there will be changes to telephone numbers in the UK. The only numbers affected in the manual are London numbers. Those listed which start 0171 and 0181 will become 0207 and 0208 respectively. Whilst every care has been taken to ensure every contact number or internet address is correct at the time of going to press, the author and publisher cannot be held responsible for subsequent changes.

UK

Tony Abel, Model Racing Yachts, 'Highnoon', Petersfinger Road, Salisbury, Wiltshire, SP5 3BY.
Tel/Fax: +44(0)1722 324677
Yacht kits, specialist fittings, sail winches and radio equipment including twin-stick TX systems (see Chapter 9).

Whirlwind Winches,
26 Sebert Road,
Bury St Edmunds,
IP32 7EB.
Tel/Fax: +44(0)1284 704482.
Email: keithskipper@mcmail.com
Sail winches, batteries and chargers.

AsTec (Model Electronics),
6 Strickland Close,
Clevedon,
North Somerset, BS12 5EX.
Tel: +44(0)1275 878125.
Email: alan@astec44.freeserve.co.uk
or www.astec44.freeserve.co.uk
Electronic Speed Controllers, Amix Multi Mixer, Power Switches, high-grade power cable, motors and matched nicads.

David Swain,
31 Beech Croft Road,
Oxford, OX2 7AY.
Tel: +44(0) 1865 550548.
Frequency Flags.

K. Bits.
20 Queens Road,
Eastbourne,
East Sussex, BN23 6JT.
Tel/Fax +44(0) 1323 725817.
Email: kenbinks@mistrral.co.uk
Futaba equipment including winches and high spec. servos. Nicads, NiMHs and chargers including the MainLink range. Accessories include high quality ball type Kwik links, replacement TX aerials and aerial/eye protectors. Catalogue on request.

MAPLIN ELECTRONICS,
Freepost, SMU94
PO Box 777,
Rayleigh
Essex, SS6 8LU.
World Service Tel: +44 (0) 1702 554000. Fax: +44 (0) 1702 551229 or http://www.maplin.co.uk   Email <recipient> @ maplin.co.uk
Note: Maplin have 50 retail outlets in the UK as well as a Mail Order service. Electronic components, materials, tools, test instruments and a small number of marine modelling items.

Catalogue published twice a year available direct, Maplin shop or any branch of W H Smith or Menzies.

RS Components UK
PO Box 99,
Corby,
Northants, NN17 9RS.
Tel: +44(0) 1536 201234.
Fax: +44(0) 1536 405678 or
http://wwwrs-components.com/rs/
Note: RS deals primarily with trade customers.
Electronic components, materials, tools and test instruments. A set of catalogues available direct at cost.

Squires Model and Craft Tools,
100 London Road,
Bognor Regis,
West Sussex PO21 1DD.
Tel: +44(0) 1243 842424.
Fax: +44(0) 1243 842525.
Large range of craft tools, soldering irons and soldering materials, work assistance tools, materials and a Limited range of electronic/electrical components. Catalogue available on request.

Tandy retail outlets nationwide – details:
Tandy Antika Retail Ltd.,
Tandy Centre,
Leamore Lane, Walsall,
West Midlands, WS2 7PS.
Tel: +44(0) 1922 434000.
Fax: +44(0) 1922 710789.
Note. Tandy UK is independent of Tandy in Europe, USA or Canada etc., Electronic tools and components.

ACTion,
140 Holme Court Avenue,
Biggleswade,
Bedfordshire, SG18 8PB.
Tel: +44(0) 1767 314732 or
http://members.aol.com./actionkit
Probably the largest range of marine-orientated self-build or built-to-order kits available. From ESs, sirens and mixer amplifiers to morse code, asdic and Big Gun Sound simulator. Range includes lamps and motors. Catalogue on request.

Bob's Models Ltd,
99 Hobs Moat Road,
Solihull,
West Midlands, B92 8JI
Tel: +44 (0) 21 742 3949.
MSCs – VARISPEED Motor Control Boards (Bob's Boards)

MainLink Systems,
1 Blunham Road,
Moggerhanger,
Bedford, MK44 3RD.
Tel/Fax: +44(0) 1767 640242.
Email: chris@mainlink.demon.co.uk
or http.//www.mainlink.demon.co.uk
Design and manufacture of chargers, analysers including DIGILISER 2000.

Allied Battery Technologies
14 Bates Industrial Estate,
Wycombe Road,
Stokenchurch,
Bucks, HP14 3RJ.
Tel: +44(0) 1494 484050.
Fax: +44(0) 1494 482161 or
Email: colin@argosycable.demon.co.uk
Manufacture under an 'Improving' licence of Rechargeable Alkaline Manganese – RAM – batteries and chargers. Available from Maplin, Boots, Comet and Index.

The Yearbook & Buyers Guide from the Low Power Radio Association, Brearley Hall, Luddenden Foot, Halifax, HX2 6HS
Tel: +44(0) 1422 886463.
Fax/voice mail +44(0) 1422 886950
Email: info@lpra.org
Internet: http://www.lpra.org
RF modules for use in Model Telemetry Band. See Appendix 1.

GEMINI ELECTRICAL SERVICES,
123 Merlin Park Road,
Portishead,
Avon, BS20 8RL.
Tel: +44(0) 1275 844112.
GEMINI GES-7W Multi Memory
System. See Chapter 14.

PJ SAILS
1, Courtney Road,
Poole,
Dorset, BH14 0HD
Tel/Fax: +44(0) 1202 744101
Yot Pots – Waterproof containers for
receivers. Also stocks yacht fittings.

Eden Model Submarine Workshop
121 Spar Road,
Orpington,
Kent, BR6 0QP
Tel/Fax: +44(0) 1689 835149
Submarine kits and fittings.

The Best of the U-Boats
Unit 9, Wat Tyler Country Park,
Wat Tyler Way,
Pitsea,
Essex
Tel: +44(0) 1268 559377
Fax: +44(0) 1702 713984
Submarine kits and fittings.

ELECTRONIZE DESIGN
2 Hillside Road,
Sutton Coldfield,
B74 4DQ
Tel/Fax: +44(0) 121 308 5877
Electronic Speed Controls, 2- and
4-way switchers and motors.

ANTEX (Electronics) Ltd.
2 Westbridge Industrial Estate,
Tavistock,
Devon, PL19 8DE
Tel: +44(0) 1822 613565
Fax: +44(0) 1822 617598
www.antex.co.uk
Email: sales@antex.co.uk
Soldering irons (electric and gas).
Soldering systems.

DEAN'S MARINE
Conquest Drove,
Farcet Fell,
Peterborough, PE7 3DH
Tel/Fax: +44(0) 1733 244166
Sole importer and European dis-
tributor for Model Control Devices
(Canada) (see below).

Vitelec Electronics Ltd.
Vitelec Works,
Station Road,
Bordon, Hants
Tel: +44(0) 1420 488661
Fax: +44(0) 1420 488014
www. Vitelec.co.uk
Email: sales@vitelec.co.uk
SMA Connectors
Bulkhead Jack – 142-0303-411
Straight Clamp Type Jack –
142-0103-011
Straight Clamp Type Plug
– 142-0203-011

GEE DEE HOBBIES &
MODELS
21 Heathcote Street,
Nottingham, NG1 3AF
Tel: +44(0) 115 9412211
Fax: +44(0) 115 9417717
Email: hobbies@gee-dee.co.uk
www. gee-dee.co.uk
Specialist supplier of the robbe
Futaba F series equipment includ-
ing expansion modules and servos. Also
robbe kits and ancillary RC com-
ponents.

Morgan's Technical Books Ltd.
PO Box 5,
Wotton-under-Edge,
Gloucester, GL12 7BY
Publishers of *A Seaman's Guide to
THE RULE OF THE ROAD*
(ISBN 0-948254-00-9)

Tomahawk Products
RAF Sopley,
Merryfield Park,

Sopley,
Christchurch, BH23 7AU
Tel/Fax: +44(0) 674474
Electronic Smoke Units and High-output Diesel Sound Generators.

SHESTO LTD
Unit 2, Sapcote Trading Centre,
374 High Road,
Willesden,
London, NW10 2DH
Tel: +44(0) 20 8451 6188
Fax: +44(0) 20 8451 5450
Email: sales@shesto.co.uk
Tools and equipment including magnifiers.

HUNTER SYSTEMS
24 Aspen Road,
Eastbourne,
East Sussex, BN22 0TG
Tel/Fax: +44(0) 1323 847771
Email: info@huntersystems.co.uk
www.huntersystems.co.uk
Motors and Sound Units. RD accessories including rare 'grain of wheat' 1.4mm diameter, 1.5V tungsten lamps. (Four in series = 6V. See Chapter 13.)

USA

Tandy, RadioShack and TechAmerica. Electronic components including switches, connectors, tools and service aids. Headquarters.
100 Throckmorton Street,
Suite 1800,
Fort Worth,
TX 76102.
Telephone: 817 415 3700

Radio Shack Customer Relations.
200 Taylor Street, Suite 600,
Forth Worth. TX 76102.
Telephone: 817 415 3200.
Fax: 817 415 32440.
Email: rscusre101@tandy.com
Product Support Center. (address as above)

Tel: 1 800 THE SHACK
Computer Fax: 817 415 6804.
Consumer Fax: 817 415 6880
Email: support@tandy.com

Tandy Corporation & TechAmerica Customer Relations.
100 Throckmorton Street, Suite 700,
Fort Worth,
Texas 76102.
Email: tacusre101@tandy.com
Product Support Center
200 Taylor Street, Suite 600,
Fort Worth,
Texas 76102.
Tel: 1 800 876 5292.
Email: support@tandy.com

Vitelec SMA Connectors are available in the USA from:
Johnson Components, Inc.
299 Johnson Avenue,
Waseca,
MN
Tel: 800 247 8256
Fax: 507 835 6287
Email: rfmarket@johnsoncomp.com
or http://johnsoncomp.com/partners.htm
Most States and Canada have distributors who can be accessed via Johnson Components. The part numbers listed in the Vitelec UK entry above are compatible with International stocks.

Canada

Electronic components including switches, connectors, tools and service aids. Radio Shack Canada, Division INTERTAN CANADA LTD, 279 Bayview Drive, Barrie, Ontario, L4M 4W5. Tel: 705-728-6242. Fax: 705-728-2012.
Note: At the time of writing the Tandy chain of retail outlets was coming under new ownership. Enquire locally for the nearest outlet.

Model Control Devices, PO Box 173, 18 Reid Street, Bobcaygeon, Ontario, Canada. KOM 1AO. HELP and Fax: 705-738-1335.

This company supplies ESCs, SWITCH 8 and SWITCH 16 Accessory Control Systems. Both sys-tems arrived too late on the author's bench for testing and inclusion in Chapter 14. Each system converts one function into either eight or sixteen key pad options for latched or momentary switching at the TX. The key pads are connected to the selected function potentiometer disconnected wiring as described in Chapter 14. The keypads are located externally on the TX. The decoder unit is plugged into the selected RX output and will switch a 6 to 16V supply 3amps continuous – 10amps peak. Either system is factory calibrated for most makes of equipment or it can be recalibrated from suppliedinstructions. There is a delay between keypad operation and response at the RX as the system skips to the requested output. This delay can be lengthened to improve interference rejection. There is also a choice of fail safe operation in the event of loss of signal. Sole European importer and distributor is DEAN'S MARINE (see above).

North America marine workers will find The Tower Hobbies 1999 Catalog of interest. For more information: https://www2.towerhobbies.com/cat alog.html or Tower Hobbies, DEPT. WWW, PO Box 9078, Champaign, IL 61826-9078 or tel: in U.S. 800-637-44989 toll free or outside U.S. 217-398-3636.

Vitelec. See Johnson Components listing above.

Appendix 3
Formulae and Useful Information

Ohms Law

Where E = Voltage, I = Current (A), R = Resistance in ohms & W = Watts then:- $E=I \times R$. $I=E/R$. $R=E/I$. $W=E^2/R$. $W=I \times E$. $W=I^2 \times R$.
Note: 1ma=1 thousandth of one Ampere. 1mV=1 thousandth of one Volt.

Capacitors

Capacitor values in suppressor circuits can be expressed either as pF, nF or mF(mF) – for example 47000pF or 47nF or 0.047mF or 0.047mF. Note that all capacitors used for electric motor suppressors are non-polarised. Electrolytic capacitors are polarised and should never be used for suppressor circuits.

Resistor colours

Black = 0, Brown = 1, Red = 2, Orange = 3, Yellow = 4, Green = 5, Blue = 6, Violet = 7, Grey = 8, White = 9.
Colours are grouped to one end to read from that end. The first and second colours are digits. The third is zeros. There may be a fourth tolerance colour. Red = 2 per cent, Gold = 5 per cent, Silver = 10 per cent, None = 20 per cent. A yellow, violet, orange, none = 47,000 ohms 20 per cent resistor, or 47kilohm or 47k.

Diodes

A diode is a solid-state component which can only pass a direct current in one direction. It is similar in appearance to a resistor and has a solid-coloured band at one end identifying the negative or kathode lead. The other lead is the positive anode. For its use see Chapter 14.

Light emitting diodes

LEDs cannot be connected to a supply without a series resistor to limit the current through the device. Some LEDs will be listed as having a series resistor built into the package for a particular voltage supply. For those without the user is required to calculate the series resistor from:-

$$R = \frac{Vs - Vf}{If}$$

Where: Vs is the supply voltage
Vf is the forward voltage
If is the forward current in amps
ie 20mA = 0.020A
Vf and If can be found in suppliers catalogue tables
if unknown assume Vf = 2.2V
& If = 0.020A

Note: Insert the resistance into the positive lead – the anode connection. Negative to kathode. The kathode connection is indicated by the short lead and a flat on the LED body.

Current capacity of cables

Maximum current is determined by the nominal cross sectional area of the conductor. A conductor can be 'solid' or made up of 'strands', *eg* 1/0.6mm diameter or 32/0.2mm diameter. To find the cross sectional area of a conductor multiply half the diameter by itself and multiply this answer by 3.1416 (radius$^2 \times 3.1416$). For example the 1/0.6mm above is $0.3 \times 0.3 \times 3.1416$ = 0.28mm^2 and 32/0.2mm is $0.1 \times 0.1 \times 3.1416 \times 32$ = 1.0mm^2. Maximum current carrying capacity can now be found from the following table for PVC insulated cables.

Cable Size	Max. Current
0.28mm^2	1amp
0.5mm^2	3amps
0.75mm^2	6amps
1.0mm^2	10amps
1.5mm^2	15amps
2.5mm^2	20amps
4.0mm^2	25amps

Note. These are conservative current ratings taking into account that when installed in a model boat the ambient temperature can be extremely high which when added to the heat generated within a high current carrying conductor increases the volt drop between battery and motor. However, there is available from specialist suppliers 2.5mm^2 silicone-insulated Extra Flexible cable made up of 462 strands $\times$ 0.08mm diameter rated at 32 amps. It has a small bend radius and is stable over a wide temperature range. This cable is ideal for power wiring in confined spaces.

UK Model Boating Contacts

*M.P.B.A.**
Jane Garner, 14 Orchard Street, Boston, Lincolnshire, PE2 8PL.
Tel/Fax: +44(0) 1205 368264.
Eight sections including Scale, Electric Racing, Circuit Racing, Hydroplanes etc. Membership is either as an individual member of the Countrywide Club or via an affiliated club. Membership includes Public Liability Insurance.

Size, weight, voltage and capacity of Sealed Lead Acid batteries

Size	Weight	Voltage	Capacity
51 × 55 × 42mm	250g	6V	1Ah
97 × 54 × 25mm	300g	6V	1.2Ah
134 × 64 × 34mm	560g	6V	2.8Ah
70 × 108 × 34mm	850g	6V	4.0Ah
151 × 98 × 33mm	1.28kg	6V	7Ah
151 × 98 × 50mm	2kg	6V	10Ah
96 × 61.5 × 25mm	350g	12V	0.8Ah
97 × 55 × 47mm	600g	12V	1.2Ah
178 × 66 × 345mm	830g	12v	2.1Ah
150 × 90 × 20mm	700g	12V	2Ah
134 × 64 × 68mm	1.1kg	12V	2.8Ah
90 × 105 × 70mm	1.75kg	12V	4Ah
151 × 98 × 65mm	2.4kg	12V	6Ah
151 × 98 × 65mm	2.65kg	12V	7Ah
151 × 98 × 98mm	4.09kg	12V	12Ah

Model Yacht Association *
Mike Hounsell, 4 Old Fire Station Court, North Street, Nailsea, BS19 2BP.
Tel: +44(0) 1275 858528.
Individual membership or via an affiliated club. membership includes Public Liability Insurance.

Electra (fast electrics)
Ian Barber, 3 Ridge Close, Portslade, Brighton, BN41 2YH.
Tel: +44(0) 1273 8800703

Scale Sail Association
Mike Taylor, 14 Palace Road, Crouch End, London, N8 8QJ.

Model Submariners Association
Dave Austin,
36 Addison Road,
Teddington,
Middlesex, TW11 9EX
Tel: +44(0) 208 255 1876

Surface Warship
George Peat BEM, 31 McNeill Terrace, Laonhead, Midlothian, EH20 9JU.
Tel/Fax: 0131 440 1939.

Compass *
Barrie Stevens, 2 Hawthorn, Crescent, Shepton Mallet, Somerset. BA4 5XR.

Tel: 01749 343017

*Are represented on the JRCUC. See Appendix 1.

USA Boating Contacts

There is a vast amount of information available on the World-Wide Web – far too extensive to list here. Instead the following web sites are recommended for further information.

Boat Clubs and Organisations
http://www.towerhobbies.com/rcwboatclub.html
Four pages including International listings.

Club Listings
http://wwh.net/iwrc/clubs.html
Eight pages covering most States. International listing includes Canada and UK.

Boat-Orientated Web Sites
http://www.towerhobbies.com/rcw.html
Three pages of marine modelling information.

R/C Magazines.
ttp://www.towerhobbies.com/rcwmags.html

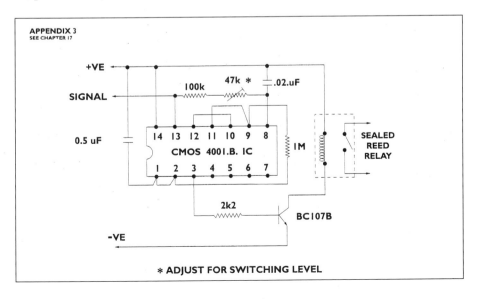

APPENDIX 3
SEE CHAPTER 17

Canadian Boating Contacts

The Canadian Radio Yachting Association
Membership Secretary: Norm Patt, 32 Woodhaven Cr. Whitby, Ontario. LIR 1R6
http://qsilver.queensu.ca/~crya/
Email:npatt@sympatico.ca

The Model Aeronautics Association of Canada has a R/C Boat Committee. Contact Andy Stishenko, 1293 Hwy 33E, Kelowna, BC. VIP 1M1. Tel: (250) 765-6888 or http://www.maac.ca/english/committees/com_boat.html

(Produced with kind permission of Dave McQue)

Reference source and magazines

A Seaman's Guide to THE RULE OF THE ROAD (ISBN 0-948254-00-9). Morgan's Technical Books (see Appendix 2).

Royal Air Force Museum
Grahame Park Way,
Hendon,
London, NW9 5LL
Information on the development of the Queen Bee radio control project between the Wars.

A large number of makers' and suppliers' catalogues and other published information has contributed to this manual so that the most comprehensive and up-to-date information and availability of equipment could be provided to the reader. The list is too long for individual recognition. The author extends his sincere thanks to all those concerned.

MARINE MODELLING INTERNATIONAL magazine
Traplet Publications,
Traplet House,
Severn Drive,
Upton-upon-Severn
Worcs. WR8 0JL
Tel: +44(0) 1684 594505
Fax: +44(0) 1684 594586
Email: general@traplet.co.uk
www.traplet.co.uk
Published monthly on about the 22nd of the preceding month. The author's column 'Airwaves' appears quarterly, plus occasional articles and reviews of RC equipment. Enquiries regarding USA and Canadian distribution should be addressed to:
Traplet Distribution USA,
3103 Tatman Court,
Suite 105,
Urbana, IL 61802
Tel: 217 328 4444
Fax: 217-328-2450

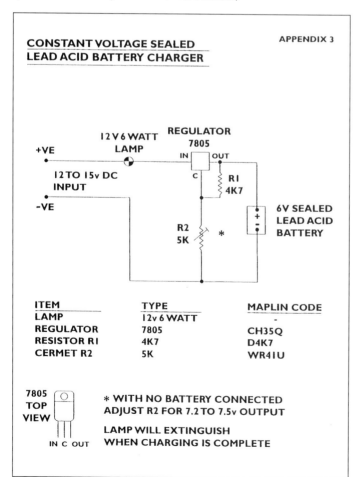

CONSTANT VOLTAGE SEALED LEAD ACID BATTERY CHARGER   APPENDIX 3

ITEM	TYPE	MAPLIN CODE
LAMP	12v 6 WATT	-
REGULATOR	7805	CH35Q
RESISTOR R1	4K7	D4K7
CERMET R2	5K	WR41U

7805 TOP VIEW
IN C OUT

* WITH NO BATTERY CONNECTED ADJUST R2 FOR 7.2 TO 7.5v OUTPUT

LAMP WILL EXTINGUISH WHEN CHARGING IS COMPLETE

INDEX